Top of the Line
Hunting Collectibles

Donna Tonelli

With a Foreword by Joe Engers

Schiffer Publishing Ltd
4880 Lower Valley Rd. Atglen, PA 19310 USA

Dedication

To Joe French, Bill Mackey, Hal Sorenson, and Will Pennington, who led the way for many decoy collectors.

Library of Congress Cataloging-in Publication Data

Tonelli, Donna.

Top of the line hunting collectibles / Donna Tonelli ; with a foreword by Joe Engers.

p. cm.

Includes bibliographical references and index.

ISBN 0-7643-416-X

1. Hunting--Collectibles--United States--Catalogs. I. Title.

NK6077.5.T66 1998

799'.075--dc21 98-10730

CIP

Designed by Bonnie M. Hensley

IowanOldSt Blk BT/Times New Roman

ISBN: 0-7643-0416-X

Printed in China

1 2 3 4

Published by Schiffer Publishing Ltd.
4880 Lower Valley Road
Atglen, PA 19310
Phone: (610) 593-1777; Fax: (610) 593-2002
E-mail: Schifferbk@aol.com
Please write for a free catalog.
This book may be purchased from the publisher.
Please include $3.95 for shipping.

Try your bookstore first.

We are interested in hearing from authors with book ideas on related subjects.

Foreword

Top of the Line Hunting Collectibles, the first compilation of all the many facets of hunting memorabilia, will prove to be a one-stop reference for all who collect and enjoy these wonderful artifacts from the golden age of waterfowling. And for its author, Donna Tonelli, this book is the accomplishment of a long-time goal.

About ten years ago, while putting together a survey book on North American decoys, I was introduced to Donna. I was told that her husband, Joe, was the authority on Illinois River decoys, but it was Donna who accumulated, researched, and recorded the history they uncovered. Since many of the fine hunting artifacts they collect were gathered from the source, we are fortunate that their attention to this important provenance was so meticulously applied.

Joe and Donna have been totally immersed in hunting (as well as fishing) collectibles for over 35 years. In many ways, it was a life-long passion as well as a livelihood. As a decoy collector, I was familiar with the many fine birds in their collection. But a visit to their home is more like a stop at a "sporting collectibles" museum. While many collectors focus on one aspect of collecting—decoys, duck calls, shot shell boxes, etc.—the Tonellis collect and enjoy them all.

Due to their interest in the many varieties of sporting collectibles, few others would be as qualified to write this book. Since they've bought and sold in this arena for years, they also have an acute awareness of the value of these items. While many of the collectibles pictured are from their personal collection, their long-time involvement in the hobby and personal friendships with other collectors have allowed them to include top quality examples from some of the finest collections nationwide. These are all presented in beautiful, full-color photographs.

If you enjoy *Top of the Line Hunting Collectibles* as much as I do, I'm sure you'll enjoy this book. How appropriate that it was produced by a couple of "top-of-the-line collectors."

Joe Engers
Publisher, Decoy Magazine

Tibbits.

Contents

Acknowledgments

Fellow decoy collectors have often told Joe and I, "You should write a book." When I started this project I had no idea how much work and dedication it would require. I certainly never would have been able to finish without help from many people. First and foremost was Joe Tonelli who was a constant source of information and support. Driven by a consuming passion for waterfowling, hunting artifacts, and folklore, Joe has compiled an impressive all-around collection and filled my files with irreplaceable information over the last thirty some years. During this time we have built a social network that revolves around collecting, and it was these friends who came forward to assist with this project.

One person who had a profound impact on our lives was James R. Cook. When he hired Joe as a decoy consultant and manager of his private waterfowl refuge, Willossippi, he opened our horizons beyond the small town where we both grew up. Jim has an appreciation for the hunting decoys that reaches beyond their investment value to a deep appreciation of their beauty and history. His decoy collection ranks among the most comprehensive and best in the country and provided many one-of-a-kind examples for this project.

I am indebted to Alan and Elaine Haid for far more than their act of opening up their collection and supplying excellent photography. Alan is an established, authoritative decoy broker and collector and author of two major decoy books, *Decoys of the Mississippi Flyway* and *Mason Decoys*. He was the first person to seriously assure me that I was capable of compiling a decoy book.

Most of the photographs of old collections and decoy carvers were lent to this project by Joseph B. French. Joe, who has been our friend for more years than either of us would like to count, shared his priceless decoy archives with no reservations. As Joe French is fond of saying, he is one of the last old-timers. He bought decoys out of barns and boathouses by the gunny sack and, aware of the history embodied in them, he donated decoys unselfishly to numerous museums, helping to preserve a bit of American folk art for all of us.

Joe French shares his dedication to this cause with three other men who were instrumental in ensuring that the decoy earned a creditable place in the realm of American folk art: William Mackey, Hal Sorenson, and Willis Pennington. They opened the world of collecting to us and to countless other collectors. William Mackey was considered the dean of decoy collecting when we met him, yet he took time to expose Joe to East Coast decoys and broadened our collecting experience. Mackey brought decoy collecting to a greater level of appreciation each time his decoys were exhibited in museums and at art shows, which was often.

The Decoy Collectors Guide was the brainchild of Hal Sorenson and the first publication devoted exclusively to vintage hunting decoys. With this quarterly publication, produced entirely by Hal and his wife, Barbara, collectors were able to access information about the newly recognized decoy carvers and their decoys. Barbara Sorenson deserves a special thanks for sharing her late husband's *Decoy Collectors Guide* files and her special support.

Few of the newer collectors know of Willis Pennington, but those of us who knew him were infected by his love of decoys and decoy dealings. Decoy collecting was a bartering man's heaven during the 1960s and no one was better at it than Pennington. Before the decoy collecting network existed, Pennington traveled throughout the Midwest buying and trading decoys and creating new collectors along the way.

From the beginning of this project, Joe and I wanted it to be more than just another decoy book. Gene and Shirley Konopasek, who have one of the finest collections of advertising art, patiently allowed us to invade their home to photograph his extensive collection. Lee Schultz and Rick Simpson brought portions of their advertising collections to us to be photographed. Ron Willoughby, recognized as the leading authority on shotgun shell boxes, provided photographs of extremely rare examples from his collection. James McCleery, one of the finest gentlemen I know, is responsible for sharing the finest shot shell box in any collection. Howard Harlan, author of *Turkey Calls—An Enduring American Folk Art* and *Duck Calls—An Enduring American Folk Art*, hand delivered selected game bird calls to be photographed. The game call section was rounded off with examples of turkey calls from George Campbell's collection, duck calls from Gary Reiker, and snipe whistles from Alan Haid. Dean Dashner provided Duck Unlimited buttons, badges, license buttons, and embroidered patches.

While our decoy collection is recognized as fairly well-rounded, several collecting friends helped fill in the blanks: Tommy O'Connor shared his superb Cobb Island decoys, with special thanks to Artie Johnson for the photography. Richard McIntyre of Collectible Old Decoys in Fripp Island, South Carolina, provided outstanding Carolina decoys. Joe Engers, owner/publisher of *Decoy Magazine*, sent photographs of Chincoteague decoys. I was especially excited to expose other collectors to the wonderful Wisconsin decoys. Folks like Herb Desch, Dean and Shirley Dashner, Tom Bosworth, John Reinfenrather, and Ladd Zidek allowed us to photograph many excellent examples that haven't received the attention they deserve until recently. The same can be said about the decoys from Minnesota.

My acknowledgments wouldn't be complete without thanking all the folks who have shared bits and pieces of waterfowling history with us over the years. Men like Malcolm Clark, Morton Smith, Jr., Jim Goodrich, Enoch Reindahl, and Stephen Havara of the Illinois Natural History Survey, gave me old hunting photographs and detailed information about hunting in diverse regions like southern Illinois and Heron Lake, Minnesota. And then there are the family members like Dotty Pennington, Norma Johnson, James Kucaba, Mrs. T. Bailey, Mrs. M. Homme, and Mrs. Robert Donaldson who provided old photographs, and individuals who supplied odd examples to help complete this project like Ron Adamson, John Herman, Dr. S. Kolwaski, Bill Rigsbee, Robert Summerfield, Todd Hoffman, Tim Melcher, Gene and Linda Kangas, authors of *Decoys* and *Decoys: a North American Survey*. I also want to say thanks to the thousands of people who sold us pieces over the years. Unknowingly they provided the nostalgia that gives special meaning to collecting old hunting memorabilia. And lastly, I want to thank Randy Root, John Delph, Frank Schmidt, Gary Guyette, Charles Bruno, Jim Julia, Dorothy Whaley, and all our fellow collectors who have made collecting more than a hobby for us.

Finally I would like to thank Doug Condon-Martin of Schiffer Publishing for his patience and excellent photography work, and also Joy Ng of Schiffer Publishing, who photographed James Cook's collection for this project, and also my editor, Tina Skinner of Schiffer Publishing, for her attention to details.

Preface

Top of the Line Hunting Collectibles is a tale of collecting and the collectors, a pictorial history of waterfowling, and a price guide to related waterfowling collectibles. An extensive bibliography in the back provides the names of numerous books that can provide more detailed information about specific hunting practices and artifacts. In an effort to present the most complete pictorial record of several hunting-related areas of collecting, written text will be minimal. It has been my experience that most collectors would rather see good photography of quality collectibles and their values. To this end I have drawn from some of the finest collections, past and present, to illustrate the diversity of waterfowling decoys, including examples from each of the major hunting regions. Game bird calls used for shorebird, goose, duck, crow, and turkey hunting; gunning collectibles such as shell boxes, reloading tools, glass target balls, advertising posters and calendars, die-cut cardboard displays, pin backs; specialty items like Ducks Unlimited buttons, hunting license pins, wardens' badges, live decoy holders, and duck stamps, represent the varied selection of related collectibles that are also discussed in *Top of the Line Hunting Collectibles*.

Chapter 1

Collectors' Gallery

I met Joe Tonelli more than thirty years ago, when he beaned me with a snowball in the parking lot of our high school hangout, the Igloo. I soon learned that Joe was an avid hunter. Even that night he had been dressed in camo! Not long after that, I found a beautiful carving in the trunk of his car. Joe explained that it was a turned head sleeper decoy carved by Charles Perdew. I had no idea what a hunting decoy was, or what a mallard was for that matter, but I loved the graceful lines and muted coloration of the piece, which captured a mallard hen with her head resting on her back as if sleeping. I insisted that he keep that mallard hen and put it in our new home after we were married.

Joel Barber (1877–1952) of Wilton, Connecticut, is called the father of decoy collecting. (*Photo by Joseph French*)

Joel Barber was one of the first to use his favorite decoys to decorate his home. Joseph French of Marathon, Florida, visited most of the major decoy collectors during his many years of collecting and made a point of capturing parts of his visits on film. (Photo by Joseph French)

We have been collecting decoys and related artifacts ever since. During the 1960s, decoy collecting was just emerging as a viable field of antiquing. If an antique dealer brought any decoys to a show, they were usually stashed under his table. Most decoy collectors were hunters who brought home discarded wooden decoys as they were being replaced with lighter weight, more durable plastic and paper mâche models. I'll never forget the first time we went to a fellow collector's home and were amazed that he had a special room designed to display his duck decoys. Most of us kept our collections in the garage or maybe the basement of our homes.

Joe and I were fortunate to have lived in one of the greatest waterfowling regions of the country, the Illinois River Valley near the "Big Bend" where the river turns sharply south and creates a natural loafing area for migrating waterfowl. During the heyday of duck hunting, master decoy carvers like Charles Perdew, Robert Elliston, Bert Graves, Charles Schoenheider, and Charles Walker had lived within fifty miles of our home. We could buy great decoys for little or nothing. Joe built our decoy collection by buying rigs of decoys and selling extras to other collectors to pay for the birds he wanted to keep. It may be hard to believe, but we would drive along the Illinois River knocking on doors, buying original paint decoys at five to ten dollars each and have a hard time finding someone to buy them for $15 or $25. Some of these same decoys are valued in the tens of thousands today. During this time, Joe became known as a decoy source. On any given day of the week, a stranger would be knocking on our door announcing that he was looking for old hunting decoys. As young kids from a small Illinois River town, decoys made it possible for us to meet and develop lasting friendships with people throughout the United States, from all walks of life, because we shared a common bond—a love of vintage hunting decoys.

William Mackey of Bedford, New Jersey, was accepted as the guru of decoy collecting. Most collectors dreamed of visiting his legendary collection before his death in 1972.

Decoy collecting was a fun time then. Individual collectors started to find each other and organize in the various regions where waterfowling was popular. Individual collectors hosted backyard picnics and other casual gatherings where the collectors could have discussions and barter for decoys. The early collectors amassed decoys, trading among themselves with little regard for monetary value: Illinois River decoys were swapped for East Coast or Michigan decoys, usually one for one. With the help of men like Joel Barber, William Mackey, Joseph B. French, Willis Pennington, and Hal Sorenson, decoy collecting spread and gained popularity. Joel Barber established himself as the father of decoy collecting when his book, *Wild Fowl Decoys*, was published in 1934. Mackey was the first major decoy dealer. He promoted the hunting decoy as an American folk art by selling decoys to individuals and several major museums, judging at the decoy carving competitions, and showing his collection at early hunting decoy exhibitions. William Mackey's home became a Mecca for decoy collectors. When Joseph French started collecting decoys in the 1950s, he realized the importance of documenting the decoy. He recorded on film the various major collections that he visited during his travels. He also donated generously to several museums throughout the Midwest in an effort to establish the decoy's place in American folklore. In 1963, Hal Sorenson of Burlington, Iowa, introduced the *Decoy Collector's Guide*, a quarterly trade publication that united decoy collectors across state lines. Sorenson's guide was instrumental in creating a network among decoy collectors that continued to grow. Willis Pennington introduced many Midwesterners to the joys of decoy collecting simply because his enthusiasm was infectious. Pennington loved to barter. As a traveling salesman, he worked his way throughout the Midwest buying and trading decoys everywhere he went. In the days before the computer, he carried a card file in his station wagon that listed every collector, their preferences, wants, and what decoys they owned.

Collectors began to follow the contemporary decoy carving contests that became popular during the 1960s, bringing along their extra decoys. Regional groups organized gatherings by staying at a common motel near the decoy contests. This led to actual shows to promote decoy collecting and provide opportunities to obtain decoys. Collectors converged from all parts of the United States and Canada. The shows usually opened to the public, but the collectors came a day or two early to visit and barter in their motel rooms. For years Joe Tonelli would tote his old hunting blocks to these shows in gunny sacks.

The Midwest Decoy Collectors' Association began when Hal Sorenson, Willis Pennington, and Ralph Leoff decided to put together a large meeting in Ottawa, Illinois, and invited collectors from the Midwest to attend using Sorenson's mailing list from the Decoy Collectors' Guide. The Midwest Decoy Collectors was chartered as a non-profit, educational organization in 1966, and is considered by most collectors to be a national organization. Today there are active decoy collecting organizations in most areas where waterfowling was practiced. Most of these groups hold annual meetings that educate and encourage new collectors.

Many decoy collectors including Joe and I, stumbled upon other interesting artifacts as we searched the back roads and antique shops for decoys. Soon we found ourselves collecting game bird calls, shell boxes, and advertising items. Rather than buy a new print, we were hanging old gunpowder company's calendars and posters on our walls. Gunpowder tins were put on the shelves with decoys to create a more attractive display. Some collectors started to specialize in these related fields of waterfowling memorabilia. Like decoy collectors, they organized clubs and started to sponsor shows to share their collections, do a little swapping, and support growing interest among other collectors. These fields are now as active as decoy collecting.

William Mackey's house became a Mecca for collectors across the country who dreamed of seeing his decoy collection.

As young men, Joe Tonelli and Randy Root had no idea decoy collecting and duck hunting would have such a major impact on their lives. They just loved decoys and thought they were in "duck heaven" in Mackey's basement. 1969. (*Photograph by William Mackey*)

Joseph French of Marathon, Florida, is one of the few collectors who has experienced firsthand the thrill of meeting the master decoy carvers. As one of the pioneer Midwest decoy collectors, French was able to special order the widgeon decoys he likes to focus his collecting on directly from men like Charles Perdew. His generous donations to many major museums helped give the simple decoy credibility as a major American folk art form.

Hal Sorenson (1924–1992) of Burlington, Iowa, probably did more than any single person to document and promote the value of decoys with his publication, *The Decoy Collector's Guide*. Sorenson's expertise and guidance helped untold numbers of collectors, and insured that the decoy would be accepted as a viable field in the world of antiques. (Photo Courtesy of Joseph French)

Willis Pennington of LaGrange, Illinois, traveled throughout the Midwest promoting decoy collecting during the 1950s, '60s, and '70s.

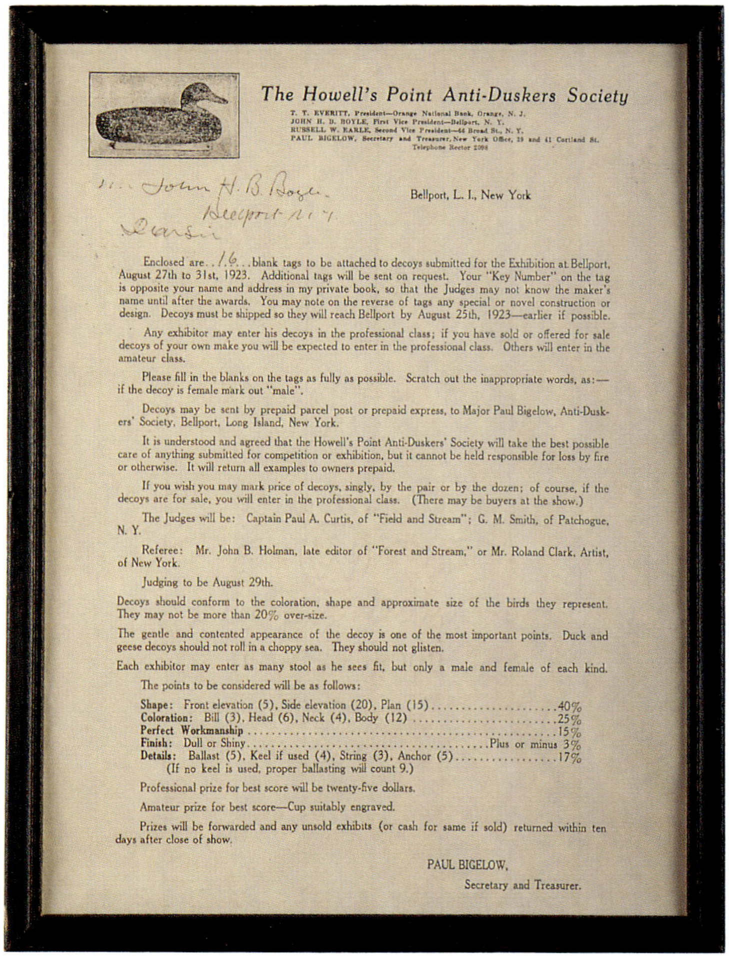

The Howell's Point Anti-Duskers Society

T. T. EVERITT, President—Orange National Bank, Orange, N. J.
JOHN H. D. BOYLE, First Vice President—Bellport, N. Y.
RUSSELL W. EARLE, Second Vice President—44 Broad St., N. Y.
PAUL BIGELOW, Secretary and Treasurer, New York Office, 39 and 41 Cortland St.
Telephone Rector 2098

Bellport, L. I., New York

Enclosed are . . 16 . . . blank tags to be attached to decoys submitted for the Exhibition at Bellport, August 27th to 31st, 1923. Additional tags will be sent on request. Your "Key Number" on the tag is opposite your name and address in my private book, so that the Judges may not know the maker's name until after the awards. You may note on the reverse of tags any special or novel construction or design. Decoys must be shipped so they will reach Bellport by August 25th, 1923—earlier if possible.

Any exhibitor may enter his decoys in the professional class; if you have sold or offered for sale decoys of your own make you will be expected to enter in the professional class. Others will enter in the amateur class.

Please fill in the blanks on the tags as fully as possible. Scratch out the inappropriate words, as:—if the decoy is female mark out "male".

Decoys may be sent by prepaid parcel post or prepaid express, to Major Paul Bigelow, Anti-Duskers' Society, Bellport, Long Island, New York.

It is understood and agreed that the Howell's Point Anti-Duskers' Society will take the best possible care of anything submitted for competition or exhibition, but it cannot be held responsible for loss by fire or otherwise. It will return all examples to owners prepaid.

If you wish you may mark price of decoys, singly, by the pair or by the dozen; of course, if the decoys are for sale, you will enter in the professional class. (There may be buyers at the show.)

The Judges will be: Captain Paul A. Curtis, of "Field and Stream"; G. M. Smith, of Patchogue, N. Y.

Referee: Mr. John B. Holman, late editor of "Forest and Stream," or Mr. Roland Clark, Artist, of New York.

Judging to be August 29th.

Decoys should conform to the coloration, shape and approximate size of the birds they represent. They may not be more than 20% over-size.

The gentle and contented appearance of the decoy is one of the most important points. Duck and geese decoys should not roll in a choppy sea. They should not glisten.

Each exhibitor may enter as many stool as he sees fit, but only a male and female of each kind.

The points to be considered will be as follows:

Shape: Front elevation (5), Side elevation (20), Plan (15) 40%
Coloration: Bill (3), Head (6), Neck (4), Body (12) 25%
Perfect Workmanship 15%
Finish: Dull or Shiny . . . . Plus or minus 3%
Details: Ballast (5), Keel if used (4), String (3), Anchor (5) 17%
(If no keel is used, proper ballasting will count 9.)

Professional prize for best score will be twenty-five dollars.

Amateur prize for best score—Cup suitably engraved.

Prizes will be forwarded and any unsold exhibits (or cash for same if sold) returned within ten days after close of show.

PAUL BIGELOW,
Secretary and Treasurer.

Howell's Point Anti-dusking Society sponsored one of the first decoy carving competitions to bring conservation issues to the attention of the sportsmen, mainly the damage that shooting waterfowl after dark can do. This competition was held in 1923, in Bellport, Long Island, New York.

Sale bill from a decoy auction, 1973. $50.

Exhibit from the International Decoy Contest at The Great 1968 Mississippi Valley Fair in Davenport, Iowa. (*Photo by Alex Gray*)

Small local shows were organized by individuals as social functions and to provide opportunities to trade with other collectors, 1967.

The Wildfowl Decoy: An American Tradition exhibition, presented by the Rockford Art Association in Rockford, Illinois in 1965, was a collection of more than 150 exceptional waterfowling decoys assembled from collectors in Illinois and Wisconsin.

The Wild-Fowl Decoys exhibition presented by the American Sportsmen of New York City in 1924 was one of the earliest exhibitions of its kind. The Exhibition Committee included noted sportsmen like Joel Barber, Roland Clark, R. H. Boyd, and Major Paul Biglow.

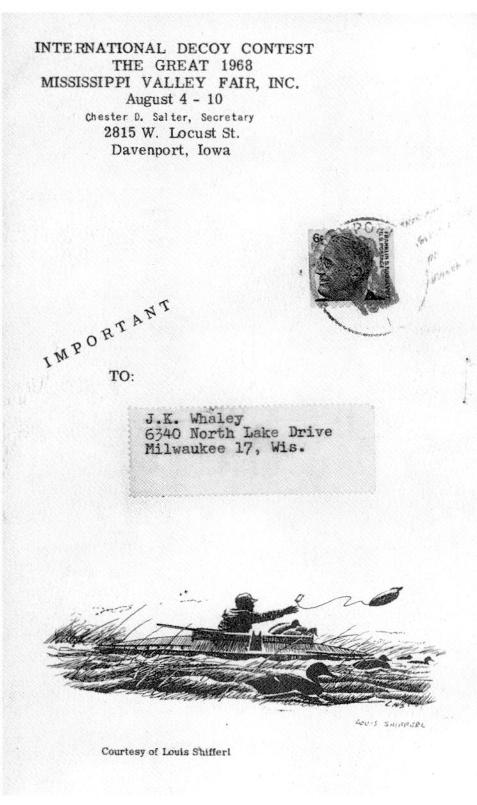

The International Decoy Contest held in conjunction with The Great Mississippi Valley fair, Davenport, Iowa drew the major decoy collectors to the Blackhawk Motel to deal and talk decoys during the 1960's and 70's.

The Midwest Decoy Contest and Collectors Meet in Rockwood, Michigan, was one of the favorite early decoy collectors' gatherings, held in conjunction with the Michigan Duck Hunters' Tournament in Monroe, Michigan. Various competitions including a carving contest were staged on the grounds of the Pointe Mouille State Game Area.

Many collectors wish they could go back to the early shows and buy every decoy on display. Left to right: Joe Tonelli of Lake Andes, South Dakota; Gene Konopasek of Fox River Grove, Illinois (Midwest Decoy Collectors' Association chairman, 1976–1995); Randy Root of Spring Bay, Illinois; and Tommy O'Connor of Virginia Beach, Virginia, at the Drake Oakbrook MDCA show, circa 1968.

John Delph of Pointe Vedra, Florida, is shown with a display of decoys at the Monroe Michigan Decoy Show in 1975. He remains one of the major players in the decoy collecting market and has authored *New England Decoy, Firearms & Tackle Memorabilia: A Collector's Guide*, and *Factory Decoys of Mason, Stevens, Dodge, and Peterson*. (Photo Courtesy of Joseph French)

Alan Haid of Darien, Connecticut, has displayed at the major decoy shows since the 1970s and has established himself as one of the country's top decoy broker/collectors. Among Haid's literary credits are *Mason Decoys* and *Decoys of the Mississippi Flyway*, benchmark publications that detail his dedicated study of decoy history. Here he is pictured at the Monroe Michigan Decoy Show in 1985. (Photo Courtesy of Joseph French)

John Hillman and Bud Ward (1922–1997) are two icons of the decoy collecting world. The late John Hillman (left) was a collecting contemporary of William Mackey. When his collection was sold by the Guyette/Schmidt Auction house in 1996, it pushed the total auction sales passed all past decoy auctions with a single auction gross of $2,708,825. Bud Ward's room was famous at decoy shows for his great hunting and decoying tales. (*Photograph by Joseph French*)

Joe Tonelli's passion for waterfowling in evident in his decoy room, circa 1980. (*Photo Courtesy of Joseph French*)

James R. Cook of Minneapolis, Minnesota, has a museum-quality display room which houses his collection, one of the finest in the country and is a far cry from the garage and basement settings where most decoys were displayed by the early collectors. (*Photo Courtesy of Mitchell Anderson*)

Randolph Root is the owner/operator of Mallard Farms in Metamora, Illinois, possibly the finest contemporary waterfowling club in the country. When he was most active in decoy collecting, Randy compiled an impressive collection of Mason Factory decoys, circa 1980. (*Photo Courtesy of Joseph French*)

The late Harold Haertel built his collection of old hunting decoys by trading his own delicate carvings for old decoys. (*Photo Courtesy of Joseph French*)

Don Clark, who specializes in collecting decoys by his personal friend, the late Charles Perdew, hosts the Henry Decoy Show in his hometown of Henry, Illinois, which still retains the flavor of the old decoy gatherings. (*Photo Courtesy of Joseph French*)

The late Edward Moore of DeKalb, Illinois, actively collected decoys during the 1960s and 70s. He also served as co-chairman of the Midwest Decoy Collectors Show in 1968. (*Photo Courtesy of Joseph French*)

Above: At one time, Sandy Schmidt of Rockford, Illinois, owned more G. K. Schmidt rig decoys carved by Charles Perdew than any one else. Circa 1970. (*Photo Courtesy of Joseph French*)
Below: The late Charles Klopp and his wife, Isabelle, hosted a yearly backyard picnic for local decoy collectors at their western Chicago home that led to the formation of the Midwest Decoy Collectors' Association. (*Photo Courtesy of Joseph French*)

Virgil Lashbrook of Rio Hondo, Texas, is one of the few surviving classic hunting decoy carvers. Circa 1971. (*Photo Courtesy of Joseph French*)

The late George Ross Starr Jr. was one of the top collectors in the country before his death in 1985. (*Photo Courtesy of Joseph French*)

Left: Hal Evans has been one of the major collectors in the East Coast decoy market since the 1960s. (*Photo Courtesy of Joseph French*)

Ray Davis owned the 1807 House in New Jersey where many collectors knew they could find a good decoy during the early days of collecting. (*Photo Courtesy of Joseph French*)

Right: Somers Headley of New Jersey drew on his personal shorebird hunting experiences when he co-authored *Shorebirds: The Birds, the Hunter, the Decoys* with John M. Levinson. (*Photo Courtesy of Joseph French*)

Dick Brust of Minneapolis, Minnesota, specializes in collecting teal decoys and was instrumental in the formation of the Minnesota Decoy Collectors Club, which meets yearly at a winter decoy show and features a classic Minnesota decoy exhibition, an antique decoy contest, and a collectors' show. (*Photo Courtesy of Joseph French*)

James McCleery of Pasadena, Texas, one of the true gentlemen of decoy collecting, was one of the first collectors to establish the present value of the hunting decoy by paying the before-unheard-of price of $10,000 for a Bill Bowman Curlew in the William Mackey estate sale in 1973. It was quite a bargain by today's rates! The McCleery collection exhibits one of the most diverse selections of pristine waterfowling decoys and was featured in a Houston Museum of National History exhibit and hard cover publication, *Call to the Sky* by Wm. Shaw. (*Photo Courtesy of Joseph French*)

The late Stan Glassmeyer of Ohio was a grassroots collector, a man who loved to hunt ducks and started to bring decoys into his home to enjoy. (*Photo Courtesy of Joseph French*)

The late Hy Dahlka, was a major force among decoy collectors in Michigan for many years. He is pictured here in his basement with James Foote, premier contemporary decoy carver of the 1970s and a fellow collector from the Detroit area. (*Photo Courtesy of Joseph French*)

Phyllis Elliston (1911–1991) of Michigan was one of the few women who collected decoys during the 1960s. She housed her collection in an old church building. (*Photo Courtesy of Joseph French*)

During the 1970s, Edward DeNavarre of Detroit, Michigan, had one of the finest collections of Michigan and St. Clair Flats decoys in the country. (*Photo Courtesy of Joseph French*)

Chapter 2
Waterfowling

The North American continent bypassed all the restrictions of the old world. In this new land, settlers found breathtaking vistas populated by abundant wildlife, and they believed that wildlife belonged to all of the people, not just the wealthy and royal. Common men took to the field to feed their family. These hunters often ignored waterfowl and game birds in favor of big game because birds were too small and hard to kill for the average hunter. Waterfowling was left to the market hunters who devised methods of killing birds as they rafted on the water in huge flocks using large 8-gauge or battery guns resting across the stern of a sneak boat. A single volley from these cannon-like guns would down whole flocks. As the gunner gathered up the dead game, he would finish off disabled birds with a smaller gun—hardly sporting, but gunning for the market was a respectable occupation then and not an easy job. For an average shoot, the professional hunter needed to have at least two-hundred shells. Most hunters hand loaded empty brass or paper shell casings sold by the ammunition companies with black powder to save money even after pre-loaded shells were available. The black powder was sold in wooden kegs and small tins that were usually decorated with company logos and graphics. The earliest examples of gunpowder tins were decorated with stenciled designs. As printing became more affordable, the tins were imprinted with graphics or printed paper labels were applied to the cans. Printed labels were often glued unto the ends of wooden and metal powder kegs. While there is a strong following of sporting tin collectors, many collectors of related items find these small colorful tins make great accenting pieces for their collections.

Shooting ducks, shorebirds, geese, and swans with no restrictions other than human endurance, the market hunter would kill a hundred or more birds on a good day. Usually working in teams, market hunters spent several days at a campsite. Their day began well before sunrise to insure a prime hunting spot. When the shooting was done, the day's kill was taken back to the campsite to be sorted, cooled, bundled, and tagged. The birds were then stored in an ice house until they could be shipped via the railroad to the commission brokers of the major cities. Wild game was a popular dinner item and sold to the general public and restaurants. The average prices for birds ranged from ten cents for small shorebirds to three dollars for the succulent canvasback.

Etching by Richard Bishop, circa 1930, $300.

Improvement in weaponry resulted in shotguns with choked barrels that increased the effectiveness of shot to ranges of forty yards. Birds could now be shot in flight by the average marksman, even with lighter, smaller-gauge guns. Inexpensive, pre-loaded shells were introduced and aggressively marketed by a growing number of ammunition companies. A representative of the gun industry testified before the United States House of Representatives that sixty-six factories were producing firearms and ammunition in 1911, according to *Our Vanishing Wildlife* by William T. Hornaday.

Black powder was replaced by smokeless powder. A hunter no longer had to duck under a heavy cloud of noxious white smoke to see if he made his shot. In 1897, Winchester Arms Company offered the hunter an affordable pump shotgun that would change waterfowling so greatly that early conservationists cautioned that the new pump shotgun, which allowed the hunter to pump seven shells through the firing chamber without reloading, would result in the extinction of all game birds.

Waterfowling took on a different slant. It became a gentlemanly sport—a tradition that was handed down from father to son. As more men learned the thrill of waterfowling for sport, individuals joined together to control the better hunting areas. Clubs were formed that became fraternities. Clubhouses were built to accommodate members. The newly developed railroad systems made it possible for a hunter from almost any major city to board a train, have dinner, play a few hands of cards in a club car, retire to his Pullman car for the evening, and arrive at a prime hunting region the next day. Locals provided services to make the hunters' visit more pleasant. Club caretakers would prepare the grounds for hunting, pick the hunters up at the station, and transport them to the clubhouse. Local guides or "pushers" made a living push-poling a small skiff into a hunting pothole, providing a good hunting spot, and retrieving dead birds. The ladies would fix meals and clean the game. The hunters would often stay at the clubhouse for a week or two, gathering in the evening for drinks and cards as they shared their hunting tales. When locals found much of the hunting grounds were being controlled by outsiders, they too banded together to form clubs. Today most hunting sites are under the control of private clubs or state and federal governments.

Print on canvas of waterfowling scene, circa 1920, $150.

Print of hunter shooting over dogs, typical of 1900 commercial wildlife art, $150.

A market hunter poses with a day's kill of canvasbacks on Heron Lake, Minnesota, circa 1910. Today's conservationists cringe at sights like this, but market hunting was a respectable occupation at the turn of the century. Wild game graced the tables of fine restaurants as well as the family dinner table. (*Photograph Courtesy of Morton Smith, Jr.*)

Heron Lake is the site of an ambitious multi-million dollar project to reverse damage caused by years of pollution, carp infestation, and farm runoff. The project encompasses a complete watershed area and is spearheaded by joint state, federal, and private efforts. Hopefully waterfowl population will return to the 1920 levels when this photo was taken. (*Courtesy of Morton Smith, Jr.*)

Morton Smith and a friend pose with day's kill from Heron Lake, Minnesota. Canvasback shooting on Heron Lake was so phenomenal that the area was known as "the Chesapeake of the West" until the 1920s when pollution, siltation, and the introduction of carp destroyed the wild celery beds that drew the canvasback to Heron Lake each spring and fall. (*Courtesy of Morton Smith, Jr.*)

Leather Von Lengerke & Antoine gunning box with hand-loaded shells for Douglas Moseley, decoy carver and charter member of the Princeton Fish and Game Club, circa 1920. $750.

A. F. & Co., Golden Pheasant gunpowder tin, $850.

Assorted pin backs: Remmington-UMC, auto loading and pump shotguns, $75-100 each; Remmington bears, $100-125 each; Remmington Quail, $30; Remmington Grouse, $30; Laflin & Rand Infallible, $30 each; Miscellaneous DuPont powder, $25 each; Daisy Manufacturing Company, Air Rifle, $75; Miscellaneous powder companies, $35-50; circa 1930-40

Wooden carrying case for brass casings with compartment for reloading tools, circa 1910, $400.

Eight-gauge, empty pre-primed paper shotgun shell casings, $75 each.

Rare Winchester Repeating Arms Co. 4-gauge shotgun shell casings, brass, $300 each; and paper, $150 each. The brass shell extractor was used when repeated firings made the spent casings too hot to handle. $250.

American Powder Mills, Boston, Massachusetts, tin gunpowder keg, Dead Shot Sporting Powder, 5 pound, circa 1880, $400.

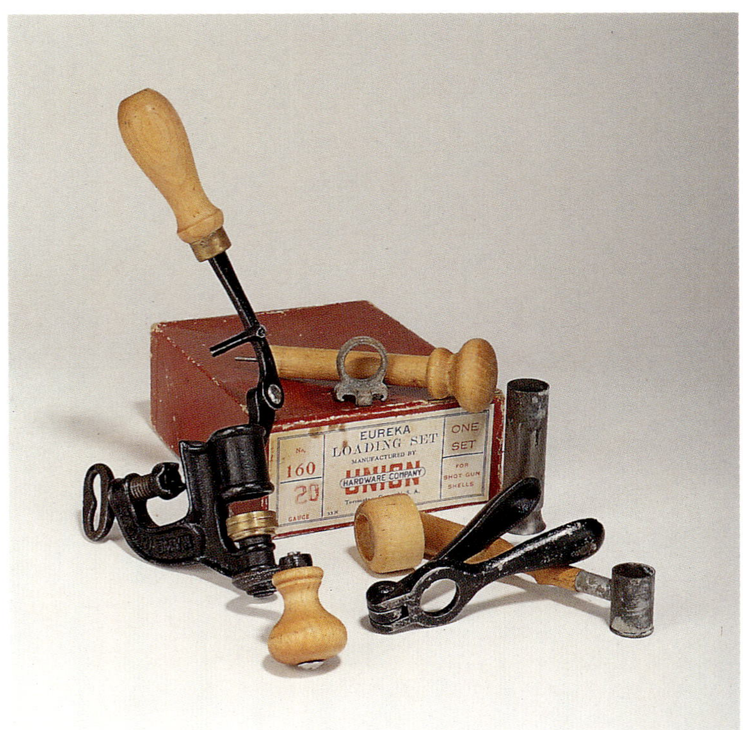

Eureka reloading tool kit, Union Hardware Co., 20 gauge, $100.

American Powder Mills Dead Shot gunpowder tins: Left, one-pound tin, $350; five-pound tin, rare, $1,000.

American Powder Mills collectibles, left to right: Dead Shot Sporting powder tin, $250; Dead Shot, $350, and Wing Shot Powder, $350.

American Powder Mills, variations of Dead Shot gunpowder tins, left to right: large red can, $300; small red can, $200, and rare black and white label, green can, $500.

Hand and Bench Crimper #7, Bridgeport Gun Implement Co., Bridgeport, Connecticut, 1883 patent application, $100.

Handmade wooden shotgun shell reloading box with miscellaneous tools, $200.

Handmade wooden shotgun shell box with miscellaneous reloading tools, $100; Union Metallic Cartridge Co., Bridgeport, Connecticut, gun wads, $10; Winchester #4 primers, Winchester Repeating Arms Co., New Haven, Connecticut, $10; paper shotgun shell casings 4-gauge, $100 each, and Winchester brass shotgun shell casings, 4-gauge $200 each.

Shotgun shell box closed.

Canadian Industries Ltd., Snap Shot Black Sporting Powder, two sizes of front and back labels, $150 each.

Back label of Honker can.

Curtis & Harvey's Honker gunpowder tin, extremely rare, circa 1900, $2,500.

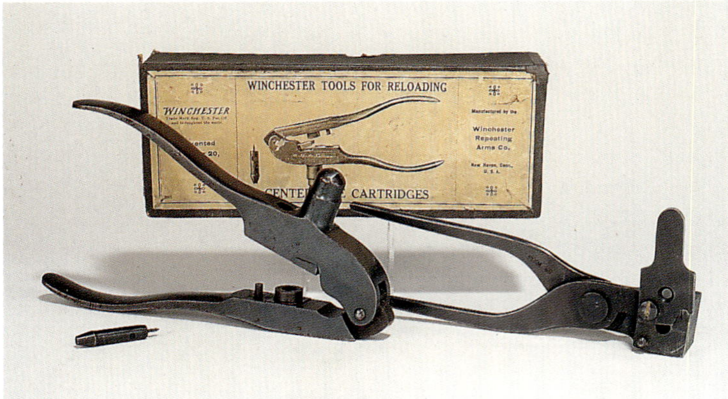

Winchester reloading tool for center fire shells, Winchester Repeating Arms Co., New Haven, Connecticut, $150 each.

Miscellaneous gunpowder advertising pins, $25-50 each. *(Courtesy Collection of Rick Simmons)*

Winchester metal store plaque, circa 1900, $200; and Winchester Repeating Arms Co. gun oil can, $35.

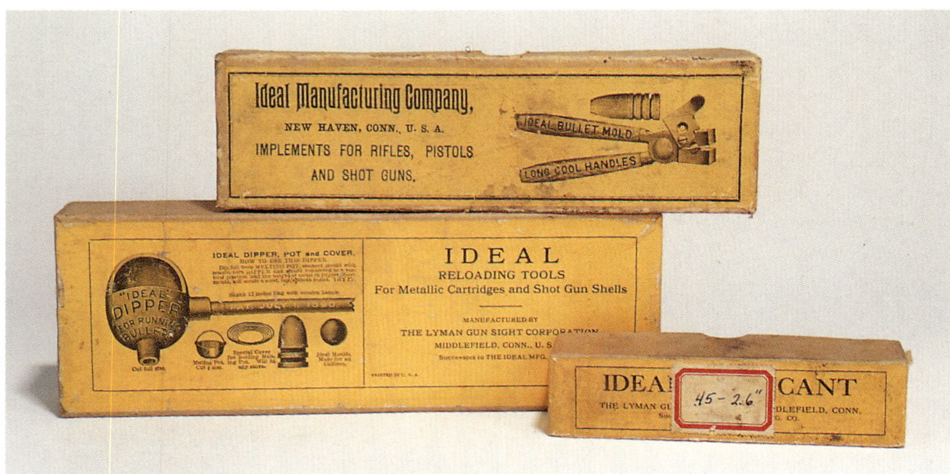

Ideal reloading kits, Ideal Manufacturing Co., New Haven, Connecticut, top to bottom: lead bullet mold, $50; dipper, pot, and cover for metallic and shotgun shells, $50, and gun lubricant, $10.

Ideal Manufacturing Co. bullet reloading kit with bullet holders, $200.

Shot shell advertising box inserts, E. I. DuPont de Nemours & Co., $100 each.

E. I. DuPont de Nemours & Co., Wilmington, Delaware, tin gunpowder keg, 5 pounds, Smokeless Powder, circa 1920, $400.

Left to right: E. I. DuPont de Nemours & Co., Schultze Gunpowder tin, $400; United States Sporting Co., San Francisco, California, Gold Dust Shot Gunpowder tin, $300, and Nobel's Empire smokeless powder, Nobel's Explosives Co., London, England, $200.

Shot shell box insert, E. I. DuPont de Nemours & Co., safety warning, $25.

Left to right: E.I. DuPont de Nemours & Co., Eagle Gunpowder Tin (Note: label is always ripped because an opening pull-string was glued under the label), rare, $700.

Handmade gunning box with gun rest used on Lake Koshkonong, Wisconsin, unknown maker, $150.

Boxed reloading kit for Ballard rifle bullets, $500; Winchester 32-caliber grooved bullets, $50; Marlin Firearms Co., Buffalo, New York, Ballard Rifle bullets, 32-caliber, $50; Peters Cartridge Co. grooved bullets, 32 caliber, $50.

Handmade gunning box with gun rest, unknown maker, from Lake Poygon, Wisconsin, $300.

Left to right: Hazard Powder Co., Duck Shooting Powder tin, $400; Warren Powder Mills, Boston, Massachusetts, Snap Shot Powder tin, $600, and Brackett's Sporting Powder, Westchester, Massachusetts, stenciled curlew, rare, circa 1860, $1,200.

Hazard Powder Co., extremely rare square powder tins, three-part set: Smokeless Rifle Powder, $2,000; 30 Caliber Smokeless Powder, $2,000, and Smokeless Rifle Powder #2, $2,000. (*Courtesy Collection of Ron Willoughby/Photography by Ron Willoughby*)

Hazard Powder Co., New York, New York, tin gunpowder keg, Sea Shooting Powder, 5 pounds, circa 1890, $250.

Hazard Powder Co., tin gunpowder keg, five pounds, Duck Shooting powder, circa 1880, $700.

Hazard Powder Co., wooden gunpowder keg with wooden bands, five pounds, Sea Shooting powder (duck size), circa 1880, $800.

Left to right: Imperial Powder tin, New Hampshire, circa 1900, $400; Imperial Gunpowder tin, circa 1900, $400, and Nobel's Empire, England, smokeless sporting powder, circa 1920, $175.

Left to right: Laflin & Rand Powder Co., New York, New York: Orange Rifle Powder tin, $800; Hazard Powder Co., American Sporting Gunpowder tin, $800, and American Powder Mills, Boston, Massachusetts, Duck and Sea Shooting Gunpowder tin, $600.

Left to right: Indian Rifle Gunpowder tin, circa 1920, $200; Hazard Powder Co. Duck Shooting Gunpowder tin, $400, and Kings Powder Co., Kings Mills, Ohio, Quick Shot Gunpowder tin, $600.

The Winter Brothers Co., which operated a meat locker in Spirit Lake, Iowa, was one of several commission brokers who hired local men to hunt waterfowl for the market. This group from the communities surrounding Heron Lake, Minnesota, including Morton W. Smith on the far right, was captured on film after a day of shooting ducks on Heron Lake, known as the "Chesapeake of the West" because of its fabled canvasback hunting. The hunters were given gunpowder and shot to load their shells and paid per bird: 50 cents for canvasbacks, 40 cents for mallards, and 20 cents for teal and bluebills. Circa 1900. (*Courtesy of Morton Smith, Jr.*)

Left to right: Laflin & Rand Powder Co., Orange Ducking Powder tin, $400; Hamilton Powder Co., Ontario Canada, Snapshot powder tin, $250, and American Powder Mills, #3 Ducking gunpowder tin, $200.

Left to right: Oriental Powder Co., South Windham, Maine, Oriental Smokeless Gunpowder tin, $400; Hazard Powder Co., Hazard Smokeless gunpowder tin, $500, and A.C. Thompson Co. Ltd., Sydney, Australia, American Rifle powder tin, $400.

Mathewson's Superior Rifle Powder tin, five pounds, circa 1900, $500.

Tom Palmer and Morton Smith are shown preparing birds for the market, circa 1900. Sorted by species, bundled, and hung to cool, the birds would later be transferred to an icehouse to be frozen and then shipped by rail to Minneapolis. (*Photo Courtesy of Morton Smith, Jr.*)

Market tags were usually supplied by the commission brokers listing the species they would buy. (*Courtesy of John Herman*)

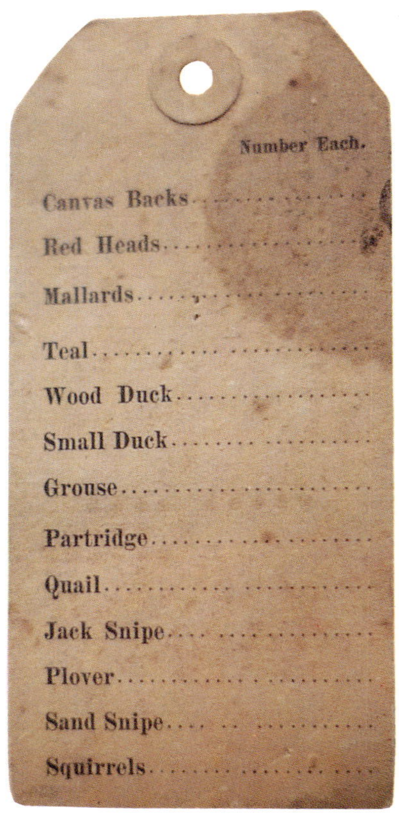

Game tag for commission broker dealing in waterfowl, circa 1920.

Andrew Bierbrodt (1928–1997) of Spring Valley, Illinois, had this picture taken on his fifth birthday after his father and uncles took him to the West End Gun Club to hunt ducks. Notice his new "pint-sized" double-barrel shotgun. Circa 1933.

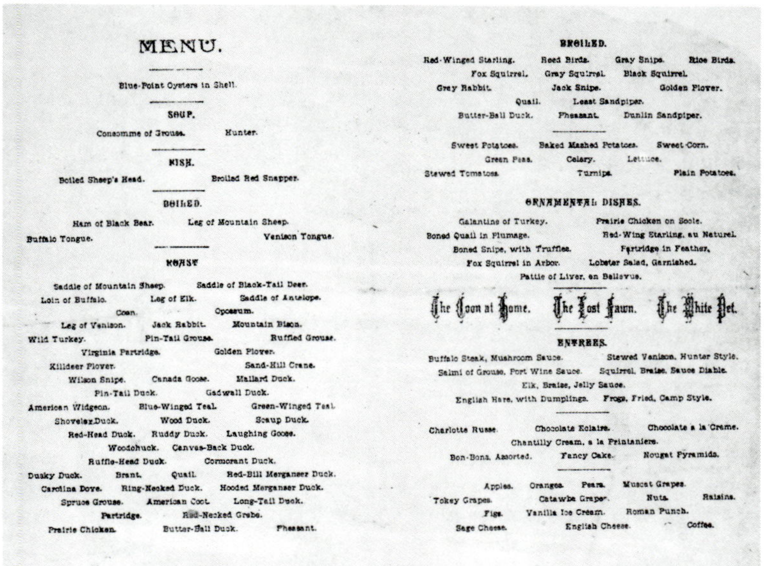

MENU.

Blue-Point Oysters in Shell.

SOUP.

Consomme of Grouse. Hunter.

FISH.

Boiled Sheep's Head. Broiled Red Snapper.

BOILED.

Ham of Black Bear. Leg of Mountain Sheep.
Buffalo Tongue. Venison Tongue.

ROAST

Saddle of Mountain Sheep. Saddle of Black-Tail Deer.
Loin of Buffalo. Leg of Elk. Saddle of Antelope.
Coon. Opossum.
Leg of Venison. Jack Rabbit. Mountain Bison.
Wild Turkey. Pin-Tail Grouse. Ruffled Grouse.
Virginia Partridge. Golden Plover.
Killdeer Plover. Sand-Hill Crane.
Wilson Snipe. Canada Goose. Mallard Duck.
Pin-Tail Duck. Gadwall Duck.
American Widgeon. Blue-Winged Teal. Green-Winged Teal.
Shoveler Duck. Wood Duck. Scaup Duck.
Red-Head Duck. Ruddy Duck. Laughing Goose.
Woodchuck. Canvas-Back Duck.
Ruffle-Head Duck. Cormorant Duck.
Dusky Duck. Brant. Quail. Red-Bill Merganser Duck.
Carolina Dove. Ring-Necked Duck. Hooded Merganser Duck.
Spruce Grouse. American Coot. Long-Tail Duck.
Partridge. Red-Necked Grebe.
Prairie Chicken. Butter-Ball Duck. Pheasant.

BROILED.

Red-Winged Starling. Reed Birds. Gray Snipe. Rice Birds.
Fox Squirrel. Gray Squirrel. Black Squirrel.
Grey Rabbit. Jack Snipe. Golden Plover.
Quail. Least Sandpiper.
Butter-Ball Duck. Pheasant. Dunlin Sandpiper.

Sweet Potatoes. Baked Mashed Potatoes. Sweet Corn.
Green Peas. Celery. Lettuce.
Stewed Tomatoes. Turnips. Plain Potatoes.

ORNAMENTAL DISHES.

Galantine of Turkey. Prairie Chicken on Socle.
Boned Quail in Plumage. Red-Wing Starling, au Naturel.
Boned Snipe, with Truffles. Partridge in Feather.
Fox Squirrel in Arbor. Lobster Salad, Garnished.
Pattie of Liver, en Bellevue.

The Coon at Home. The Lost Fawn. The White Pet.

ENTREES.

Buffalo Steak, Mushroom Sauce. Stewed Venison, Hunter Style.
Salmi of Grouse, Port Wine Sauce. Squirrel, Braise, Sauce Diable.
Elk, Braise, Jelly Sauce.
English Hare, with Dumplings. Frogs, Fried, Camp Style.

Charlotte Russe. Chocolate Eclaire. Chocolate a la Creme.
Chantilly Cream, a la Printaniere.
Bon-Bons, Assorted. Fancy Cake. Nougat Pyramids.

Apples. Oranges. Pears. Muscat Grapes.
Tokey Grapes. Catawba Grapes. Nuts. Raisins.
Figs. Vanilla Ice Cream. Roman Punch.
Sage Cheese. English Cheese. Coffee.

Wild game was a popular fare at most of the better restaurants. The Grand Pacific Hotel in Chicago used this menu for their annual game dinner held on November 22, 1879.
(*Courtesy of Morton Smith, Jr.*)

Railroad lines offered special rates and accommodations for sportsmen traveling to prime waterfowling areas. It was not uncommon for a gentleman from a major city to belong to a distant hunting club where he would go waterfowling several times a year.

Hunters at West End Gun Club captured a day of hunting on film, circa 1930.
(*Courtesy of Andrew Bierbrodt*)

BY-LAWS

THE WEST END GUN CLUB
(Incorporated)
Spring Valley, Illinois

June 1, 1926

GAZETTE PRINT SPRING VALLEY

Rule book of the West End Gun Club, located on Turner Lake (locally known as Mud Lake) in Putman County, Illinois. The club is still operated by forty shareholders.

Sons learned the thrill of waterfowling early. Duck hunting was an important part of life in a river town. (*Courtesy of George Campbell*)

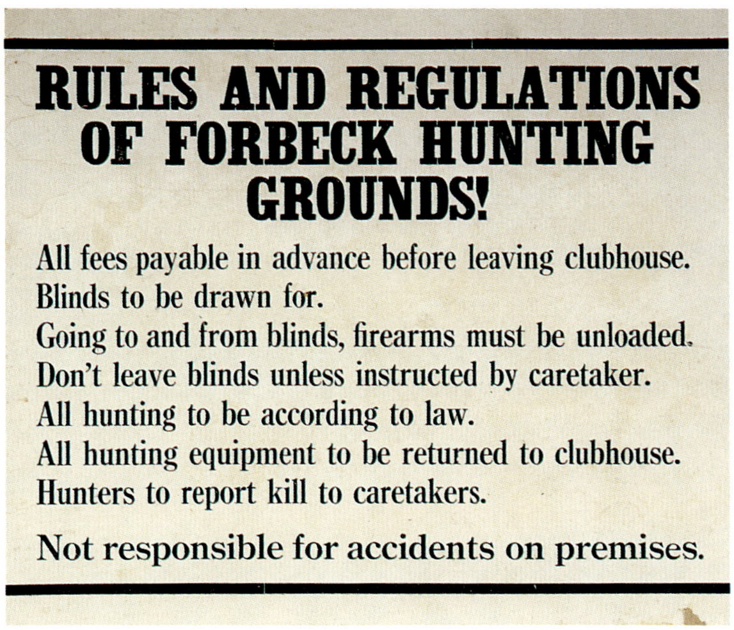

RULES AND REGULATIONS OF FORBECK HUNTING GROUNDS!

All fees payable in advance before leaving clubhouse.
Blinds to be drawn for.
Going to and from blinds, firearms must be unloaded.
Don't leave blinds unless instructed by caretaker.
All hunting to be according to law.
All hunting equipment to be returned to clubhouse.
Hunters to report kill to caretakers.

Not responsible for accidents on premises.

Posting from Forbeck Hunting Grounds.

Ted Bailey and his father shared many pleasurable moments at the Princeton Game and Fish Club. Ted bought his own share in this famous gunning club and hunted there until his death. (*Courtesy of Mrs. T. Bailey*)

Many duck hunting clubs used a houseboat as a portable clubhouse because they concentrated their hunting in different areas depending on the season, spring or fall. This is the Hennipen Shooting Club houseboat moored on east shore of Illinois River below Hennipen, Illinois. Circa 1880. (*Courtesy of the Putman Historical Society*)

Advertising mirror, Greenwing Gun Club, Bureau County, Illinois, circa 1920, $250.

Hennipen Shooting Club in Hennipen, Illinois, was incorporated in 1887 by a group of Chicago businessmen. It was one of the earliest organized hunting clubs on the Illinois River, located by Hennipen on the "Big Bend" of the river. Here the river turned southward and spread over its banks each spring, creating a honeycomb of backwater ponds and marshes that drew migrating waterfowl by the tens of thousands. Circa 1880.

N. E. Simonsen, President
2243 Orrington Ave.
Evanston

George C. Davis, Vice President
422 Milwaukee Ave.

C. P. Zacher, Sec'y-Treas.
1842 E. 79th Street
7955 S. Ashland Ave
Vincennes 9300

Office of Secretary - Treasurer

Senachwine Club

1842 E. 79th Street
7955 S. Ashland Ave.
Phone South Shore 5050
Vincennes 9300
Chicago

Directors
N. E. Simonsen
George C. Davis
C. P. Zacher
Chas. E. Carson
Harry Severson
A. L. Wilcoxson
Gerald W. Peck

Grounds: Putnam, Ill.

Letterhead from the Senachwine Club, Putman County, Illinois, circa 1930.

Hennipen Shooting Club sign off of original clubhouse boat, circa 1890, $1, 500, and an extremely rare carved duck call with unusual leaf and vine relief carving by George Cunningham (1842–1923) of Hennipen, Illinois, first caretaker and guide at Hennipen Shooting Club, circa 1892, his own Glodo-style call with metal bands, circa 1880, $8,000.

Rule book from the Hennipen Shooting Club.

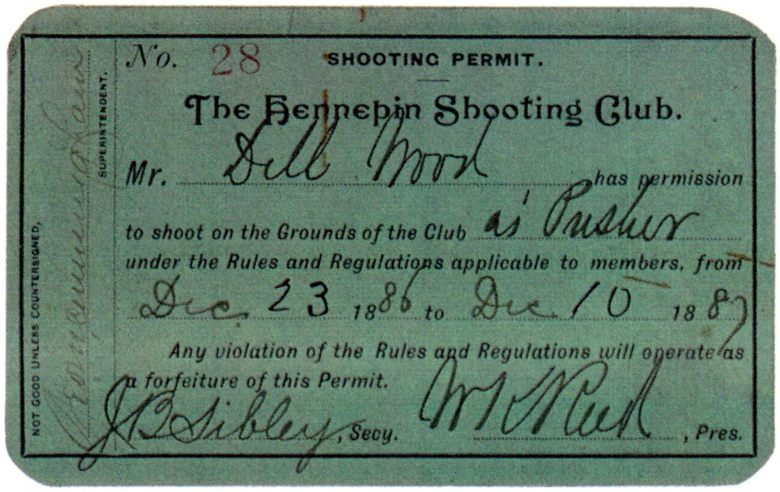

No. 28 SHOOTING PERMIT.

The Hennepin Shooting Club.

Mr. Dell Wood has permission to shoot on the Grounds of the Club as Pusher under the Rules and Regulations applicable to members, from Dec 23 1886 to Dec 10 1887

Any violation of the Rules and Regulations will operate as a forfeiture of this Permit.

J B Sibley, Secy. , Pres.

NOT GOOD UNLESS COUNTERSIGNED, SUPERINTENDENT.

Shooting pass from the Hennipen Shooting Club, issued to Dell Wood, pusher and one-time caretaker of the club.

When the Chicago Drainage District started their extensive drainage program, which eventually reversed the flow of the Chicago River, the hunting grounds of the Hennipen Shooting Club on the east banks of the Illinois River were completely drained and the club disbanded and reformed as the Senachwine Club. Incorporated in 1902, the Senachwine Club abuts the southern boundaries of the Princeton Game and Fish Club on Goose Pond on the opposite side of the Illinois River.

Rule book for the Mallard Club, established during the late 1800s and still owned and controlled by the Miller family in Bureau County, Illinois.

The West End Gun Club in Putman County, near Spring Valley, Illinois, was formed by local hunters when out-of-towners started to gain control of the better hunting grounds along the Illinois River. Commonly called Mud Lake, West End Club still operates today and remains a blue-collar club. The club's main hunting areas were on the land-locked Turner Lake. The houseboat was used as rest stop when members hunted grounds on both sides of the river. Circa 1933. (*Courtesy of Andrew Bierbrodt*)

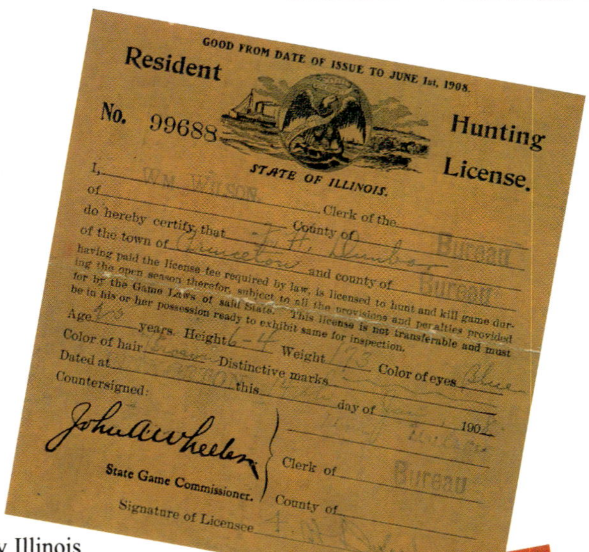

GOOD FROM DATE OF ISSUE TO JUNE 1st, 1908.

Resident Hunting License.

No. 99688

STATE OF ILLINOIS.

I, W. M. Wilson, Clerk of the County of Bureau do hereby certify that ... of the town of Princeton and county of Bureau having paid the license fee required by law, is licensed to hunt and kill game during the open season therefor, subject to all the provisions and penalties provided for by the Game Laws of said State. This license is not transferable and must be in his or her possession ready to exhibit same for inspection.

Age ... years. Height 6-4 Weight 173 Color of eyes Blue

Color of hair ... Distinctive marks ...

Dated at ... this ... day of ... 190...

Countersigned: John A. Wheeler, State Game Commissioner.

Clerk of Bureau County of ...

Signature of Licensee ...

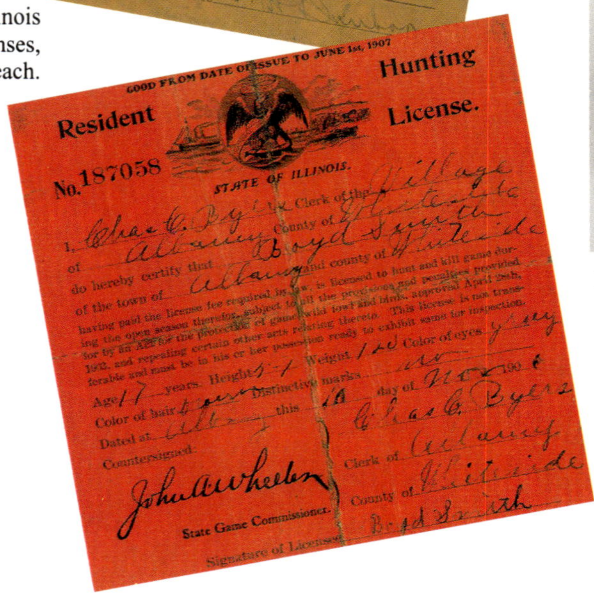

GOOD FROM DATE OF ISSUE TO JUNE 1st, 1907

Resident Hunting License.

No. 187058

STATE OF ILLINOIS.

I, ... Clerk of the ... County of ... do hereby certify that ... of the town of ... and county of ... having paid the license fee required by law, is licensed to hunt and kill game during the open season therefor, subject to all the provisions and penalties provided for by an Act for the protection of game ... This license is not transferable and must be in his or her possession ready to exhibit same for inspection.

Age ... years. Height ... Weight ... Color of eyes ...

Color of hair ... Distinctive marks ...

Dated at ... this ... day of ... 190...

Countersigned: John A. Wheeler, State Game Commissioner.

Clerk of ... County of ...

Signature of Licensee ...

Early Illinois waterfowling licenses, $200 each.

Miscellaneous embroidered patches, circa 1930–40, $25-35 each. (*Collection of Dean Dashner*)

Belonging to Princeton Game and Fish Club meant being a part of a fraternity of Bureau County's elite. This remains one of the most prestigious hunting clubs in the country. Here everyone gathers in front of the clubhouse after breakfast to have a club picture taken by a professional photographer on opening day, which was reserved for members-only hunting. (*Courtesy of Dr. S. Kolwalski*)

Rule book of the Princeton Game and Fish Club in Bureau County, Illinois.

Princeton Game and Fish Club minutes document a month-long stay in 1914 by William Schmedigan, a professional wildlife illustrator. This painting of canvasbacks over Rousseau Lake on the club grounds hung in the clubhouse for many years.

Ted Bailey, Richard Fuller, and Marion Black on boat landing of Princeton Fish and Game Club, circa 1947. (*Courtesy of Mrs. T. Bailey*)

Miscellaneous Wisconsin buttons; guide, hunting license, and warden badges, and a trapping permit, circa 1950, $100-300 each. (*Collection of Dean Dashner*)

Guides at Illinois River hunting clubs were often called "pushers" because one of their responsibilities was to push-pole the hunting skiff through the shallow backwaters to a hunting hole where a stationary platform blind was situated on the edge of patch of water cleared of aquatic plants. Decoys would be arranged in the clearing to attract ducks. (*Courtesy of Malcolm Clark*)

Duck hunters could easily conceal themselves and hunt in relative comfort in their blinds. This Illinois River hunter patiently awaits the next flight of timber mallards, circa 1930. (*Courtesy of Malcolm Clark*)

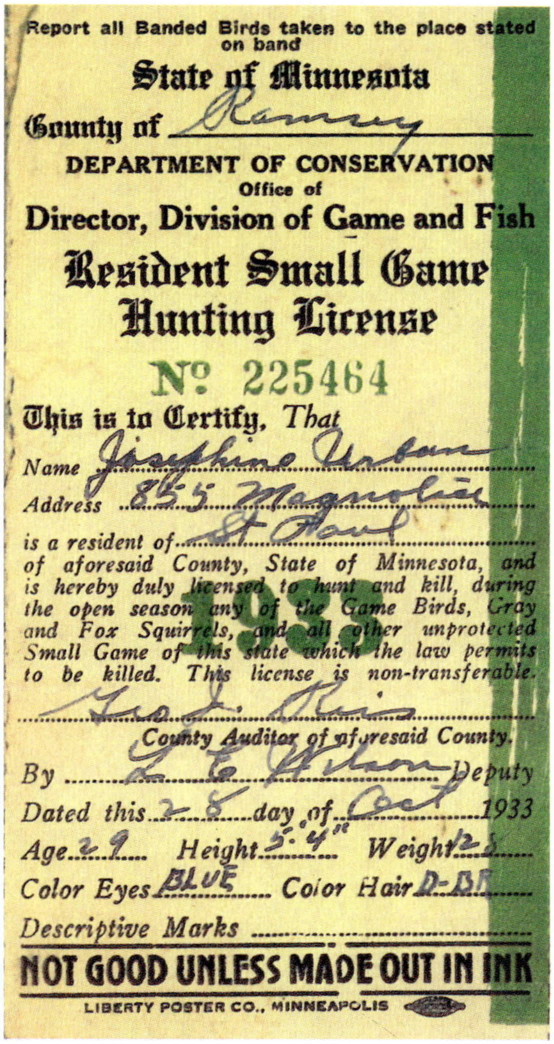

Report all Banded Birds taken to the place stated on band

State of Minnesota

County of Ramsey

DEPARTMENT OF CONSERVATION

Office of

Director, Division of Game and Fish

Resident Small Game Hunting License

No. 225464

This is to Certify, That

Name Josephine Urban

Address 855 Magnolia

is a resident of St Paul

of aforesaid County, State of Minnesota, and is hereby duly licensed to hunt and kill, during the open season any of the Game Birds, Gray and Fox Squirrels, and all other unprotected Small Game of this state which the law permits to be killed. This license is non-transferable.

1933

County Auditor of aforesaid County.

By .... Deputy

Dated this 28 day of Oct 1933

Age 29 Height 5'4" Weight ....

Color Eyes BLUE Color Hair D-BR

Descriptive Marks ....

NOT GOOD UNLESS MADE OUT IN INK

LIBERTY POSTER CO., MINNEAPOLIS

Hunting license from the State of Minnesota, 1933. $10.

Hunters relax outside the clubhouse at The Ranch, a noted hunting club on Heron Lake, Minnesota. Circa 1910. (*Courtesy of Morton Smith, Jr.*)

Boyd's "Hotel" was moored on the Illinois River near Beardstown, Illinois, another of that state's famed hunting regions. (*Courtesy of Malcolm Clark*)

Local ladies would always be willing to clean a hunter's birds for a price. (*Courtesy of Andrew Bierbrodt*)

Prior to federal legislation prohibiting baiting fields with feed, wild ducks and geese were drawn miles from their natural feeding areas into harvested corn fields that were baited. (*Photograph by Bob Becker, Chicago News Tribune staff writer, 1946/Courtesy of the Illinois Natural History Survey*)

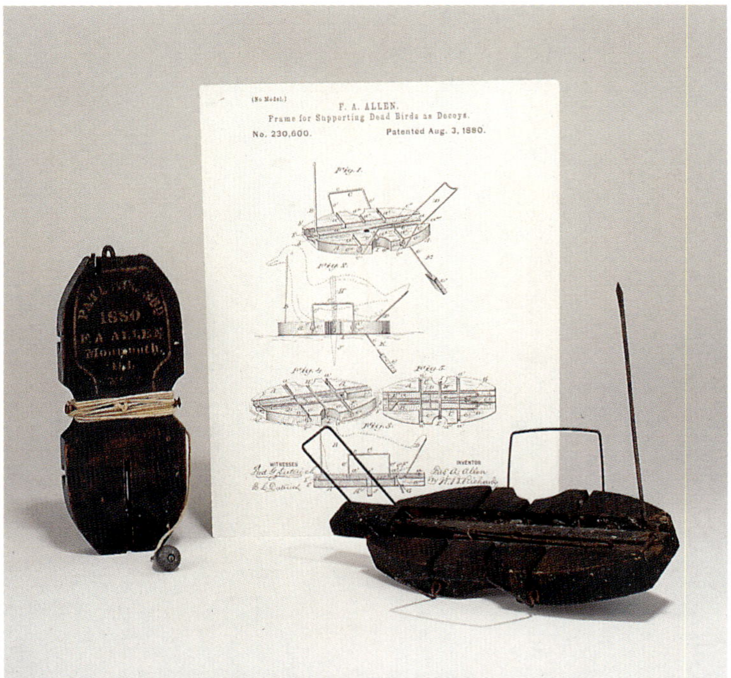

Fred Allen of Mommouth, Illinois, patented his decoy duck frame, a collapsible wood and wire frame that turned a dead bird into a floating decoy, in 1880. It was available in two sizes. $250 each.

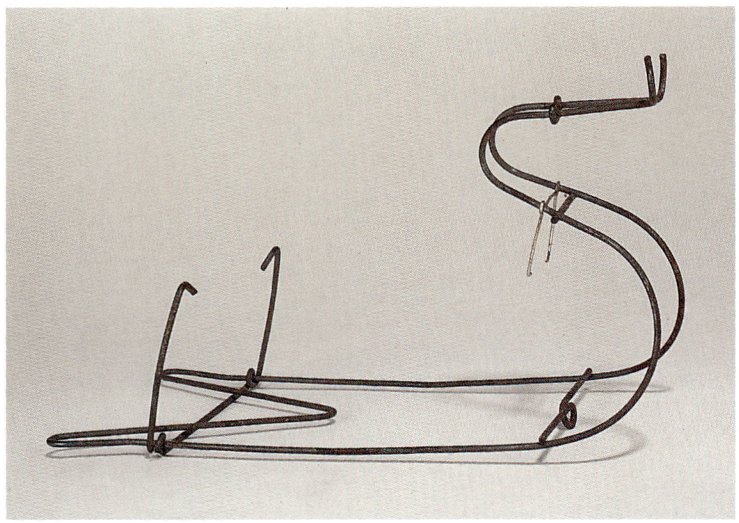

Little is known about this duck frame, which obviously was used for decoying. Circa 1930. $250.

John N. "Newt" Rule operated his hunting camp on Muscooten Bay at the convergence of the Sangamon and Illinois Rivers near Beardstown, Illinois, circa 1920. By 1930, his son-in-law, Warren Smith, joined him in his guiding operation. (*Courtesy of Mrs. R. Donaldson*)

Brochure promoting hunting near Beardstown.

When baiting was banned in southern Illinois, Newt Rule produced several dozen corn decoy. With individual kernels notched out for added realism, Rule's ears are the best known examples of working corn decoys. $500 each.

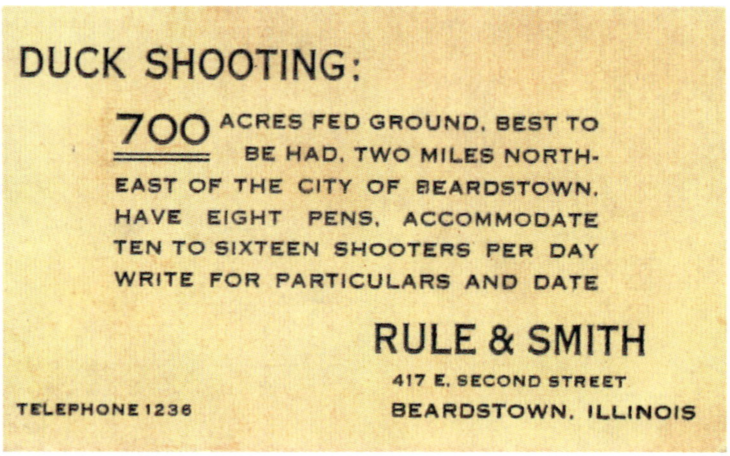
DUCK SHOOTING:

700 ACRES FED GROUND, BEST TO BE HAD, TWO MILES NORTH-EAST OF THE CITY OF BEARDSTOWN. HAVE EIGHT PENS, ACCOMMODATE TEN TO SIXTEEN SHOOTERS PER DAY WRITE FOR PARTICULARS AND DATE

RULE & SMITH
417 E. SECOND STREET
BEARDSTOWN, ILLINOIS

TELEPHONE 1236

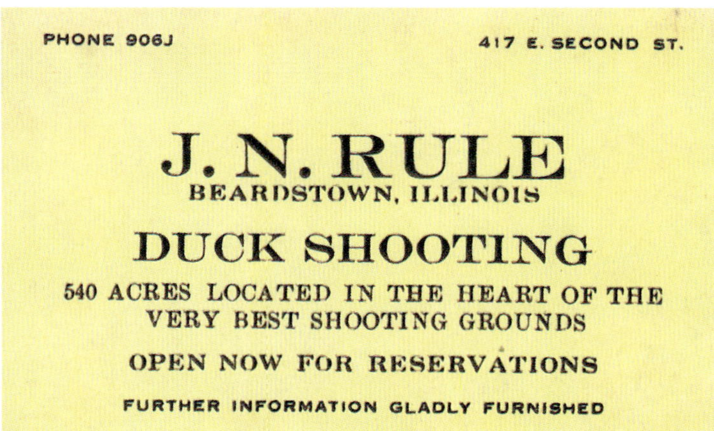
PHONE 906J

417 E. SECOND ST.

J. N. RULE
BEARDSTOWN, ILLINOIS

DUCK SHOOTING

540 ACRES LOCATED IN THE HEART OF THE VERY BEST SHOOTING GROUNDS

OPEN NOW FOR RESERVATIONS

FURTHER INFORMATION GLADLY FURNISHED

Newt Rule's business card.

The Carry-Lite Decoy Co. of Milwaukee manufactured a line of paper mâche corn decoys, which were shipped in a cardboard carton that held three dozen ears with graphics that showed a hunter shooting Canada geese in a field over Carry-Lite corn decoys, $40 each.

Advertising for Carry-Lite corn decoys.

Miscellaneous handmade wooden corn decoys, Illinois River region, makers unknown. $200 each.

Miscellaneous handmade wooden corn decoys used in Nebraska, South Dakota, and Illinois, $200 each.

Cobbe Corn Decoys came by the dozen in a printed canvas bags. Manufactured by Bedard & Morency Mill Co., Oak Park, Illinois. Ears $200 each, complete set with bag, $2,500.

NEW DUCK DECOY

Will not fail to bring the birds. Hunt with this new lawful decoy. Exact replica of Cob Field Corn. It Floats. Will last for years. Packed 12 to a box, assorted sizes. If your dealer cannot supply you send $9.75. Box of 12 will be sent postpaid.

BEDARD & MORENCY MILL COMPANY
101 No. Lombard Ave.
Oak Park, Ill.

Patent Applied For

Cobbe Corn Decoy ad.

Signs were posted in areas where live decoys were being used to protect the birds from other hunters. A bird handler often tied a red ribbon to his decoy's leg so it could be seen in flight.

Smaller English mallards crossbred with wild mallards were considered the best live decoys by most hunters. Even wild birds were easily imprinted and trained using corn. Feeding the live decoys in a hunting boat induced the birds to head straight for the skiff when they were released. circa 1930. (*Courtesy of Malcolm Clark*)

Often one of the duties of the club caretaker was to tend to the live decoys on the club grounds. Good decoys were so valued that they were usually taken home during the off season by the caretaker and members.

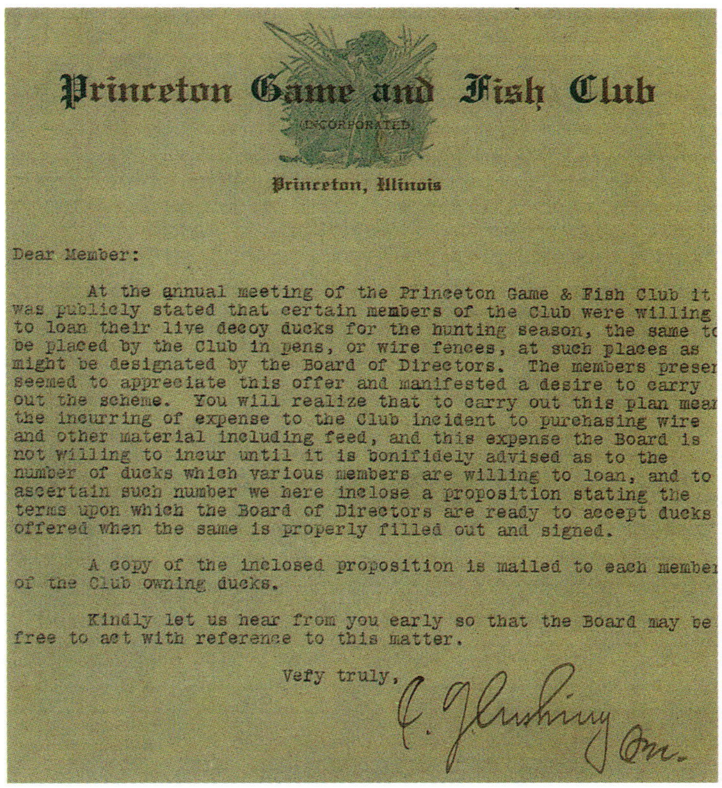

Princeton Game and Fish Club
(INCORPORATED)
Princeton, Illinois

Dear Member:

At the annual meeting of the Princeton Game & Fish Club it was publicly stated that certain members of the Club were willing to loan their live decoy ducks for the hunting season, the same t be placed by the Club in pens, or wire fences, at such places as might be designated by the Board of Directors. The members prese seemed to appreciate this offer and manifested a desire to carry out the scheme. You will realize that to carry out this plan mea the incurring of expense to the Club incident to purchasing wire and other material including feed, and this expense the Board is not willing to incur until it is bonifidely advised as to the number of ducks which various members are willing to loan, and to ascertain such number we here inclose a proposition stating the terms upon which the Board of Directors are ready to accept ducks offered when the same is properly filled out and signed.

A copy of the inclosed proposition is mailed to each membe of the Club owning ducks.

Kindly let us hear from you early so that the Board may be free to act with reference to this matter.

Very truly,
C. J. Cushing Pm.

Letters discussing the use of live decoys on Princeton Game and Fish Club grounds.

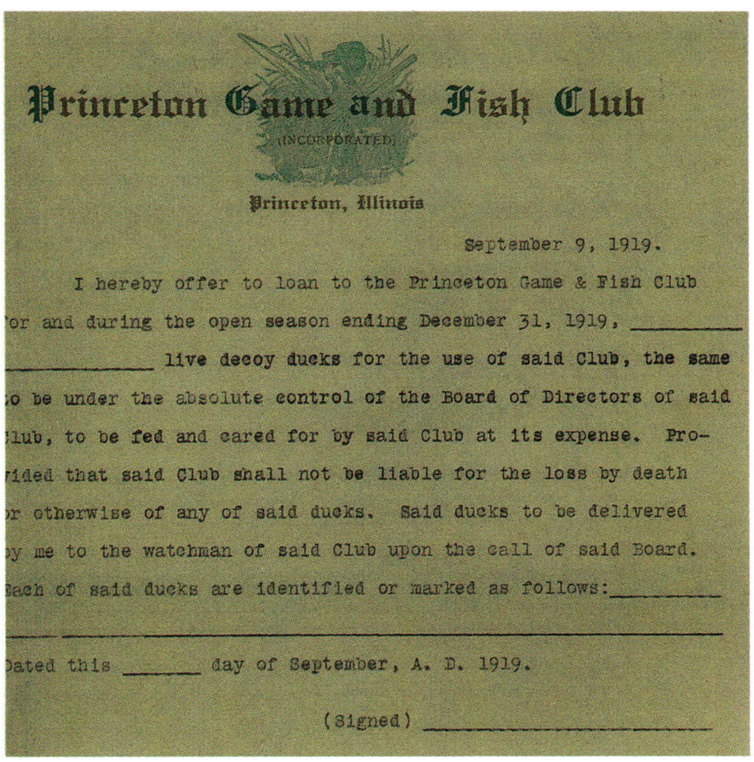

Princeton Game and Fish Club
(INCORPORATED)
Princeton, Illinois

September 9, 1919.

I hereby offer to loan to the Princeton Game & Fish Club 'or and during the open season ending December 31, 1919, _________ _________ live decoy ducks for the use of said Club, the same o be under the absolute control of the Board of Directors of said lub, to be fed and cared for by said Club at its expense. Pro- ided that said Club shall not be liable for the loss by death r otherwise of any of said ducks. Said ducks to be delivered y me to the watchman of said Club upon the call of said Board. Each of said ducks are identified or marked as follows:________

Dated this ______ day of September, A. D. 1919.

(Signed) ____________________

A small flock of tame ducks is penned off out of sight of the tethered decoy, making the ducks call back and forth loudly to attract passing wild ducks. (*Photo by Bob Becker, Chicago News Tribune, circa 1936/Courtesy of the Illinois Natural History Survey*)

It was pretty obvious that Albert "Stub" Lind's live decoys were comfortable in a hunting situation. Lind hunted Lake Poygon near Tustin, Wisconsin. Circa 1935. (*Courtesy of Dean Dashner*)

A hunter with well trained live decoys was usually a very successful hunter, but it took hours of patience and year-round care to create a good decoy. (*Courtesy of Malcolm Clark*)

Red Ideus, a guide and caretaker at the Schuler Gun Club, and a customer flank a live decoy standing on its carrying crate. Circa 1935. (*Courtesy of Malcolm Clark*)

Carrying crates like this were used to tote trained ducks to one's hunting hole. The homemade box fit between the hunter's legs on the bottom of his boat so he could reach in, grab his duck, and attach a harness easily. $500.

If you look closely in this carrying crate, you can see a mallard hen calmly waiting to be carted to the duck blind. $300. (*Courtesy of Dean Dashner*)

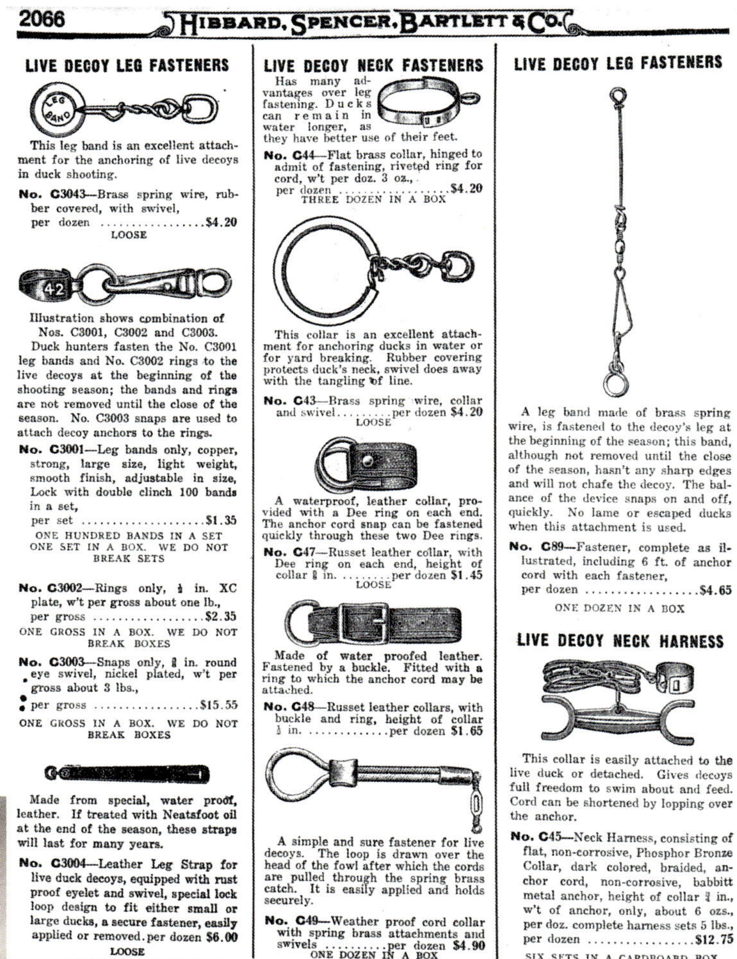

2066 HIBBARD, SPENCER, BARTLETT & CO.

LIVE DECOY LEG FASTENERS

This leg band is an excellent attachment for the anchoring of live decoys in duck shooting.

No. C3043—Brass spring wire, rubber covered, with swivel, per dozen $4.20
LOOSE

Illustration shows combination of Nos. C3001, C3002 and C3003.

Duck hunters fasten the No. C3001 leg bands and No. C3002 rings to the live decoys at the beginning of the shooting season; the bands and rings are not removed until the close of the season. No. C3003 snaps are used to attach decoy anchors to the rings.

No. C3001—Leg bands only, copper, strong, large size, light weight, smooth finish, adjustable in size, Lock with double clinch 100 bands in a set, per set $1.35
ONE HUNDRED BANDS IN A SET ONE SET IN A BOX. WE DO NOT BREAK SETS

No. C3002—Rings only, ½ in. XC plate, w't per gross about one lb., per gross $2.35
ONE GROSS IN A BOX. WE DO NOT BREAK BOXES

No. C3003—Snaps only, ⅜ in. round eye swivel, nickel plated, w't per gross about 3 lbs., per gross $15.55
ONE GROSS IN A BOX. WE DO NOT BREAK BOXES

Made from special, water proof, leather. If treated with Neatsfoot oil at the end of the season, these straps will last for many years.

No. C3004—Leather Leg Strap for live duck decoys, equipped with rust proof eyelet and swivel, special lock loop design to fit either small or large ducks, a secure fastener, easily applied or removed. per dozen $6.00
LOOSE

LIVE DECOY NECK FASTENERS

Has many advantages over leg fastening. Ducks can remain in water longer, as they have better use of their feet.

No. C44—Flat brass collar, hinged to admit of fastening, riveted ring for cord, w't per doz. 3 oz., per dozen $4.20
THREE DOZEN IN A BOX

This collar is an excellent attachment for anchoring ducks in water or for yard breaking. Rubber covering protects duck's neck, swivel does away with the tangling of line.

No. C43—Brass spring wire, collar and swivel.........per dozen $4.20
LOOSE

A waterproof, leather collar, provided with a Dee ring on each end. The anchor cord snap can be fastened quickly through these two Dee rings.

No. C47—Russet leather collar, with Dee ring on each end, height of collar ⅝ in. ....per dozen $1.45
LOOSE

Made of water proofed leather. Fastened by a buckle. Fitted with a ring to which the anchor cord may be attached.

No. C48—Russet leather collars, with buckle and ring, height of collar ¾ in. ....per dozen $1.65

A simple and sure fastener for live decoys. The loop is drawn over the head of the fowl after which the cords are pulled through the spring brass catch. It is easily applied and holds securely.

No. C49—Weather proof cord collar with spring brass attachments and swivels ....per dozen $4.90
ONE DOZEN IN A BOX

LIVE DECOY LEG FASTENERS

A leg band made of brass spring wire, is fastened to the decoy's leg at the beginning of the season; this band, although not removed until the close of the season, hasn't any sharp edges and will not chafe the decoy. The balance of the device snaps on and off, quickly. No lame or escaped ducks when this attachment is used.

No. C89—Fastener, complete as illustrated, including 6 ft. of anchor cord with each fastener, per dozen $4.65
ONE DOZEN IN A BOX

LIVE DECOY NECK HARNESS

This collar is easily attached to the live duck or detached. Gives decoys full freedom to swim about and feed. Cord can be shortened by lopping over the anchor.

No. C45—Neck Harness, consisting of flat, non-corrosive, Phosphor Bronze Collar, dark colored, braided, anchor cord, non-corrosive, babbitt metal anchor, height of collar ¾ in., w't of anchor, only, about 6 ozs., per doz. complete harness sets 5 lbs., per dozen $12.75
SIX SETS IN A CARDBOARD BOX

Hibbard, Spencer, Barlett & Co. in Chicago, Illinois, was one of the major suppliers of hunting and fishing equipment. Circa 1920.

Some hunters transported three or more live decoys in a box with a sliding lid for easy access. The notches on the crate's lid were added for gun rests. $500. (*Courtesy of John Herman*)

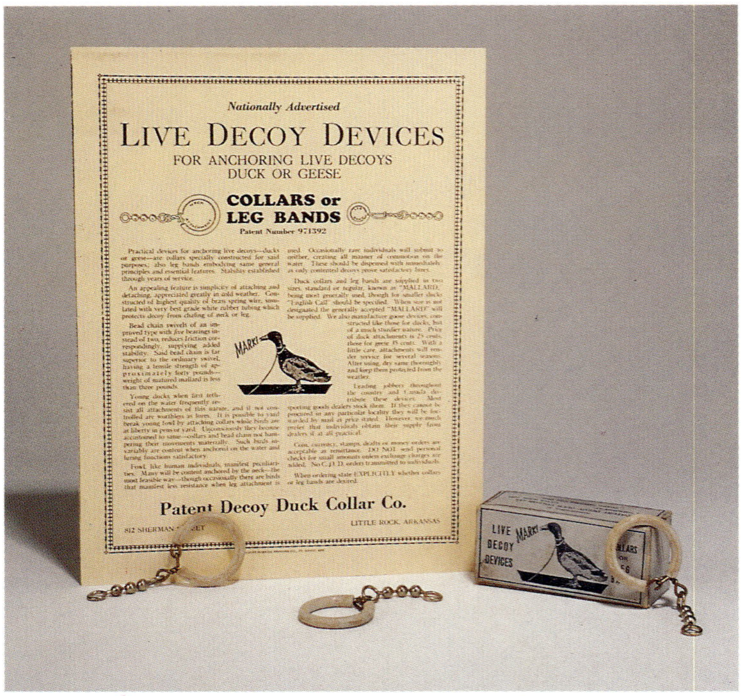

Patent Decoy Duck Collar Co. produced neck collars and leg bands for live decoys. Their patented design (Patent #971392) included bead chain swivels and white rubber tube covering over the brass wire collars to provide extra comfort and freedom of movement for the birds, circa 1925. $35 each.

William Pratt Decoy Co. in Joliet, Illinois, constructed their decoy harness out of heavy white cording with an adjustable brass clip. Circa 1930. $50 each.

Cook Live Decoy Holder, Springfield, Illinois, circa 1910, $40 each. Unknown leather duck collar with homemade shotgun brass filled with lead for anchor weight, $75 each.

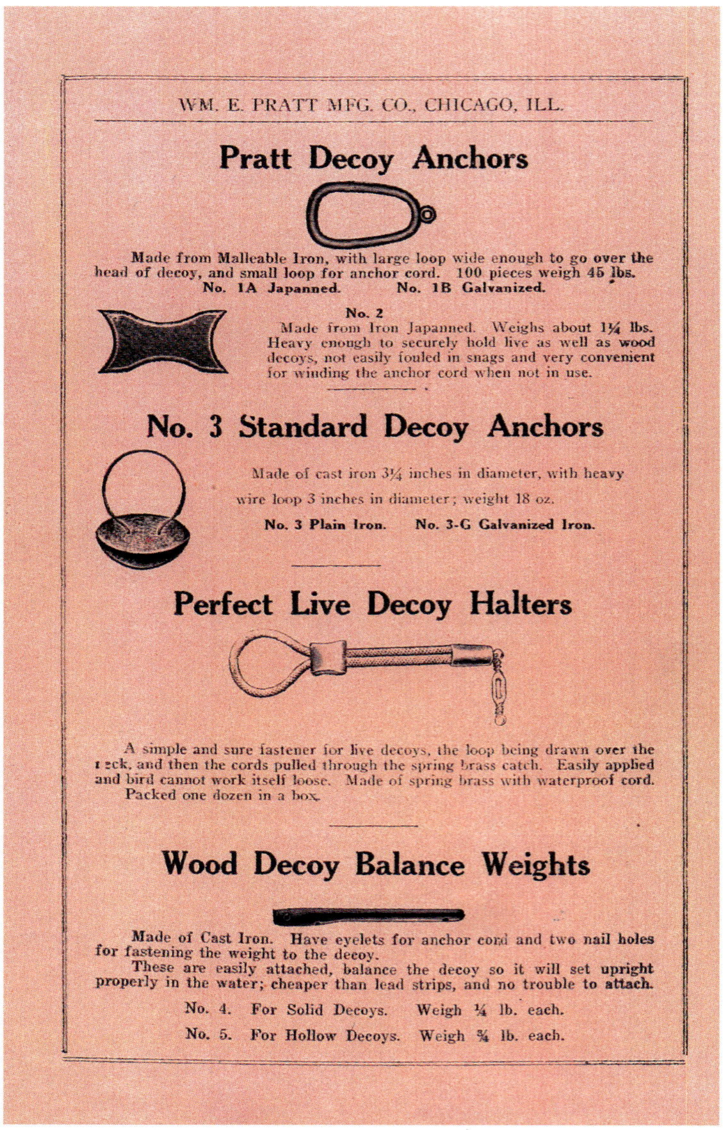

Advertising for Pratt decoy harnesses.

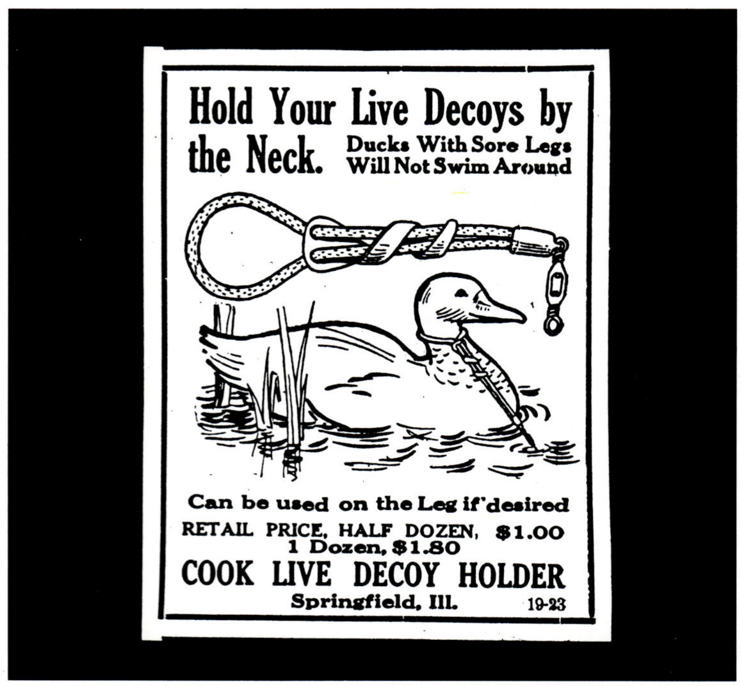

Cook Live Decoy Holder.

Miscellaneous decoy harnesses, circa 1920, $40-75 each.

Miscellaneous decoy harnesses, circa 1920, $40-75 each.

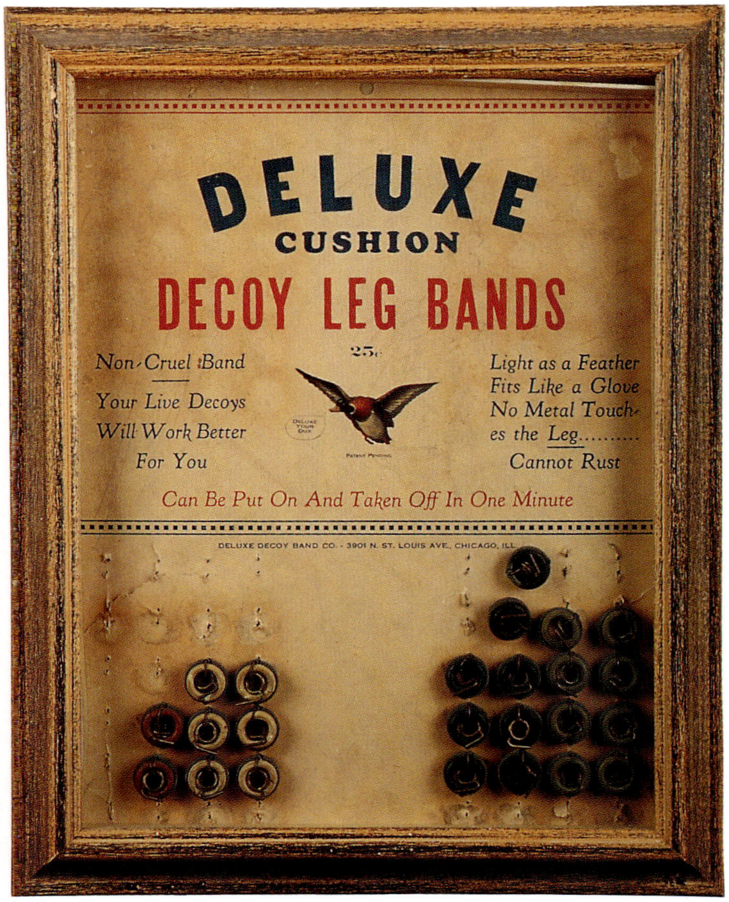

A display card with cushioned leg bands from the Deluxe Decoy Band Co. of Chicago, Illinois, circa 1915, $500.

Framed collection of live decoy holders including warning sign once posted at the West End Gun Club in Putman County, Illinois. Clockwise from top left: Perfect Live Decoy Holders, Wm. Pratt Decoy Co., Joliet, Illinois; Patent Decoy Duck Collar Co., Little Rock, Arkansas, two leg bands; Samuel Humane Live Duck Fastener; unknown commercial leather duck collar with metal ring; Delux Decoy Band Co., Chicago, Illinois; Patent Decoy Duck Collar Co., two neck collars; Perfect Live Decoy Holder, Wm. Pratt Decoy Co., Joliet, Illinois; Cook Live Decoy Holder, Springfield, Illinois; Patent Decoy Duck Collar Co., Little Rock, Arkansas; Hill & Rafter Co. copper neck harness, Eddie Rafter, Spring Valley, Illinois; unknown handmade copper neck holder; Hill & Rafter Co. copper neck harness; unknown handmade copper neck holder; unknown commercial rubber-coated brass leg clip holder; Patent Decoy Duck Collar Co. leg band; and Cook Live Decoy Holder. $50-100 each; framed set, $1, 200.

Advertising for Samuel Humane Duck Fastener.

Right to left: Samuel Humane Live Duck Fastener, jointed neck collar with weight, $75; letter informing members of rules for using club's live decoys, circa 1933; Cook Live Decoy Holder, Chicago, Illinois, with weight, $50; forming jig used by Eddie Rafter to produce his copper duck neck harnesses, $50.

Live Decoy Duck Collar-Anchor from Happe Manufacturing Co. in Kirkwood, Missouri, with "Happe Mfg. Co., Kirkwood Mo." embossed on lead casted anchor, with original box, circa 1920, $100. (*Collection of Todd Hoffman*)

Ed Rafter with a 1908 bag limit.

Edward Rafter of Spring Valley, Illinois, was a small man with a big reputation as a superb waterfowler and market hunter. Circa 1908.

This Hill & Rafter advertisement illustrates a handmade copper neck harness commonly known as Eddie Rafter's live decoy holder; Spring Valley, Illinois, circa 1930.

Patent Decoy Duck Collar

Most Practical Device for Anchoring Live Decoys (Ducks or Geese)

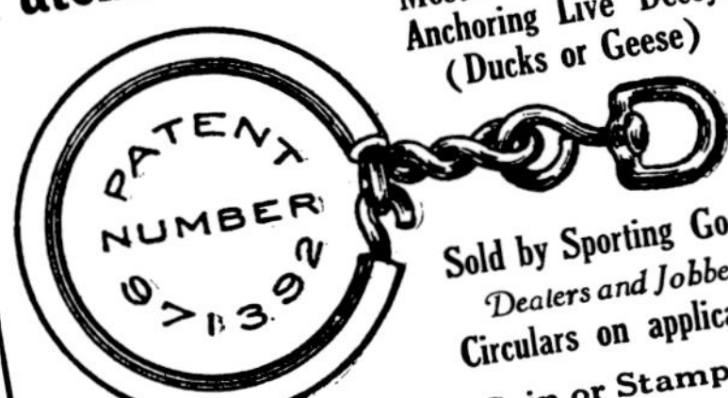

Sold by Sporting Goods Dealers and Jobbers
Circulars on application

Sample by Mail 25c. Coin or Stamps
PATENT DECOY DUCK COLLAR CO.
812 Sherman St. LITTLE ROCK, ARK.

OLT'S Superior Live Decoy Setout,

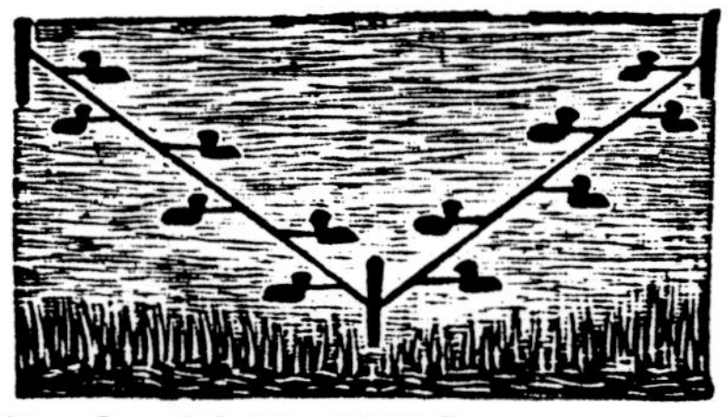

the quickest and cheapest, placed out in a few minutes. 84 ft. in length, contains 12 crossline box swivels every 6 ft. apart, to which 12 sturgeon Decoy Fasteners are attached. No possible chance of tangling. Holds 12 Live or Wood Decoys. Price is only $4.75. Make Duck Hunting Duck Shooting. Write for Literature.

P. S. OLT, MFG. PEKIN, ILL.

Field and Stream—September, 1929

Duck AND Goose HUNTERS

Pat. Aug. 19, 1924
BILL DARTON'S Merrymeeting Bay Duck and Goose Strap
will hold your live decoys. Made from special leather equipped with rustless swivel and eyelet
Duck straps $3.75 per dozen; $2.00 half dozen.
Goose straps $5.70 per dozen; $3.25 half dozen.
Postage paid
Dealers ask for circulars and prices
W. B. DARTON, 24 Clifton St., Portland, Me.

DECOYS & CALLERS

ENGLISH Call Ducks; pair $5.50; trio $7.50; Mallards $3.50 pair; trio $5.00; good callers. F. T. Smith, Gueydan, Louisiana.

LIVE DECOY DUCKS—200 English Grey Call Ducks, $2.00 each; $4.00 pair; $6.00 trio; weight 2½ lbs. each; good callers, mated perfectly; guaranteed to please. Charles Squire, [illegible] E. Jefferson Street, Havana, Illinois

DUCKLINGS

From domesticized Wild Mallard Ducks

$30. per hundred; $145. for 500. Make fine decoys for hunting. Cute pets, are unsurpassed as a table bird.
Send for free catalog
MAC'S DUCKERY
805 N. Sheridan Road Peoria, Illinois

Field and Stream—September, 1929

Miscellaneous ads for live decoy holders.

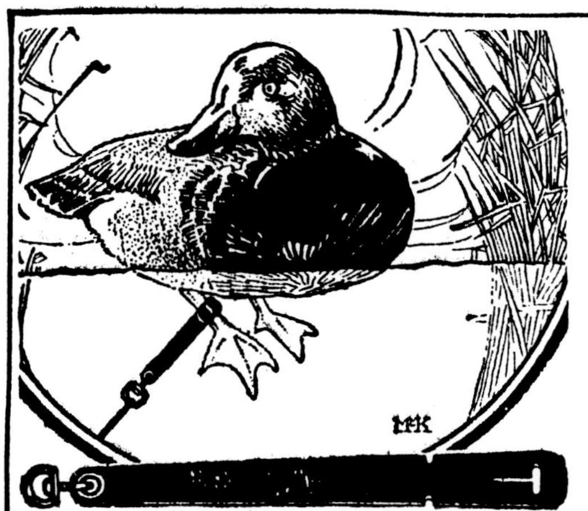

Duck AND Goose HUNTERS

Pat. Aug. 19, 1924
BILL DARTON'S Merrymeeting Bay Duck and Goose Strap
will hold your live decoys. Made from special leather equipped with rustless swivel and eyelet
Duck straps $3.75 per dozen; $2.00 half dozen.
Goose straps $5.70 per dozen; $3.25 half dozen.
Postage paid
Dealers ask for circulars and prices
W. B. DARTON, 24 Clifton St., Portland, Me.

Decoys

OLDING DUCK, OWL, CROW DEcoys cheap. Write, Renolds Recoy Facry, Forest Park, Illinois. (3-10)

MALL ENGLISH CALLERS $3.00 PAIR, $4.50 trio, trained with flyers shoter. C.O.D. Mallard $1.00 each. Canaan Geese $10.00 pair. C. G. Coffman, rthage, Illinois. (3-11)

'ILL GEESE! DUCKS! CALL THEM without fail. The Goosehonker talks oose language, giving clear, true note th simple movement of hand. No blowg . . . no mistakes. The Duckquacker beautiful, handmade walnut call—one u will be proud to possess. Both tuned noted hunter. Absolute satisfaction aranteed. Either $2.00 Postpaid. Goosenker Company, Memphis, Tenn.

EATHERWEIGHT DECOYS DESIGNed to be realistic and practical 90¢. eese of Balsa shavings $1.50. Folding angular ducks $1.00. No literature. ices F.O.B. Penoyar Planes, Seabright, lif.

UARANTEED—LIVE DECOYS! Genuine Midget Calls—Wild Canada Geese Wild Mallards, Pure-bred, trained stock asonable. Also Pheasants — Quail. ILD LIFE NURSERIES, Box 71P10, hkosh, Wisconsin. (2-11)

MALL ENGLISH CALLERS AND MALlards, $2.00 pair, $10.00 dozen. Wm. illiams, R. 1, Marissa, Ill.

UARANTEED MIDGET CALL, DUCKS, mallards, Canada geese, duck calls; ul Lieb, Anna, Ill.

"PerFecT" Live Decoy Harness

Will not slip or bind. Does not interfere with decoys' natural action, so you can attach "PerFecT" Harness at opening of the season and leave it on 'till season closes. Fully adjustable to any decoy.
Size "A" for Ducks..............30¢ each
Size "B" for Geese..............40¢ each
Money back guarantee.
THE "PerFecT" LIVE DUCK DECOY HARNESS CO.
130 North Fifth Street, Salina, Kansas

UNEXCELLED • FULL FLIGHT
RINGNECKS
QUAIL • DECOYS
Complete satisfaction guaranteed
ORDER NOW
BRUFFS ISLAND GAME FARM
John G. Alley Easton, Maryland

Decoys—Callers—Trained Birds

(Shot over often 1931-32-33)

Wild Decoy Mallard—$4.00, $3.00 pair
English Callers—$8.00, $7.00, $6.00, $5.00 pair
Black Mallard—$10.00, $8.00, $7.00 pair
Belgian Callers—$12.50, $10.00 pair

Old—young trained Canada Geese. New low prices. 1933 Canvas-back, Wood, other ducks. Flyers for restocking. ⅔ grown. (Stay where put.) 100 lots. Duck book 25c. Goose booklet 25c. Safe arrival. Order at once.

Breman Co., Danville, Ill.

MARK! LIVE DECOY DEVICES FOR

HUMANELY TETHERING DECOYS, DUCKS OR GEESE

Sold by Sporting Goods Trade. Circular Free.
Sample-Duck, 25c. Goose, 35c
PATENT DECOY DUCK COLLAR CO.
812 Sherman St., Dept, H-T Little Rock, Ark.

Trained geese where staked out in corn fields to call in passing Canada geese. Stakes with Cook Live Decoy Holders attached, $100.

Hunters made their own small, weedless anchor weights to restrain live decoys without endangering them. If an anchor weight became entangled in submerged brush the decoy could drown. Spent brass shotgun shells used as containers for molten lead created interesting weights.

W. A. GIBBS & SON, CHESTER, PA. 17

Gibbs Live Duck Decoy Anchor Attachment

HUNTING is associated with trapping, and duck hunting especially with marsh, lake and river trapping and live decoys are an invaluable asset to duck shooting when they work properly.

This they will do in most cases if they are anchored so they cannot get snarled up, hurt or scared, but it is more difficult than it would seem to make a device to accomplish this purpose successfully.

Mr. Gibbs has always enjoyed duck shooting and has tried every anchoring device for live decoys that he has ever seen without being able to find a successful one. Consequently, for his own use he devised one which is the best thing of the kind that we have ever seen and it is also inexpensive.

Nothing is more disagreeable on a duck hunt than to have a live decoy become frightened through getting snarled up in its anchor line or otherwise, or to be unable to detach the duck from the anchoring device when one has been in the blind for a long time and become cold and chilled.

The Gibbs device takes all of these points into consideration and is a successful device for the purpose for which it is intended.

A ring is permanently installed on the duck's leg to which the anchor line snaps on and off. No frightened or injured ducks and no escaped ducks when this device is used.

Try Them. You will be pleased with results.

The pans on all Gibbs traps are always steady and in the middle of the traps. An exclusive Gibbs feature of great value to the trapper.

Page from trap producers W.A. Gibbs & Sons catalog describing their live decoy anchor attachment.

Advertisements for Gibbs' Live Duck Decoy Anchor Attachment

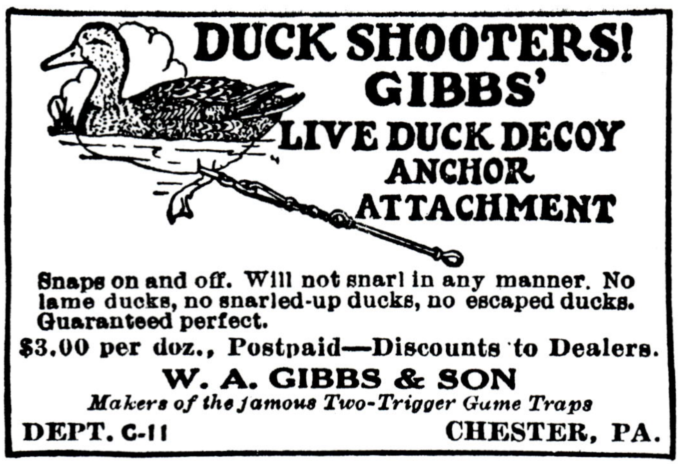

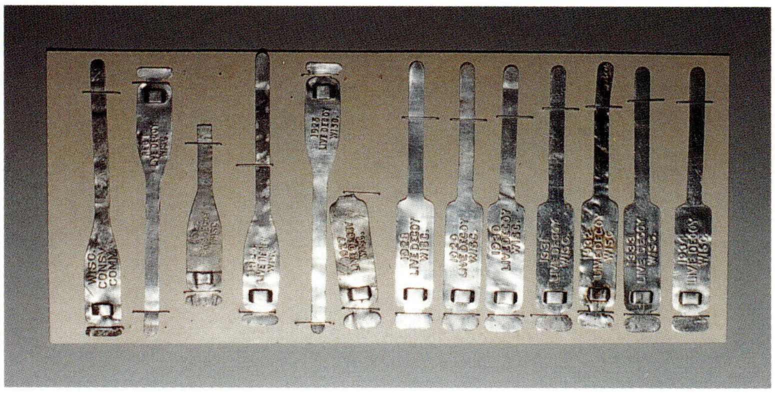

Before live decoys were banned completely, state governments limited their use. As early as 1922, Wisconsin's Conservation Commission required metal tags be placed on live decoys' legs. Leg tags, dated, $75 each.

Mushroom duck anchor weights, circa 1940: South Bend Bait Co., Indiana, $50; Acme Foundry, Minnesota, $25; Duck-In, Wizard Co., Missouri, $20, and unknown foundry, $15.

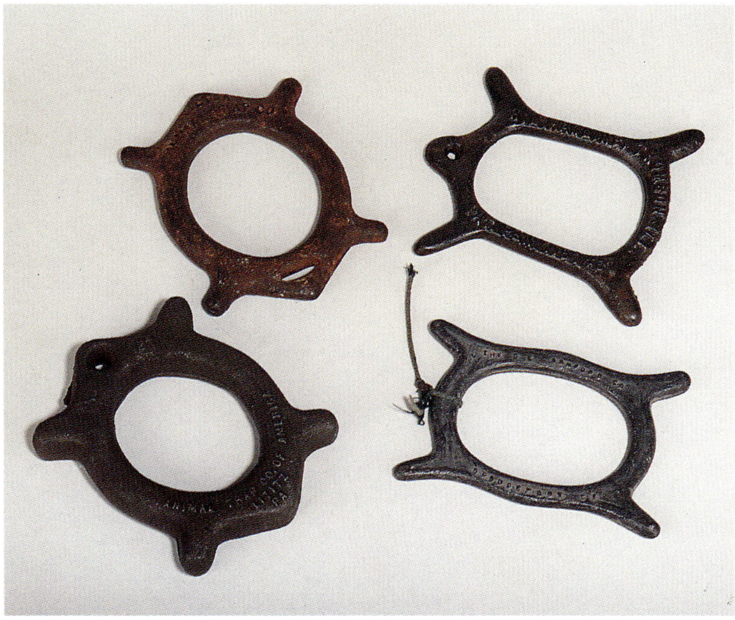

Decoy anchor weights: top left, Animal Trap Co., circa 1930, duck weight, $25; lower left, Animal Trap Co., Pennsylvania, goose weight, $35; top right, Rowlings Decoy Anchor, Thompson, Illinois, circa 1920, $25; and lower right, C. L. Stanford Co., Bridgeport, Connecticut, $25.

Miscellaneous anchor weights from Illinois, Wisconsin, $25-30 each.

Keel decoy weights and decoy anchor weights, $50-100 each.

Miscellaneous decoy anchor weights, left to right: Herter's Inc., Minnesota, $15; green cast iron, unknown foundry, $15, and unknown decoy weights. $15 each.

Mason Decoy Co. decoy weights with catalog listing. Catalog, $200. Left, ring weights, $25 each, and lead tear-drop weights, rare, $50 each.

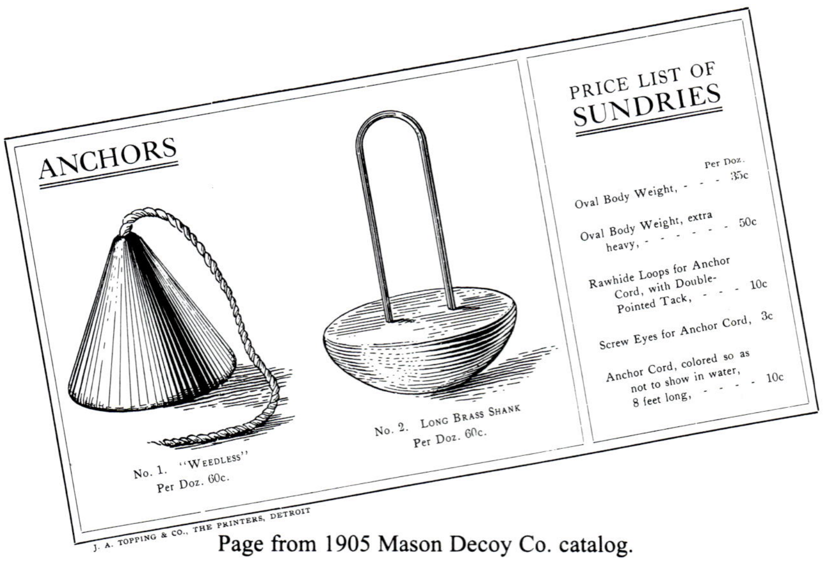

ANCHORS

No. 1. "Weedless"
Per Doz. 60c.

No. 2. Long Brass Shank
Per Doz. 60c.

PRICE LIST OF
SUNDRIES

	Per Doz.
Oval Body Weight, - - -	35c
Oval Body Weight, extra heavy, - - - - - -	50c
Rawhide Loops for Anchor Cord, with Double-Pointed Tack, - - -	10c
Screw Eyes for Anchor Cord,	3c
Anchor Cord, colored so as not to show in water, 8 feet long, - - - -	10c

J. A. TOPPING & CO., THE PRINTERS, DETROIT

Page from 1905 Mason Decoy Co. catalog.

Decoy weights, counter-clockwise from top left: Herter's Incorporated, Minnesota, goose weight, $20; Herter's Inc. duck weight, $25; Bergman/VanDyke, $20, and V. L. & A. Sporting Goods, decoy weight, rare $50.

Chapter 3

WaterfowlingDecoys

Long before hunting decoys were created, primitive hunters propped up birds that they had killed to draw more birds within striking distance. Some modern day hunters devised portable holders that held fresh kills on a small platform that could be floated. The best hunting decoy is the live decoy. Prior to the 1935–36 hunting season, using live birds to draw wild game was legal. Waterfowl, especially mallards, blackducks, and Canada geese, were fairly easily trained to lure passing birds into shooting range. Various styles of harnesses were produced to tether the live birds so they could swim freely among the decoy spread. Another luring technique used by early waterfowlers was baiting with fresh grains. When combined with live decoys, baited fields could draw waterfowl miles away from their nature flight patterns to open fields. Since corn was the favored bait, carvers tried to create corn decoys that could dupe passing ducks when baiting was outlawed. Obviously these corn decoys were not very productive since few were produced. However the corn decoy is an interesting collectible.

Wooden hunting duck and goose decoys are as varied as the carvers who made them. The most logical way to organize collectible hunting decoys is by the flyway in which they were used because the different hunting conditions determined the basic style and form of most working decoys. One of the least recognized yet fundamental facets of the waterfowling decoy is how it relates to the water. Hunting blocks that were used on large bodies of water were usually wide and heavy so they could ride the swells and waves without tipping. On the marshes and smaller lakes, decoys could be hollowed out so they would be lighter to carry. Ballasting keel weights and stringed anchor weights held the decoys in the hunting hole, yet allowed the decoy to gently sway among the water vegetation. Once classified as belonging to one of the four major migration flyways—the Atlantic, the Mississippi, the Central, or the Pacific—decoys are more easily evaluated by different criteria. For example, collectors of decoys used in salt water are more tolerant of wear and overpaint, whereas collectors of Illinois River decoys want to find birds in pristine original condition.

Wildlife refuge sign, painted wood, circa 1960, $50.

Oil painting on canvas, water spaniel, unsigned, circa 1900, $1,000.

Enamel sign, Department of the Interior, circa 1960, $200.

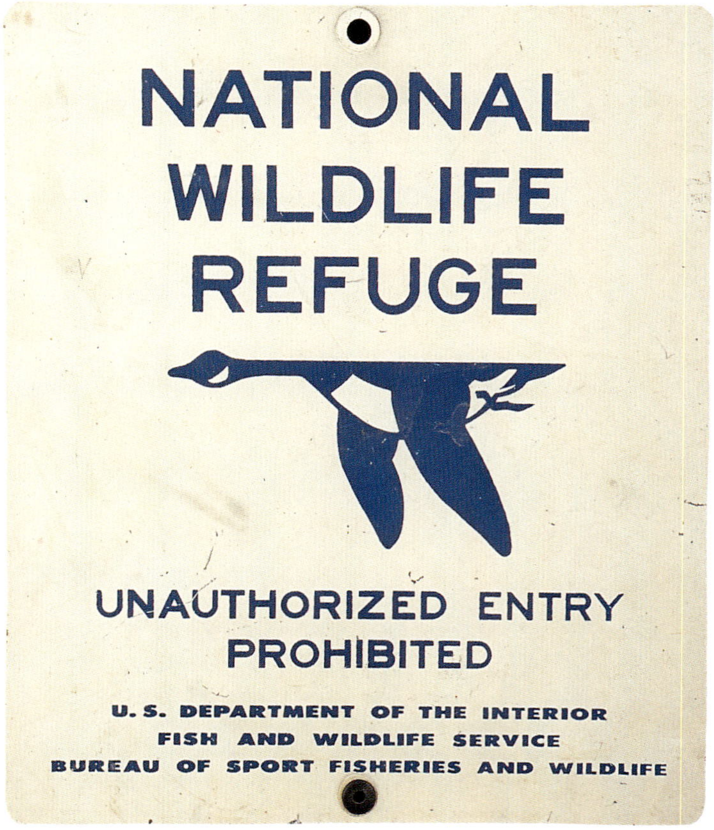

Enamel sign, National Wildlife Refuge, circa 1960, $200.

State Game Refuge sign, painted wood, circa 1970, $100.

Enameled sign, Waterfowl Protection Area, circa 1975, $150.

Decoys of the Atlantic Flyway

Migrating waterfowl funnel down the Atlantic flyway from Northeast Canada through the maritime provinces and southward to winter, stopping off to rest and feed in the states of Maine, New Hampshire, Massachusetts, Rhode Island, Connecticut, New York, New Jersey, Delaware, Pennsylvania, Maryland, Virginia, South Carolina, and North Carolina. The hunting conditions in these areas are by far the most diverse, ranging from shooting of sea ducks and shorebirds in the sheltered coastal coves to gunning divers on the Mid-Atlantic back bays or decoying puddle ducks to the marshes and small ponds of the inland rivers. Gunners bagged Canada geese, brant, shorebirds, sea duck, diver ducks, and puddle ducks.

Heavy cast iron decoys were placed on platforms that extended on all sides of a float blind, commonly known as a sink box. The weight of these decoys would help stabilize the blind and lower the platform into the water so only the hunter's head could been seen above the horizon and other decoys could be spread out on the platform and appear to be floating. Redhead drake, cast-iron "wing duck," maker unknown, circa 1880, $750.

In the maritime provinces of Nova Scotia, Prince Edward's Island, and New Brunswick, hunters shot Canada geese in the fields over full-bodied goose decoys and brant, eider, scoters, American mergansers, and red-breasted mergansers in the shelter coves using heavy decoys that were often highly stylized with great sculptural forms. Repainting is common because saltwater destroys even the strongest marine paint, usually in a single hunting season. Sea ducks were also heavily hunted in Maine. Sea hardy men shot out of batteries, sink boxes, or layout boats. These water blinds allowed only the hunter's head to rise above the waterline. On platforms that spread off each side of these blinds, decoys were arrange so they appeared to be floating. Heavy cast iron wing ducks helped to lower the blind into the sea and stabilize this awkward sea craft.

Prior to legislation that started to limit the destruction of the various species of shorebirds, the Atlantic seaboard was the center of shorebird shooting. Because flocks of shorebirds would circle and continue to return to a decoy rig until they were all killed, entire species were threatened with extinction including the Eskimo Curlew, which became extinct in 1929. Legislation like the Migratory Bird Act of 1918 began to limit shorebird shooting. By 1928, all shorebird hunting was illegal, so most working shorebird decoys predate the 1930s. There are several established carving schools along the Atlantic flyway—Delaware River decoys, Stratford school of Connecticut, Chesapeake Bay decoys, and Carolina decoys—as well as various factory produced decoy lines.

The Atlantic flyway was the center of shorebird hunting during the 1800s. This photo was taken on Shinnecock Bay, Long Island, New York, circa 1900. Note the fine silhouette of the Mason decoy company's rare long-billed curlew decoys. (*Courtesy of Barbara Sorenson*)

Red-breasted merganser drake, swimming style, Fred Nickerson (1902–1980) of Villagedale, Nova Scotia, circa 1930, $4,000. (*Collection of James R. & Diane Cook*)

Oil painting on canvas by B. Baldwin, circa 1930. Coastal hunters often built blinds along the shore among the sea grass.

American merganser hen, unknown Canadian carver, circa 1910, $2000.

Red-breasted merganser drake, Gus Wilson style, unknown maker, Maine, $10,000.

Decoys carved by Augustus "Gus" Aaron Wilson (1880–1940) of Portland, Maine, exhibit a variety of life-like positions—he made sleepers, preeners, swimmers, and feeding birds holding shells and fish in their bills. Red-breasted merganser, swimming style, circa 1920, $10,000. (*Collection of Alan and Elaine Haid/Photography by Alan Haid*)

Red-breasted merganser with sea grass by Gus Wilson of Portland, Maine, circa 1920, $6,000. (*Private collection*)

Blackduck, preening style, by Gus Wilson of Portland, Maine, circa 1920, $7,000. (*Collection of Alan and Elaine Haid/ Photography Alan Haid*)

Eider hen, preening, Gus Wilson, Portland, Maine, circa 1920, $6,500. (Collection of Joseph Engers)

Hurley Conklin, (1913–?) of Mananhawkin, New Jersey.

Hooded merganser pair by Hurley Conklin of Mananhawkin, New Jersey, circa 1960, $1,000. (*Collection of Alan and Elaine Haid/Photography by Alan Haid*)

Red-breasted merganser pair by Daniel Lake Leeds (1852–1922) of Pleasantville, New Jersey, $8,000. (*Collection of James R. and Diane Cook*)

Ruddy turnstone by Daniel Lake Leeds of Pleasantville, New Jersey, circa 1890, $8,000.

Black-bellied plover by Daniel Lake Leeds of, Pleasantville, New Jersey, circa 1890, $4,000.

Harry Van Nuckson Shourds (1871–1920) of Tuckerton, New Jersey, dominated the Tuckerton school of decoy making with his clean, distinct carving pattern.

Canada goose in rare swimming style by Harry V. Shourds, circa 1890, $50,000. (*Collection of Alan and Elaine Haid/Photography by Alan Haid*)

Redhead drake by Harry V. Shourds, circa 1890, $6,000.

Bluebill drake by Harry V. Shourds, circa 1890, $5,000.

Red-breasted merganser hen by Harry V. Shourds, circa 1890, $8,000.

Bufflehead drake by Harry V. Shourds, circa 1900, $10,000.

Bufflehead hen by Harry V. Shourds, circa 1900, $10,000.
(*Collection of Alan and Elaine Haid/Photography by Alan Haid*)

Blackduck by Harry V. Shourds, circa 1890, $8,000.

Snipe by Harry V. Shourds, circa 1900, $4,000. (*Collection of Alan and Elaine Haid/Photography by Alan Haid*)

Black-bellied plover by Harry V. Shourds, circa 1900, $3,500. (*Collection of Alan and Elaine Haid/Photography by Alan Haid*)

Sickle-bill curlew by Harry V. Shourds, circa 1900, $5,000. (*Collection of Alan and Elaine Haid/Photography by Alan Haid*)

Red-breasted merganser pair by Rhodes Turdex (?–1934) of Atlantic City, New Jersey, circa 1920, $8,000. (*Collection of Alan and Elaine Haid/ Photography by Alan Haid*)

Ruddy turnstone by unknown New Jersey maker, circa 1900, $1,000.

Ruddystone by unknown New Jersey maker, circa 1890, $2,000.

Ruddy Turnstone by unknown New Jersey maker, circa 1900, $750.

Ruddystone by unknown New Jersey maker, circa 1890, $1,000.

Long-bill curlew by unknown New Jersey maker, circa 1900, $2,500.

Ruddy turnstone by unknown, primitive New Jersey shorebirds, $500 each.

Left: Yellowlegs by unknown New Jersey maker, circa 1900, $2,000

Below: Long-billed curlew by unknown New Jersey maker, rare, circa 1900, $3,500.

Pintail drake, extremely rare, by John Dawson (1889–1959) of Trenton, New Jersey, circa 1900, $100,000. (*Collection of James R. and Diane Cook*)

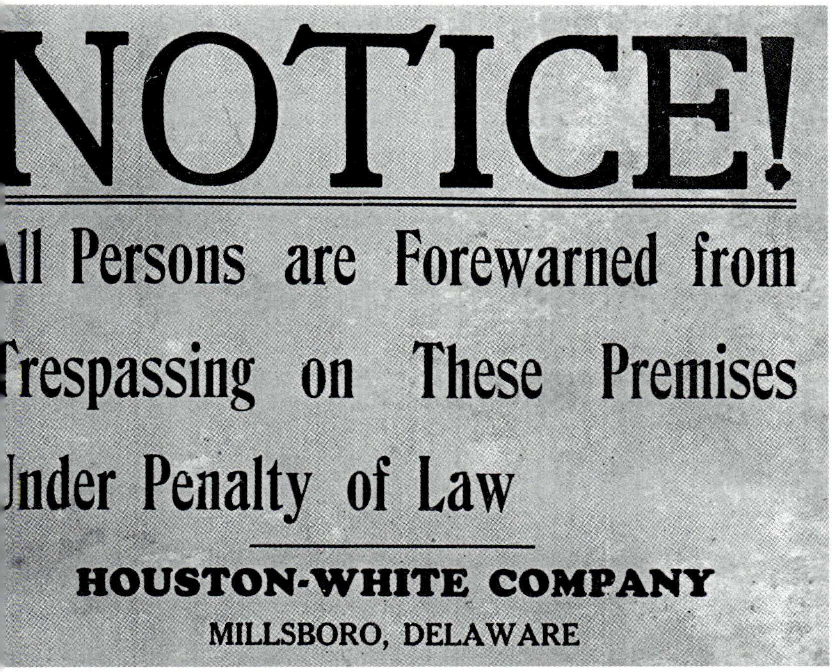

No hunting sign from the Houston-White Co. of Millsboro, Delaware, circa 1940.

Classic Delaware River decoys: mallard drake by John Dawson of Trenton, New Jersey, circa 1900, $20,000, and pintail drake by Tom Fitzpatrick (1887–1958) of Delanco, New Jersey, circa 1930, $6,000. (*Collection of James R. and Diane Cook*)

Canvasback drake by John Dawson of Trenton, New Jersey (Delaware River), circa 1920, $12,000.

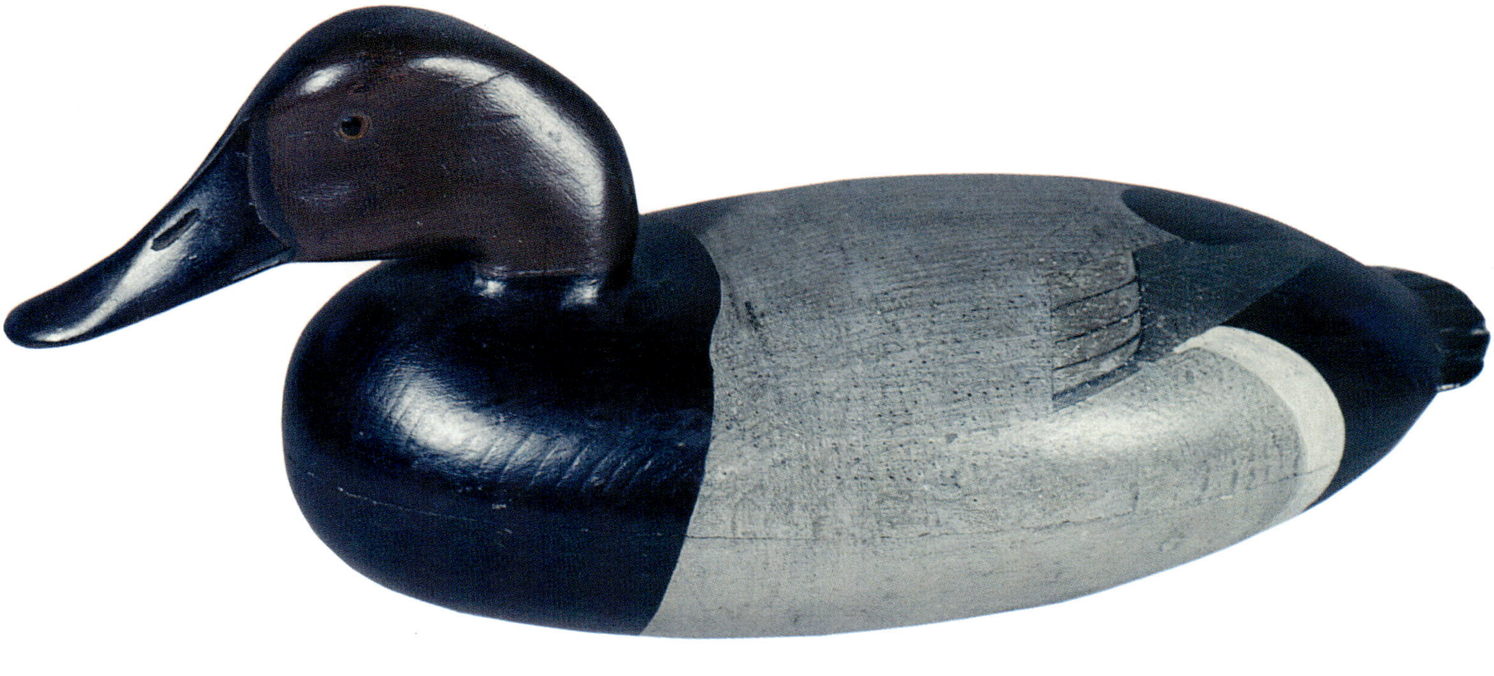

Delaware River decoys by Dan English (1883–1962) of Florence, New Jersey, circa 1900: blackduck, $20,000, and pintail hen, $25,000. (*Collection of James R. and Diane Cook*)

Delaware River decoys: blackduck by Dan English, circa 1941, $10,000, and blackduck by John English, Florence, New Jersey, circa 1880, $10,000. (*Collection of James R. and Diane Cook*)

Old squaw pair by Mark English (circa 1870–1930) of Somer's Point, New Jersey, circa 1890, $25,000. (*Collection of James R. and Diane Cook*)

Delaware River decoys: blackduck by Harry Fenimore (1886–1970) of Bordentown, New Jersey, circa 1930, $ 2,000, and blackduck by Al Rietz (1907–?) of Croyden, New Jersey, circa 1940, $3,000. (*Collection of James R. and Diane Cook*)

Widgeon pair by Jess Heisler (1891–1943) of Burlington, New Jersey, circa 1920, $25,000. (*Collection of James R. and Diane Cook*)

Red-breasted merganser pair by Stanley Grant (?–1960) of Barnegat, New Jersey, circa 1930, $8,000. (*Collection of James R. and Diane Cook*)

Bluebill pair by Nathan "Rowley" Horner (1882–1942) of Tuckerton, New Jersey, circa 1910, $20,000. (*Collection of James R. and Diane Cook*)

Mallard hen by Tom Fitzpatrick of Delmanco, New Jersey, circa 1940, $3,000.

Mallard hen by Nathan "Rowley" Horner, circa 1920, $25,000.

Blackduck by Nathan "Rowley" Horner, circa 1920, $8,000. (*Collection of Alan and Elaine Haid/Photography by Alan Haid*)

Classic Delaware River decoys by Joseph King (1909–?) of Edgely, Pennsylvania, circa 1920: blackduck, $15,000, and pintail drake, $20,000. (Collection of James R. and Diane Cook)

Pintail drake by John Blair (1881–1953) of Philadelphia, Pennsylvania, circa 1870, $50,000. (*Collection of James R. and Diane Cook*)

Blackduck by John Blair, circa 1870, $25,000. (*Collection of Alan and Elaine Haid/Photography by Alan Haid*)

Blackduck sleeper by Albert Laing (1811–1886) of Rathway, Connecticut, circa 1870, $15,000. (*Collection of Alan and Elaine Haid/Photography by Alan Haid*)

Blackduck sleeper by Louis Rathmell (1890–1975) of Stratford, Connecticut, circa 1940, $8,000. (*Collection of Alan and Elaine Haid/Photography by Alan Haid*)

Mallard hen by Louis Rathmell of Stratford, Connecticut, circa 1930, $5,000. (*Collection of James R. and Diane Cook*)

Charles "Shang" Wheeler (1872–1949) of Stratford, Connecticut, is considered the leader of the Stratford school of decoy carving. His influence and patterns spread across the country through correspondence with other carvers during the 1940s.

Blackduck sleeper by Charles "Shang" Wheeler, circa 1920. $75,000.

Red knot, winter and spring plumage, decorative carvings by Charles "Shang" Wheeler, circa 1920, $5,000

Black-bellied plover, winter and spring plumage, decorative carvings by Charles "Shang" Wheeler, cîrca 1920, $5,000.

Canada goose by Charles "Shang" Wheeler, circa 1920. This was the cover decoy on the first decoy book, *Wild Fowl Decoy*, by Joel Barber. $100,000. (*Collection of James R. and Diane Cook*)

Bluebill pair with hen sleeper by Charles "Shang" Wheeler, circa 1930. These decoys were given to Hector Whittington of Oglesby, Illinois, a noted Illinois River decoy maker who carved his personal hunting rig using Wheeler's patterns. $40,000. (*Collection of James R. and Diane Cook.*)

Mallard pair by Charles "Shang" Wheeler, circa 1930, $70,000. (*Collection of James R. and Diane Cook*)

Pintail pair by Charles "Shang" Wheeler, circa 1930, $15,000 each. (*Collection of James R. and Diane Cook*)

Shoveler (spoonbill) pair by Charles "Shang" Wheeler, circa 1930, $50,000. (*Collection of James R. and Diane Cook*)

Swan by Charles "Shang" Wheeler, circa 1930, $75,000. (*Collection of James R. and Diane Cook*)

Redhead drake, Charles "Shang" Wheeler, circa 1930, $12,000. (Collection of James R. and Diane Cook)

Connecticut decoys in classic Stratford-school style: blackduck decoy, $500; bluebill drake, unknown maker, $750.

WILDFOWLER
DECOYS
(INCORPORATED)

WILDFOWLER DECOYS
SAYBROOK, CONN.

WINNERS
1941 THROUGH 1951
NATIONAL DECOY CONTESTS

In the machine made Decoy Division, Wildfowler Decoys have won every 1st and 2nd ribbon, including, "Best Machine Made Decoy in Show," against all competition.

OLD SAYBROOK
CONNECTICUT
1956

Flyer and price list for the Wildfowler Decoys, Old Saybrook, Connecticut, circa 1956.

Edward H. Mulliken (1896–1964) owned and operated The Wildfowler Decoys Co. in Saybrook, Connecticut, producing a complete line of white pine and balsa working decoys using a multiple armed duplicating machine from 1938 until 1958, when the company was sold and moved to Quogue, Long Island. Wildfowler Decoys was sold again in 1961 and relocated in Point Pleasant, New Jersey.

Pintail pair from the Wildfowler Decoy Co, circa 1940, $700. (*Collection of Alan and Elaine Haid/Photography by Alan Haid*)

Green-winged teal pair from the Wildfowler Decoy Co., circa 1940, $700. (*Collection of Alan and Elaine Haid/Photography by Alan Haid*)

Three blackducks from the Wildfowler Decoy Co., circa 1940, $250-300 each. (*Collection of Alan and Elaine Haid/Photography by Alan Haid*)

Golden plover by William Bowman (1824–1906) of Lawrence, Long Island, New York, circa 1870, $25,000. (*Collection of Alan and Elaine Haid/ Photography by Alan Haid*)

Ruddy turnstone by William Bowman, circa 1870, $30,000.

Willet by William Bowman, circa 1860, $25,000.

Shorebirds by William Bowman, circa 1890: dowitcher, $35,000, and yellowlegs, $30,000. (*Collection of Alan and Elaine Haid/Photography by Alan Haid*)

Decoys by William Bowman, circa 1880: blackduck, $7,000, and redhead drake, $8,000. (*Collection of Alan and Elaine Haid/Photography by Alan Haid*)

Yellowlegs by William Bowman, circa 1870, $30,000.

Long billed curlew by Chief Caffey of Long Island, New York, circa 1900, $25,000.

Bluebill drake sleeper by Joel Barber (1877–1952) of Wilton, New York, circa 1930, $3,500. (*Collection of James R. and Diane Cook*)

Plover by John Dilly of Long Island, New York, circa 1880, $25,000. (*Collection of Alan and Elaine Haid/Photography by Alan Haid*)

Shorebirds by John Dilly of Quogue, Long Island, New York, circa 1890: ruddy turnstone, $40,000, and red knot, $35,000. (*Collection of Alan Elaine Haid/Photography by Alan Haid*)

Decoys by Ken Harris of New York, circa 1950: pair of widgeon, $600, and pintail drake, $200. (*Photograph by Alan Haid*)

Blackduck hen by Julius E. Mittlesteadt (1888–1957) of Buffalo, New York, circa 1930, $2,000. (*Photograph by Alan Haid*)

Bluebill pair by Julius Mittesteadt of New York, $2,000. (*Photograph Alan Haid*)

Blackduck from the Stevens Brothers Decoy Factory, owned by brothers Harvey (1847–1894) and George (1847–1905) Stevens of Weedsport, New York, circa 1890, $2,000. (*Collection of Alan and Elaine Haid/Photography by Alan Haid*)

Mallard drake by the Stevens Brothers Decoy Factory, circa 1880, $5,000.

Redhead pair from the Stevens Brothers Decoy Factory, circa 1880, $12,000. (*Collection of James R. and Diane Cook*)

Decoys from the Stevens Brothers Decoy Factory, circa 1880: blue-winged teal drake, $5,000; bluebill drake, $4,000, and widgeon drake, $6,000. (*Collection of James R. and Diane Cook*)

FOLDING TIN SNIPE DECOYS

Very light and take but little space. Packed one dozen in a box. When set up make a perfect snipe decoy.

Turnstone Golden Plover, Black Breast Plover	per doz.,	$4 00
Yellow Leg Plover	"	4 50

BLOWING HORNS

No.		Per doz.
No. 262	Blowing horn, French pattern, with metal tongue,	$6 00
265	Blowing horn, American pattern, genuine cows-horn, with open mouth, medium size	16 00
1265	Ditto, extra large	22 00

Advertisement for folding tin snipe decoys, 1894, Schoverling, Daly & Gale Sporting Goods catalog.

Shorebird, "Tinnie," Strater & Sohier Co., 1870, $200. (*Collection Alan and Elaine Haid/Photography by Alan Haid*)

Black-bellied plover from the Verity family of Lawrence, Long Island, New York, circa 1890, $3,500.

Ruddy Turnstone, "Tinnie," circa 1870, $400. (*Collection of Alan and Elaine Haid/Photography by Alan Haid*)

Curlew from the Verity family, circa 1880, $15,000. (*Collection of Alan and Elaine Haid/Photography by Alan Haid*)

Black-bellied plover, "Tinnie," stenciled "Strater, Patent c.1852," Strater & Sohier Co., $250. (*Collection of Alan and Elaine Haid/Photography by Alan Haid*)

Yellowlegs, "flattie" style, from the Verity family, circa 1880, $1,500. (*Collection of Joseph Engers*)

Black-bellied plover from the Verity Family, circa 1880, $3,500.

Peep from the Verity Family, circa 1860, $8,500. (*Collection of Alan and Elaine Haid/Photography by Alan Haid*)

Canvasback pair by Chauncey Wheeler (1962–1937) of Alexandria Bay, New York, circa 1930, $7,000. (*Collection of Alan and Elaine Haid/ Photography by Alan Haid*)

Shorebirds by Obediah Verity (circa 1850–1910) of Seaford, Long Island, New York, circa 1870: black-bellied plover, $40,000, and yellowlegs in rare feeding style, $50,000. (*Collection of Alan and Elaine Haid/Photography by Alan Haid*)

Canvasback drake, a rare flying decoy by Chauncey Wheeler, circa 1920, $8,000. (*Collection of Alan and Elaine Haid/Photography by Alan Haid*)

Mallard drake, a rare flying decoy by Chauncey Wheeler, circa 1920, $10,000. (*Collection of Alan and Elaine Haid/Photography by Alan Haid*)

Red-breasted merganser drake, attributed to Casius Smith (1850–1910) of Seaford, Long Island , New York, circa 1880, $15,000. (*Collection of Alan and Elaine Haid/ Photography by Alan Haid*)

Blackduck standing with metal legs, unknown maker from New York state, circa 1950. $2,500.

Left: Black-bellied plover by George Boyd (1873–1941) of Seabrook, New Hampshire, circa 1910, $ 2,000. (*Collection of Alan Elaine Haid/ Photography by Alan Haid*)

Above: Blackduck by George Boyd, circa 1920, $10,000. (*Collection of James R. and Diane Cook*)

Right: Red-breasted merganser pair by George Boyd of New Hampshire, circa 1890, $30,000. (*Collection of Alan and Elaine Haid/Photography by Alan Haid*)

Plover by George Boyd, circa 1900, $3,000. (*Collection of Alan and Elaine Haid/Photography by Alan Haid*)

A. Elmer Crowell (1862–1952) of East Harwich, Massachusetts, is recognized as a master carver of most aviary species. His body of work includes working duck, geese, and shorebird decoys, miniature and decorative songbird, waterfowl, game birds, and fish carvings.

A. Elmer Crowell produced sets of miniature carvings of waterfowl, songbirds, shorebirds, and game birds for the tourist trade on Cape Cod, Massachusetts.

Decoys from Dr. Phillips rig by Elmer Crowell, circa 1900: redhead drake, $35,000; canvasback drake, $25,000. (*Collection of James R. and Diane Cook*)

An extremely rare preening pintail drake by Elmer Crowell, circa 1900, made for Dr. Philip's hunting rig. Dr. Phillips was a personal friend of Crowell and many of the finest examples of Crowell's work were made especially for him. This decoy holds the world's record price for a duck decoy—$316,000—from RWO Auction House of July 1986.

Green-winged teal pair, Elmer Crowell, East Harwich, Massachusetts, extremely rare from Dr. Phillips rig, circa 1900, $60,000. (*Collection of Alan and Elaine Haid/Photography by Alan Haid*)

Sickle-billed curlew, maker unknown. This exceptional shorebird measuring 21-1/2 inches holds the world record decoy auction price—$335,000 bid in July 1997 at Guyette/Schmidt Decoy Auction House. Circa 1890, from Dr. Philips' personal hunting rig. (*Courtesy of Gary Guyette and Frank Schmidt Auction House*)

Widgeon drake, extremely rare preening style from Dr. Phillips rig by Elmer Crowell of East Harwich, Massachusetts, circa 1890, $75,000. (*Collection of James R. and Diane Cook*)

Mallard drake by Elmer Crowell, circa 1920, $15,000.

Decoys from Dr. Phillips rig by Elmer Crowell, circa 1900: Bluebill drake, $20,000; Blue-winged teal drake, $30,000. (*Collection of James R. and Diane Cook*)

Wood duck drake by Elmer Crowell, circa 1900, $50,000. (*Collection of James R. and Diane Cook*)

Goldeneye drake, extremely rare raised wing preening style, by Elmer Crowell, circa 1900, from Dr. Phillips rig, $75,000. (*Collection of James R. and Diane Cook*)

Red-breasted merganser drake by Elmer Crowell, $15,000. (*Collection of Alan and Elaine Haid/Photography by Alan Haid*)

Blackduck, rare preening style, by Elmer Crowell, circa 1900, Dr. Phillips rig, $50,000, (*Collection of James R. and Diane Cook*)

Plover, carved-wing style, Elmer Crowell, circa 1900, $40,000. (*Collection of James R. and Diane Cook*)

Shorebirds by Elmer Crowell, circa 1900, referred to as "Dust Jacket Birds." These fat-body style decoys were used as cover birds on William Mackey's *American Bird Decoy*. Rare, carved-wing, feeding style yellowlegs, $50,000; carved-wing style plover, $50,000. (*Collection of Alan and Elaine Haid/ Photography by Alan Haid*)

Plover, extremely early, fat style by Elmer Crowell, circa 1890, $40,000. (*Collection of James R. and Diane Cook*)

Shorebirds by Elmer Crowell: yellowlegs, carved-wing style, $35,000; yellowleg, carved-wing, feeder style, $40,000. (*Collection of James R. and Diane Cook*)

Black-bellied plover, carved-wing, feeding style by Elmer Crowell, circa 1900, $45,000. (*Collection of James R. and Diane Cook*)

Joseph Whiting Lincoln (1859–1938) of Accord, Massachusetts, hand crafted his hunting blocks out of cedar logs, creating sleek decoys finished in stylized paint patterns.

Shorebirds by Elmer Crowell: dowitcher, carved-wing style, $35,000; Willet, carved-wing style, $25,000. (*Collection of James R. and Diane Cook*)

Joseph Lincoln's business card.

Old squaw hen by Joseph Lincoln, circa 1920, $20,000. (*Collection of James R. and Diane Cook*)

Canada goose by Joseph Lincoln, circa 1920, $20,000. (*Collection of James R. and Diane Cook*)

American merganser hen by Joseph Lincoln, circa 1920, $15,000. (*Collection of Alan and Elaine Haid/Photography by Alan Haid*)

Decoys by Joseph Lincoln, circa 1890: old squaw drake, $25,000; widgeon drake, $30,000. (*Collection of James R. and Diane Cook*)

Plover by Joseph Lincoln, circa 1910, $2, 500. (*Collection of Alan and Elaine Haid/Photography by Alan Haid*)

Yellowlegs in Joseph Lincoln style, from Massachusetts, circa 1900, $5,000. (*Collection of Alan and Elaine Haid/Photography by Alan Haid*)

Willet by an unknown Massachusetts maker in the Joseph Lincoln style, circa 1900, $2,500.

American merganser hen by Lothrop Holmes of Massachusetts, circa 1880, $50,000.

Red-breasted merganser pair by Franklin Pierce Wright, Cape Cod, Massachusetts, circa 1890, $10,000.

American merganser drake by an unknown maker from Cape Cod, Massachusetts, circa 1920, $5,000.

Black-bellied plover by an unknown Massachusetts maker, circa 1910, $1,500.

Red-breasted merganser by an unknown maker from Martha's Vineyard, Massachusetts, circa 1900, $5,000. (*Collection of James R. and Diane Cook*)

Black-bellied plover by an unknown Massachusetts maker, circa 1900, $750

American merganser pair, unknown maker, Cape Cod, Massachusetts, circa 1900, $40,000. (*Collection of James R. and Diane Cook*)

Swan by Captain John C. Cockey of Kent Island, Maryland, circa 1900, $20,000. (*Courtesy of Collectible Old Decoys, Fripp Island, South Carolina*)

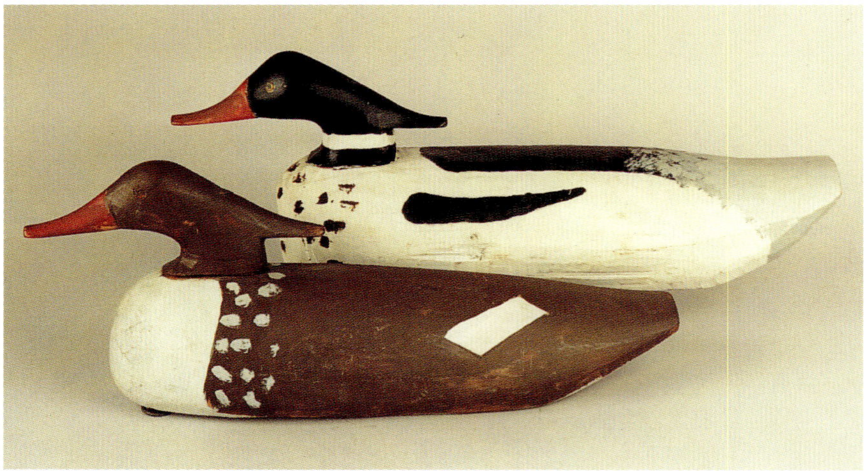

Red-breasted merganser pair by Clarence Hi "Pap" Creighton of Hopper's Island, Maryland, circa 1950, $950. (*Collection of Joseph Engers*)

Decoys by Robert F. McGaw (1879–1958) of Havre de Grace, Maryland, circa 1920: blackduck, $1, 500; canvasback, $1,000.

Canvasback drake, oversized, by Captain John Glenn of Rock Hall, Maryland, circa 1935, $2,000. (*Courtesy of Collectible Old Decoys, Fripp Island, South Carolina*)

Robert F. McGaw (1879–1958) of Havre de Grace, Maryland.

Bluebill drake by William Y. "Billy Snakes" Heverin (1860–1951) of Charlestown, Maryland, circa 1930, $850. (*Collection of Joe Engers*)

Madison Mitchell (1901-?) of Harve de Grace, Maryland, in his workshop. Taken by Joseph French, circa 1960.

Swan, gunning decoy by Madison Mitchell (1901–?) of Havre de Grace, Maryland, circa 1950, $2,500. (*Collection of Alan and Elaine Haid/Photography by Alan Haid*)

Canvasback pair by Madison Mitchell, circa 1950, $1,500. (*Collection of Alan and Elaine Haid/Photography by Alan Haid*)

Canvasback pair sleeper style by Madison Mitchell, circa 1950, $1,500. (*Collection of Alan and Elaine Haid/Photography by Alan Haid*)

Canvasback pair by Madison Mitchell, circa 1960, $1,000. (*Collection of Alan and Elaine Haid/Photography by Alan Haid*)

Blackduck, rare Eastern shore stick-up style, by Lloyd Sterling of Crisfield, Maryland, circa 1910, $7,000. (*Courtesy of Collectible Old Decoys, Fripp Island, South Carolina*)

Lemuel T. Ward, Jr.(1896–?)(pictured), and his brother, Stephen (1895–1976) , of Crisfield Maryland, carved and painted thousands of hunting blocks from 1930 through the late 1950s when they began to focus on decorative carvings. Their decoys were exemplary of the classic Maryland decoy.

Lloyd Tyler (1898–1971) of Crisfield, Maryland.

Canvasback drake by the Ward brothers, rare, circa 1932, $10,000.

Blackduck by the Ward brothers, rare, circa 1932, $10,000.

Canada goose by the Ward brothers, used at Bishop's Head Gun Club, Maryland, rare, circa 1930, $25,000.

Blackduck pair, classic 1936 style, by the Ward brothers, $50,000. (*Collection of James R. and Diane Cook*)

Decoys by the Ward brothers, circa 1930: pintail drake, $25,000; mallard drake, $20,000. (*Collection of James R. and Diane Cook*)

Green-winged teal pair by the Ward brothers, circa 1930, rare, $35,000. (*Collection of James R. and Diane Cook*)

Canvasback drake by an unknown Maryland carver, circa 1940, $500; Canvasback hen, by an unknown Maryland carver, $500.

Swan by Charles Birch, circa 1910, $75,000. (*Collection of James R. and Diane Cook*)

Canada goose by Charles Birch (1868–1956) of Chincoteague, Virginia, circa 1910, $15,000.

Black-bellied plover by Charles Clark (circa 1880) of Chincoteague, Virginia, circa 1920, $2,500. (*Collection of Tommy O'Connor/Photography by Archie Johnson*)

Black-bellied plover by the Cobb family, Cobb Island Virginia, circa 1880, $18,000. (*Collection of Tommy O'Connor/Photography by Archie Johnson*)

Robin Snipe decoys by an unknown maker from Cobb Island, Virginia, circa 1880, $7,500 each. (*Collection of Tommy O'Connor/Photography by Archie Johnson*)

Curlew by an unknown maker from Cobb Island, Virginia, circa 1880, $8,000. (*Collection of Tommy O'Connor/Photography by Archie Johnson*)

Curlew by an unknown maker from Cobb Island, Virginia, circa 1880, $35,000. (Collection of Tommy O'Connor/ Photography by Archie Johnson)

Curlew by an unknown maker from Cobb Island, Virginia, circa 1880, $10,000. (*Collection of Tommy O'Connor/Photography by Archie Johnson*)

Curlew by Nathan Cobb (1825–1905) of Cobb Island, Virginia, circa 1880, $60,000. (*Collection of Tommy O'Connor/Photography by Archie Johnson*)

Curlew by Nathan Cobb, circa 1880, $40,000. (*Collection of Tommy O'Connor/ Photography by Archie Johnson*)

Brant by Elkanah B. Cobb (1882–1943) of Cobb Island, Virginia, circa 1900, $40,000. (*Collection of Tommy O'Connor/Photography by Archie Johnson*)

Atlantic brant by Nathan Cobb, circa 1860, $40,000. (*Collection of Alan and Elaine Haid/Photography by Alan Haid*)

Atlantic brant, swimming style, by Nathan Cobb, circa 1860, $60,000. (*Collection of Alan and Elaine Haid/Photography by Alan Haid*)

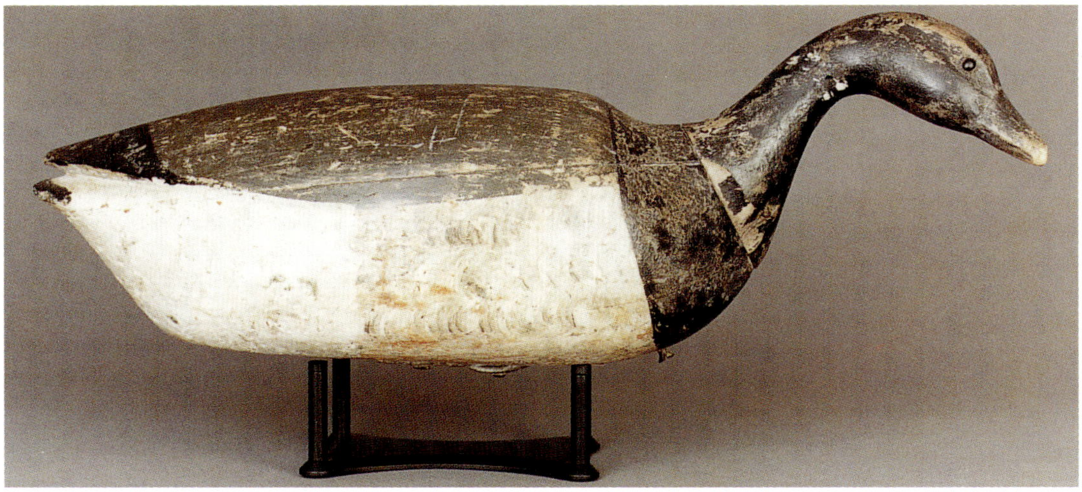

Atlantic brant, swimming style, by Nathan Cobb, circa 1860, $35,000. (*Collection of Alan and Elaine Haid/Photography by Alan Haid*)

Brant by Nathan Cobb, circa 1880, $25,000. (*Collection of Tommy O'Connor/Photography by Archie Johnson*)

Brant by Nathan Cobb, circa 1880, $25,000. (*Collection of Tommy O'Connor/Photography by Archie Johnson*)

Brant by Nathan Cobb, circa 1880, $20,000. (*Collection of Tommy O'Connor/Photography by Archie Johnson*)

Brant, reaching root head, swimming style by an unknown Cobb Island maker, circa 1900, $6,500. (*Collection of Joseph Engers*)

Redhead drake by Nathan Cobb, circa 1880, $15,000. (*Collection of Tommy O'Connor/Photography by Archie Johnson*)

Redhead hen by Nathan Cobb, circa 1880, $15,000. (*Collection of Tommy O'Connor/Photography by Archie Johnson*)

Brant by Eli Doughty of Hog Island, Virginia, circa 1880, $10,000. (*Collection of Tommy O'Connor/Photography by Archie Johnson*)

Blackduck by John Henry Downes of Smith Island, Virginia, $8,000. (*Courtesy of Collectible Old Decoys, Fripp Island, South Carolina*)

Linwood Lee Dudley (1861–1942) of Knotts Island, Virginia, advertised his Island Club in various sporting magazines staring in 1917. This brochure offered waterfowling, fishing, trap shooting, and other "rest day amusements."

Canvasback in classic Dudley style, by Linwood Lee Dudley of Knotts Island, Virginia, $20,000. (*Collection of Tommy O'Connor/Photography by Archie Johnson*)

Canada goose, hissing-head style, by Miles Hancock (1889–1975) of Chincoteague, Virginia, circa 1930, $7,000. (*Courtesy of Collectible Old Decoys, Fripp Island, South Carolina*)

Canada goose, swimmer style, by Ira Hudson, circa 1935, $15,000. (*Courtesy of Collectible Old Decoys, Fripp Island, South Carolina*)

Red-breasted merganser hen by Miles Hancock (1888–1974) Chincoteague, Virginia, circa 1940, $850. (*Collection of Joseph Engers*)

Mallard drake, standing with spread wings, by Ira Hudson, circa 1923, $20,000. (*Courtesy of Collectible Old Decoys, Fripp Island, South Carolina*)

Red-breasted merganser drake by Ira Hudson (1873–1949) of Chincoteague, Virginia, circa 1920, $15,000. (*Collection of James R. and Diane Cook*)

Yellowlegs by Ira Hudson, circa 1930, $8,000. (*Collection of Tommy O'Connor/Photography by Archie Johnson*)

Dowitcher, running, by Ira Hudson, circa 1930. Ex-Hillman collection, $15,000. (*Collection of Joseph Engers*)

Blackduck by Samuel Douglas J. Jester (1876–1961) of Chincoteague, Virginia, circa 1920, $2,000.

Curlew by Luther Nottingham of Chesapeake, Virginia (once known as Cobb's Station), circa 1890, $12,000. (*Collection of Tommy O'Connor/Photography by Archie Johnson*)

Swan by John Williams of Backbay, Virginia, circa 1909, $15,000. (*Collection of Backbay Wildfowl Guild Inc.*)

Swan pair by Perry Carawan (1910–?) of Mattamuskeet, North Carolina, circa 1930. Only four known, $25,000. *(Courtesy of Collectible Old Decoys, Fripp Island, South Carolina)*

Mallard drake carved by Caines brothers in rare preening style and decorated with West African fetish design by Eddie Roberts (former slave and hunting companion of Ball Caines). Georgetown, South Carolina, circa 1875, $80,000. *(Courtesy of Collectible Old Decoys, Fripp Island, South Carolina)*

Putting out Caines Brothers decoys, circa 1906. *(Courtesy of Collectible Old Decoys, Fripp Island, South Carolina)*

Below: Mallard pair, rare snaky-neck style by the Caines brothers, (probably Ball Caines) of Georgetown, South Carolina, circa 1900, $150,000 pair. *(Courtesy of Collectible Old Decoys, Fripp Island, South Carolina)*

Left to right: Hucks Caines with lantern, guest holding Mason Premier blackduck decoy; Sawney Caines with shotgun, guest at Hobcaw Barony, Georgetown, South Carolina, circa 1906. (*Courtesy of Collectible Old Decoys, Fripp Island, South Carolina*)

Ruddy duck by Joe Lewark of Currituck, North Carolina, circa 1910, $6,000. (*Courtesy of Collectible Old Decoys, Fripp Island, South Carolina*)

Caines brothers' homestead: right; Baruch Lodge, "Clambank" area, Hobcaw Barony, Georgetown, South Carolina, circa 1906. Note the dozen raised-wing Caines Brothers mallards in the bow of the skiff. (*Courtesy of Collectible Old Decoys, Fripp Island, South Carolina*)

Classic Carolina decoys: ruddy duck by Alvirah Wright of Currituck, North Carolina, circa 1900, $10,000; and mallard hen by the Caines brothers of Georgetown, South Carolina, circa 1900, $10,000. (*Courtesy of Collectible Old Decoys, Fripp Island, South Carolina*)

Hunting rig including Caines brothers' mallards and Premier Mason blackduck decoys in the salt marsh of Hobcaw Barony, Georgetown, South Carolina, circa 1906. (*Courtesy of Collectible Old Decoys, Fripp Island, South Carolina*)

Swan, maker unknown; found in Waterlily, North Carolina, following Hurricane Hazel, 1954. Hollow body is constructed like a "Carolina" skiff. Bill is splined through the head, reminiscent of early Virginia decoys, circa 1870, $25,000. (*Courtesy of Collectible Old Decoys, Fripp Island, South Carolina*)

Decoys of the Mississippi Flyway

Waterfowl that bred in the Delta Marsh of northern Manitoba and Saskatchewan provinces of Canada follow the rivers which flow toward the Mississippi. Each spring they migrated through the Great Lakes regions providing excellent hunting on the backwater lakes and marshes in the states of Minnesota, Michigan, Iowa, Illinois, Ohio, Mississippi, Arkansas, Tennessee, Wisconsin, and Louisiana. There are several strong schools of carving whose styles reflect the hunting conditions of the various waterfowl stopovers: The St. Clair Flats decoy bodies are usually hollowed into a thin shell and sealed with a bottom board. Hunters in this region needed to carry their decoys in small sneak boats or layout boats out onto an enormous watershed complex of marshes and landlocked lakes to shoot puddle ducks and diver ducks, which fed on the small crustaceans and aquatic plants.

Hunting large Midwestern landlocked lakes meant shooting large rafts of diver ducks; canvasback, redheads, and blue bills. The decoys were solid, broad blocks that could ride the rough lake waters without tipping over. Their tails were often "bobbed off" since diver duck tails are rarely visible on the big waters. The hunters of the Illinois River preferred colorful, hollow decoys because they gunned duck holes surrounded with heavy natural feed. The decoys, which characteristically have deep V-shaped, two-piece bodies, had to show up in this overgrowth.

The carvers of Louisiana shaped decoys following the twisting growth patterns of the Bayou cypress woods creating interesting, free-flowing puddle duck decoys that drew passing birds down into the flooded delta timbers. Because most waterfowling was done in sheltered, fresh waterways, original paint is a must for the collector of Mississippi flyway decoys and many superb examples are in collections.

Blackduck by Ken Anger, circa 1940, \$800. (*Collection of Alan and Elaine Haid/Photography by Alan Haid*)

Redhead drakes by Tom Chambers (1860–1948) of Toronto, Ontario, used at Lake St. Clair Shooting Club, circa 1880, \$5,000 each. (*Collection of James R. and Diane Cook*)

Wooduck drake by Ken Anger (1905–1961) of Dunnville, Ontario, circa 1940, \$7,000. (*Collection of James R. and Diane Cook*)

Canvasback drake by Tom Chambers, used at Lake St. Clair Shooting Club, circa 1880, \$3,000 each.

Goldeneye pair, hollow with bottom board, by William Finkel of Port Huron, Michigan, circa 1900, $5,000.

Canada geese by Robert Charles McGaffey (1863–1949) of Wallaceburg, Ontario, circa 1920, $1,000 each.

Duncan Ducharme (1912–1972) in his Portage le Prairie, Manitoba, workshop, circa 1960.

Bluebill hen by Orel LeBoeuf (1886–1980) of St. Anicet, Quebec, circa 1930, $2,500. (*Collection of Alan and Elaine Haid/Photography by Alan Haid*)

Canvasback hens by Duncan Ducharme, used by James Robinson, noted outdoor writer for *The Minneapolis Star Tribune* in Minnesota, circa 1930, $3,000.

Green-winged teal drake by the Reeves family, which was headed by Phineas Reeves and sons, John C., Charles P., and Francis. They carved decoys for the Long Point Co. Duck Club in Long Point, Ontario. Circa 1890, $700.

Bernie Smith's son, Don, hunts with a friend near Old Wife's Lake, Saskatchewan, over his father's goose decoys, circa 1955. (*Courtesy of Don Smith*)

Speckle bellied geese by Bernie Smith of Mossbank, Saskatchewan. Paper mâché, circa 1940. $500 each

Bluebill pair by Tory Ward of Portage le Prairie, Manitoba, circa 1970, $600.

Canada goose by George Warin (1830–1904) of Toronto, Ontario, circa 1880. $15,000. (*Collection of James R. and Diane Cook*)

Legend has it that these were used by the Prince of Wales (Edward VII) of England when he hunted the Delta Marsh at Galt's Duck Camp on Lake Francis during a royal visit to Canada in 1901. Decoys by John R. Wells (1880s–1953) of Toronto, branded "J R W Maker," were shipped from Toronto to Manitobe for the "royal hunt," circa 1900: top, shoveler drake, $20,000; bottom, pintail drake, $15,000. (*Collection of James R. and Diane Cook*)

Below: No hunting sign used on baiting station of Long Point Shooting Club in Ontario, circa 1930.

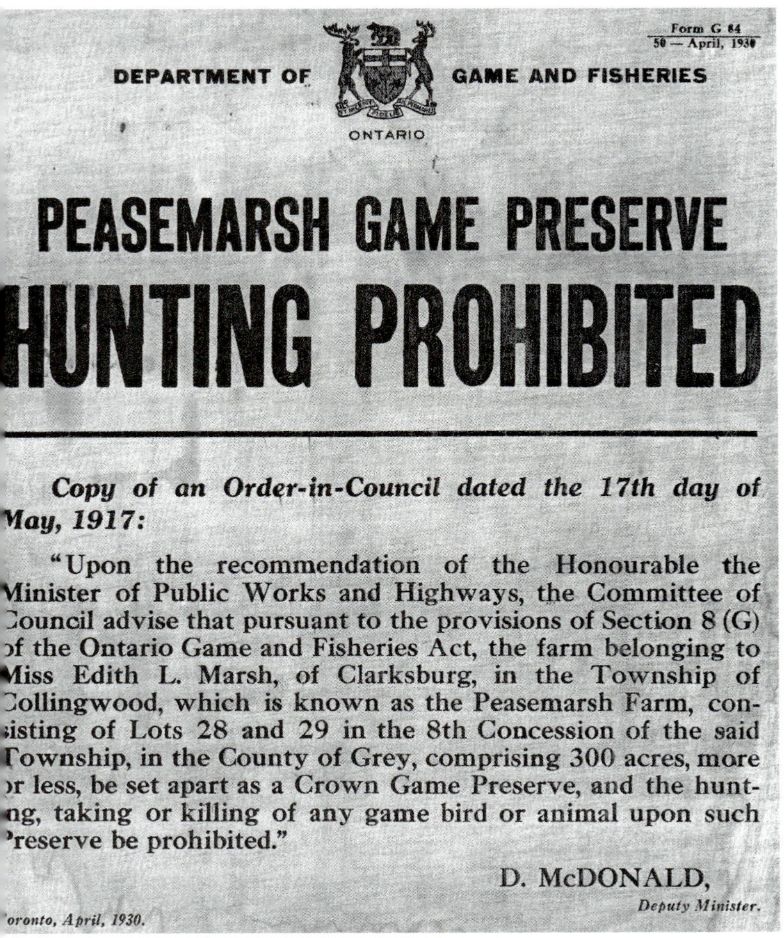

Form G 84
50 — April, 1930

DEPARTMENT OF GAME AND FISHERIES

ONTARIO

PEASEMARSH GAME PRESERVE

HUNTING PROHIBITED

Copy of an Order-in-Council dated the 17th day of May, 1917:

"Upon the recommendation of the Honourable the Minister of Public Works and Highways, the Committee of Council advise that pursuant to the provisions of Section 8 (G) of the Ontario Game and Fisheries Act, the farm belonging to Miss Edith L. Marsh, of Clarksburg, in the Township of Collingwood, which is known as the Peasemarsh Farm, consisting of Lots 28 and 29 in the 8th Concession of the said Township, in the County of Grey, comprising 300 acres, more or less, be set apart as a Crown Game Preserve, and the hunting, taking or killing of any game bird or animal upon such Preserve be prohibited."

D. McDONALD,
Deputy Minister.

Toronto, April, 1930.

Below: Canadian hunting sign from Peasemarsh Game Preserve, Toronto, circa 1930.

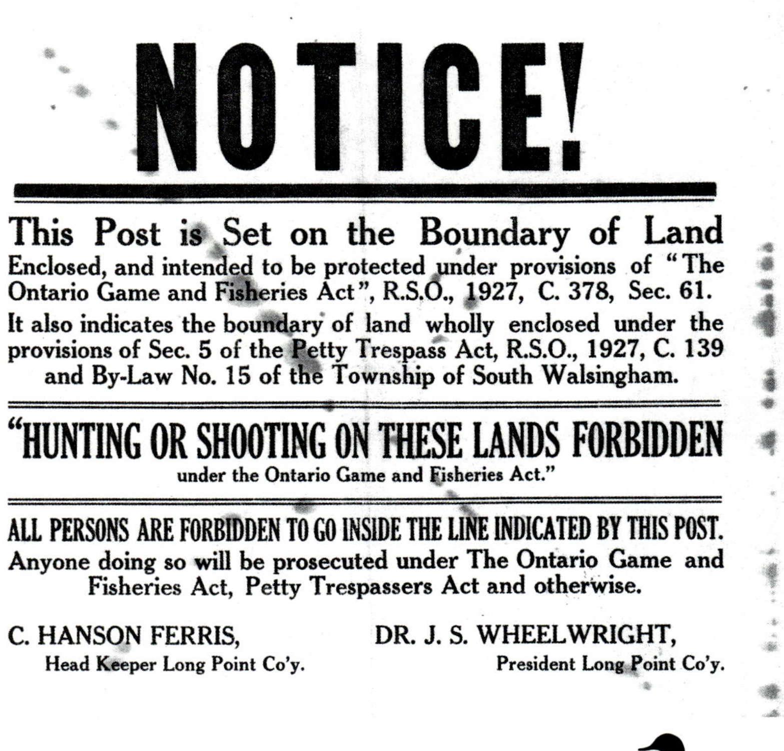

NOTICE!

This Post is Set on the Boundary of Land Enclosed, and intended to be protected under provisions of "The Ontario Game and Fisheries Act", R.S.O., 1927, C. 378, Sec. 61. It also indicates the boundary of land wholly enclosed under the provisions of Sec. 5 of the Petty Trespass Act, R.S.O., 1927, C. 139 and By-Law No. 15 of the Township of South Walsingham.

"HUNTING OR SHOOTING ON THESE LANDS FORBIDDEN under the Ontario Game and Fisheries Act."

ALL PERSONS ARE FORBIDDEN TO GO INSIDE THE LINE INDICATED BY THIS POST. Anyone doing so will be prosecuted under The Ontario Game and Fisheries Act, Petty Trespassers Act and otherwise.

C. HANSON FERRIS,
Head Keeper Long Point Co'y.

DR. J. S. WHEELWRIGHT,
President Long Point Co'y.

Redhead pair by an unknown carver from Toronto, used with Marham rig, circa 1890, $15,000. (*Collection of James R. and Diane Cook*)

Michigan offered the waterfowlers lots of great hunting in areas like the St. Clair Flats, Walpool Island, and Lake Michigan.

Michigan's master carvers, front row left to right: Ferdinand Bach (1888–1967), Benjamin J. Schmidt (1884–1968), and Charles L. Pozzini (1904–1974), all of Detroit. Back row left to right: Thomas Schroeder (1886–1976) and Ralph Johnston, taken in 1967. (*Photograph by Frank M. Cowger*)

American merganser by Ferdinand Bach of Detroit, Michigan, circa 1930, $15,000. (*Collection of James R. and Diane Cook*)

Canvasback pair by Gordon "Pecor" Fox (1914–?) of New Baltimore, Michigan, circa 1940, $800.

Canvasback pair by Ferdinand Bach, circa 1930, $10,000 each. (*Collection of James R. and Diane Cook*)

Hunting rig of Nate Quillin Decoys. The decoys, all predating 1900, include mallards, pintail, redheads, bluebills, and are blue-winged teal drake found on Pointe Mouille. Found circa 1960s.

Pintail drake, Nate Quillin , circa 1880, $3,000. (Collection of Alan and Elaine Haid/Photography by Alan Haid)

Canvasback pair, high-head style, by Ivar Gustav Fernlund of Hamilton, Ontario, circa 1910, $12,000. (*Collection of James R. and Diane Cook*)

Decoys by Nate Quillin (1839-1908) of Rockwood, Michigan, circa 1870: top; helmet style redhead hen sleeper, $6,000; bottom; regular low-head style redhead drake, $6,000.

Blue goose with hollow bottom board by Benj Schimdt (1884–1968) of Detroit, Michigan, circa 1930, $4,000.

Canada goose, hollow with bottom board, by Benj Schimdt, circa 1930, $5,000. (*Collection of James R. and Diane Cook*)

Decoys by Benj Schmidt: top, blackduck, circa 1930, $1,500; bottom, green-winged teal drake, circa 1930, $2,500.

Ringbill drake by Thomas Schroeder (1886–1976) of Detroit Michigan, circa 1930, $3,500

Redhead drake by John Unger of Detroit, Michigan, $1,000. (*Collection of James R. and Diane Cook*)

Swan by an unknown Michigan carver, used at Lake St. Clair Flats Shooting Club circa 1890, $100,000. (*Collection of Alan and Elaine Haid/ Photography by Alan Haid*)

Canvasback decoys by unknown makers from Lake St. Clair near Detroit, Michigan: top, circa 1930, $400; bottom, circa 1930, $400.

Redhead pair, bobtail style typical of Michigan decoys, solid cedar body with rounded off tail, unknown makers, St. Clair Flats, Michigan, circa 1920, $200 each.

Canvasback pair by an unknown maker from Long Point, Ontario, in style typical of this hunting area, circa 1940, $600 each.

Top: Canvasback hen by an unknown maker, used on Detroit River, Detroit, Michigan, circa 1930, $500. Bottom: Redhead drake by Dan Scriven (1880–1943) of Detroit, branded "Hy Dahlka" by this noted hunter in the Detroit River area, circa 1925, $400.

Acrylic painting, Mason Decoy Co. Montage, by Donna Tonelli, 1974, $500.

Many a hunter shot waterfowl over decoys produced by the Mason Decoy Factory in Detroit, Michigan, not only in Michigan but across the country. Founded by William James Mason in 1889, the company remained in operation until 1924. Some of the equipment, patterns, and remaining stock was sold to the Pratt Co. of Joliet, Illinois. The Mason Decoy Co. produced most species of waterfowl in several Grades—Premier, Challenge, Standard (Detroit) glass eye, Standard (Detroit) tack eye, and Fourth Grade painted eye models. Shorebird decoys were offered with glass or tack eyes. The earliest examples of shorebirds had wooden bills and later models had iron bills.

Cover of a W.J. Mason company catalog, Detroit, Michigan, circa 1905.

Standard Model Glass Eye Decoys

Any Specie $12.00 per dozen

F. O. B. Detroit

Mason's Decoy Factory

5971-5975 Milford St. and P. M. R. R.

DETROIT, MICHIGAN

1919

PRICE LIST

All Quotations F. O. B. Detroit

Subject to change without notice

Premier Model (Hollow) - -	$21.00	per	dozen
Mammoth Canvas Back (Solid)	21.00	"	"
Canada Brant - - - - - - -	30.00	"	"
11 W.-Weedless Anchors - -	2.00	"	"
11 BS-Brass Shank Anchors -	2.00	"	"
11 BW-Oval Body Weights -	1.50	"	"
11 BWX-Oval Body Weights (Extra Heavy) - - - - -	1.75	"	"
11 RHL-Rawhide Loops - -	.30	"	"
11 SE-Screw Eyes - - - - -	.15	"	"
11 AC-Anchor Cord - - - - -	.50	"	"
1 FS-Lead Balance Weight -	1.50	"	"
1 J-Iron Loop Anchor - - -	2.00	"	"
1 G-Iron Loop Anchor - - -	2.25	"	"

These prices for immediate acceptance only

MASON'S DECOY FACTORY

5971-5975 Milford St. and P. M. R. R.

DETROIT, MICHIGAN

Price list from the Mason Decoy Factory, circa 1919.

Wood duck drake, extremely rare, Challenge Grade, $35,000. (*Collection of Alan and Elaine Haid/ Photograph by Alan Haid*)

Wooduck drake, Premier Grade. One of two known examples. Considered to be the finest decoy Mason Decoy Co. ever produced. $100,000-plus.

Mallard hen, Premier Grade, $3,500.

Mallard drake, snaky head style Premier Grade, Branded "G. K. Schmidt" as part of that noted decoy rig from Rockford, Illinois, $5,000

Mallard drakes, hollow, Challenge Grade, $2,000 each.

Blackduck, early slope-breasted style, Premier Grade, $5,000; shown with Mason Decoy Co. catalog, $400.

Mallard pair, Detroit Grade, $400 each.

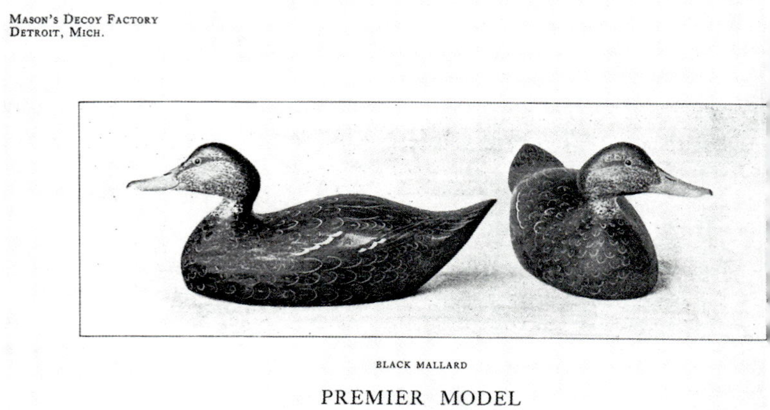
MASON'S DECOY FACTORY
DETROIT, MICH.

BLACK MALLARD

PREMIER MODEL

Entry from 1905 Mason Decoy catalog.

Mallard pair, Detroit Grade, $500 each.

Blackduck, Challenge Grade, $4,000.

Blackduck, Premier Grade, $4,000.

Pintail drakes, Premier Grade: top, very early slope-breasted style, $6,000; later style, $5,000.

Pintail drake, very early slope-breasted style, Premier Grade, $6,000.

Pintail pair, extremely rare hollow Challenge Grade, $8,000. (*Collection of Bill Rigsbee*)

Green-winged teal pair, Premier Grade, rare, $12,500. (*Collection of James R. and Diane Cook*)

Blue-winged teal pair, Premier Grade, $6,000.

Blue-winded teal drake, Premier Grade, double blue wing patch, full crescent, and exceptional crested head style, $5,000.

Blue-winged teal, snaky head style, Premier Grade, $4,000.

Bufflehead drake, Detroit Grade, $3,500.

Bufflehead hen, Challenge Grade, extremely rare, $10,000.

American merganser pair, Premier Grade, $15,000. (*Collection of James R. and Diane Cook*)

American merganser pair, Challenge Grade, $9,000.

Bluebills, Premier Grade, from the Fuller rig: top, early slope-breasted drake, $5,000; bottom, pair in low-head sleeper style, $9,000.

Bluebill pair, Premier Grade, $7,000.

Bluebill (great scaup) pair, snaky head style with extra wide bills, Challenge Grade, $4,000.

Coot, Challenge Grade, $1,500.

Redhead drakes, Premier Grade: top, early style, $4,000; bottom, late style, $2,500.

Canvasback drake, early slope-breasted style, Premier Grade, stamped "V.L.& A." (Von Lengercke & Antoine Sporting Goods, Chicago, Illinois), $5,000.

Entry from the 1905 catalog.

Brant, Challenge Grade, classic "Barron" rig, owned by the Barron Gun Club, Virginia, circa 1910, $2,000.

Entry from 1905 catalog: center bird and two left decoys are rare wooden-bill style.

Early style wooden bill shorebirds, extremely rare, circa 1905: left, dowitcher, $10,000; right, snipe, $10,000. (*Collection of Alan and Elaine Haid/Photography by Alan Haid*)

Special order wooden bill shorebirds, extremely rare: left, robin snipe, $8,000; black-bellied plover, $8,000. (*Collection of Alan and Elaine Haid/Photography by Alan Haid*)

Rare wooden bill, split-tail black-bellied plover, $8,000. (*Collection of Alan and Elaine Haid/Photography by Alan Haid*)

Entry from a 1905 Mason catalog.

Oil painting by Kingdon Hemming of Mason long-billed curlew, circa 1969, $500.

Hunters had great success this day over their Dodge pintail decoys. Note the live decoys in the foreground. Circa 1900. (*Courtesy of Morton Smith Jr.*)

Long-billed curlews: left, special-order patterned after William Bowman-style decoy with raised carved wings, $12,000; right, Standard Mason-style two-piece Glass-eye Grade curlew, $15,000. (*Collection of Alan and Elaine Haid/Photography by Alan Haid*)

Mallard hen from the J. N. Dodge Decoy Co. (1884–1894) of Detroit, Michigan, extremely rare, $1,250. (*Collection of Alan and Elaine Haid/ Photography by Alan Haid*)

Widgeon drake by J. N. Dodge Decoy Co., $4,000. (*Collection of James R. and Diane Cook*)

Blue-wing teal drake, George Peterson Decoy Co. (1873–1884), Detroit, Michigan, $2,500.

By the 1950s, molded paper mâché and plastic decoys were replacing the wooden decoy. Carry-Lite Decoy Co. of Milwaukee, Wisconsin, produced an interesting line of decoys. Early birds have large full-color labels glued to their bottoms. In mint condition, these types of decoys are becoming collectible.

Duck skiff sign from Fox Lake, Wisconsin, hung outside W. Nourse's boat building shop, circa 1930, $2,000.

Miscellaneous Wisconsin buttons: guide, hunting license, and warden badges, and a guide's patch, circa 1950, $100-300 each. (*Collection of Dean Dashner*)

Mallard pair, miniature, by Warren P. Dettman (1904–1979) of Milwaukee, Wisconsin, circa 1947, $2,500. (*Collection of T. Thompson Bosworth/ Photograph by Joanne Peterson*)

Miscellaneous Wisconsin warden badges, shoulder patches, and belt buckle, circa 1950, $100-150 each. (*Collection of Dean Dashner*)

Mallard hen by Warren Dettman of Milwaukee, Wisconsin, circa 1947, $4,000. (*Collection of T. Thompson Bosworth/Photograph by Joanne Peterson*)

Decoys by Walter Pelzer (1911–?) of Milwaukee, Milwaukee Public Museum school, circa 1940: top, bluebill hen, $3,000; bottom, ringbill hen, $3,000. (*Collection of Herb Desch*)

Bluebill pair by Pelzer/Dettman of Milwaukee, Wisconsin school, circa 1930, $8,000. (*Collection of James R. and Diane Cook*)

Pintail drake by Pelzer/ Dettman, Milwaukee, Wisconsin, circa 1930. $6,000.

Walter Evans (1872–1948) of Ladysmith, Wisconsin, started his production of hunting decoys under the Evans Decoy Co. name in the early 1920s and continued to offer canvasback, mallard, pintail, redhead, green-winged and blue-winged teal, bluebills, and coot decoys in three Grades: Mammoth, Standard, and Competitive until the mid 1930s.

Canvasback drake from the Evans Decoy Co., Standard Model, $500.

FROM

THE EVANS DUCK DECOY CO.

MANUFACTURERS OF

LIKE-LIVE DUCK DECOYS

LADYSMITH, WIS.

CONTENTS-FOURTH-CLASS MATTER-MERCHANDISE

POSTMASTER: This parcel may be opened for postal inspection if necessary

TO

1931 1932

Price List

EVANS DECOYS

LIKE LIVE

Manufactured by

EVANS DUCK DECOY COMPANY

Ladysmith, Wisconsin

LIVE BIRDS ARE OUR MODELS

PERFECTION OUR AMBITION

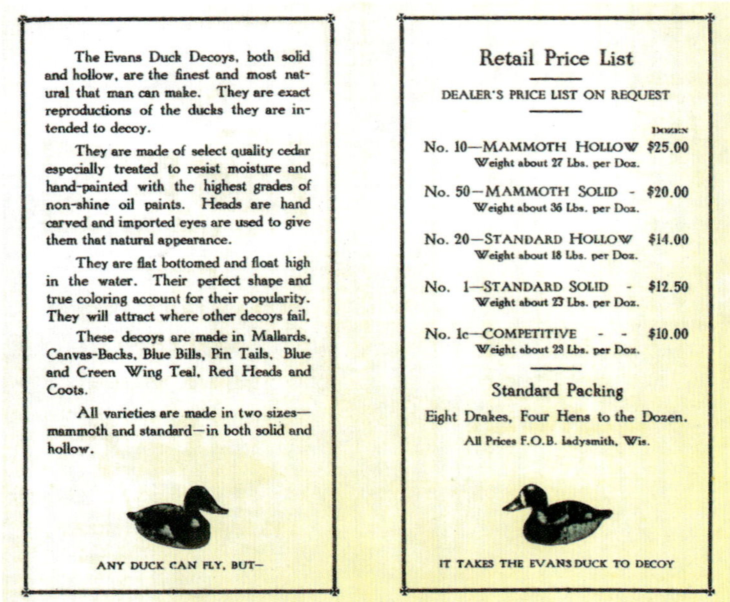

The Evans Duck Decoys, both solid and hollow, are the finest and most natural that man can make. They are exact reproductions of the ducks they are intended to decoy.

They are made of select quality cedar especially treated to resist moisture and hand-painted with the highest grades of non-shine oil paints. Heads are hand carved and imported eyes are used to give them that natural appearance.

They are flat bottomed and float high in the water. Their perfect shape and true coloring account for their popularity. They will attract where other decoys fail.

These decoys are made in Mallards, Canvas-Backs, Blue Bills, Pin Tails, Blue and Green Wing Teal, Red Heads and Coots.

All varieties are made in two sizes—mammoth and standard—in both solid and hollow.

ANY DUCK CAN FLY, BUT—

Retail Price List

DEALER'S PRICE LIST ON REQUEST

	Dozen
No. 10—Mammoth Hollow Weight about 27 Lbs. per Doz.	$25.00
No. 50—Mammoth Solid - Weight about 36 Lbs. per Doz.	$20.00
No. 20—Standard Hollow Weight about 18 Lbs. per Doz.	$14.00
No. 1—Standard Solid - Weight about 23 Lbs. per Doz.	$12.50
No. 1c—Competitive - - Weight about 23 Lbs. per Doz.	$10.00

Standard Packing

Eight Drakes, Four Hens to the Dozen.

All Prices F.O.B. Ladysmith, Wis.

IT TAKES THE EVANS DUCK TO DECOY

Packing label and 1931–1932 price list from Evans Decoy Co.

Blue-winged teal from the Evans Decoy Co., circa 1930, $1,500 each. (*Collection of Herb Desch*)

Bluebill pair from the Evans Decoy Co., hollow Standard Grade, circa 1930, $2,000. (*Collection of Herb Desch*)

Green-winged teal, hollow, from the Evans Decoy Co. Extremely rare, only known examples, circa 1925, $6,000. (*Collection of James R. and Diane Cook*)

Blackducks from the Evans Decoy Co.: top, Mammoth Grade hollow, circa 1920, $1,500; bottom, Standard Grade, circa 1920, $1,000. (*Collection of Dean Dashner*)

Mallard pair, flying miniatures on painted plaque, by Joseph Gigle of Neehan, Wisconsin, circa 1940, $1,000.

Canada geese, flying miniatures mounted on painted wooden bowl, by Joseph Gigle, circa 1940, $1,000.

Mandt Homme (1905–1964) of MacFarland, Wisconsin, circa 1935. (*Photograph by Enoch Reindahl/Courtesy of Mrs. Mandt Homme*)

Owen Gromme of Milwaukee, Wisconsin, was the leading force that propelled the Milwaukee Public Museum's P.W.A.-style decoys. Mallard hen, circa 1940, $4,000; Pintail drake, $5,000.

Canada goose by Mandt Homme, circa 1930, $20,000.

Canada geese in Owen Gromme's basement. Gromme's molds that were used to form this rig of paper mâché field decoys can be seen on the lower shelf.

Canvasback drake by Mandt Homme, circa 1940, $3,000.

Canvasback pair by Mandt Homme, circa 1930, $10,000 pair.

Below: Mallard pair with sleeper hen by Ferdinand Homme, circa 1940, $8,000. (*Collection of James R. and Diane Cook*)

Rear view of canvasbacks.

Mallard drake, sleeper style, by Ferdinand Homme of Mac Farland, Wisconsin, circa 1930, $10,000. (*Collection of Gene and Linda Kangas*)

Stencil on bottom of Homme drake.

Carvers Roy E. Discher (1899–1977) and Charles Koepsel (1898–1980) of Milwaukee, Wisconsin. This was a promotional photograph from Blatz Brewing Co.'s display of their decoys. (*Courtesy of John D. Riefenrather*)

Decoys by Koepsel and Discher, circa 1940: top, mallard drake, $500; bottom, canvasback drake, $500.

Brochure, *How to Make Decoys*, by Roy Discher and Chuck Koepsel. Was distributed at Blatz Brewing Co.'s display at the Milwaukee sport show, circa 1954. (*Courtesy of John D. Reifenrather*)

Canada goose by Discher and Koepsel, circa 1940, $1,000. (*Courtesy of John D. Riefenrather*)

Blackduck sleeper by Walter Lowry of LaCrosse, Wisconsin, circa 1930, $2,500. (*Collection of Dean Dashner*)

Mallard pair by Walter Lowry, circa 1930, $3,000. (*Collection of Herb Desch*)

Canada goose by August "Gus" Moak (1852–1942) of Tustin, Wisconsin, circa 1930, $3,000. (*Collection of Herb Desch*)

Canvasback pair, swimming style, by Gus Moak, circa 1920, $5,000. (*Collection of Herb Desch*)

Canvasback drake by Gus Moak, circa 1920, $2,000.

Mallard pair by Gus Nelow of Omro, Wisconsin, circa 1940, $2,500. (*Collection of Dean Dashner*)

Bluebill pair by August "Gus" Nelow (1882–1962) of Oshkosh and Omro, Wisconsin, circa 1940, $3,000.

Wisconsin decoys: top, unknown mallard drake, circa 1940, $500; bottom, blue-winged teal by Gus Nelow, circa 1940, $2,000. (*Collection of Dean Dashner*)

Bluebill pair by Gus Nelow, circa 1940, $2,000.

Bluebill drake by John D. Reinfenrather of Madison, Wisconsin, circa 1950, $500.

Enoch Reindahl (1904–present) of Stoughton, Wisconsin, with his personal hunting rig featured in *Sports Afield* article by Enoch Reindahl, "How to Make Decoys," August 1949. (*Photograph by Enoch Reindahl*)

Mallard hen, swimming style, by Enoch Reindahl, circa 1940, $3,000.

Pintail drake, Enoch Reindahl, Stoughton, Wisconsin, circa 1940, $6,000. Reindahl Brothers sign hung at the entrance of their lakeside camp.

Mallard drake, sleeper style, by Enoch Reindahl, circa 1940, $5,000.

Canada goose, removable head, by Enoch Reindahl, circa 1940, $20,000.

Enoch Reinhadl with his goose decoys. (*Photo by Reindahl, circa 1938*)

Mallard hen, early gunning decoy by Enoch Reindahl, circa 1930, $3,000.

Blue-winged teal by Frank Resop, circa 1930, $2,000.

Oil painting: canvasbacks over Reindahl canvasback decoys, oil on canvas by Enoch Reindahl, circa 1930, $1,000.

Canvasback pair by Frank G. Strey (1890–1966) of Oshkosh, Wisconsin, circa 1930, $1,500.

Canvasback pair by Frank Resop (1898–1962) of Berlin, Wisconsin, circa 1930, $1,500.

Redhead pair by Frank G. Strey, circa 1930, $1,500. (*Collection of Herb Desch*)

Canvasback drake, high-head style, by Joseph Seiger, Tustin, Wisconsin, circa 1920, $5,000.

Mallard pair by Frank G. Strey, circa 1940, $2,000. (*Collection of Herb Desch*)

Mallard drake in Milwaukee Public Museum school, unknown P.W.A. maker, circa 1940, hollow, $2, 500. (*Collection of Dean Dashner*)

Canvasback drakes by Sylvester "Swede" Swedesky of Neehna, Wisconsin, circa 1930, $1,000 each.

Redhead drake in Milwaukee Public Museum school, circa 1940, $3,000.

Canvasback pair, sleeper drake and a preening hen, maker unknown, from Lake Poygan area in Wisconsin, circa 1920, $3,000. (*Collection of Dean Dashner*)

Mallard pair by DeWitt Wakefield (1850–1912) of Fremont, circa 1880, $3,000. (*Collection of Herb Desch*)

Blue-winged teal by Otto Weinert (1893–1979) of Oshkosh, Wisconsin, circa 1940, $2,000.

Enamel "No Hunting Sign" used at Willossippi Refuge in Palisade, Minnesota, circa 1980, $50.

Mallard drake, rare, standing field model only, offered in catalog for three years by Herter's Inc., circa 1977, $800.

Carvings by Fred Lexow (1888–1971) of Balsam Lake Minnesota, circa 1930: bluebill drake decoy, $800; bluebill, jewelry box, $250.

Canada goose, earliest style Herter decoy, blanks were turned by Chicago Novelty Co. and finished by Herter's Inc., circa 1942, $400.

Mallard pair, rare standing field decoys, by John Tax (1894–1967) of Osakis, Minnesota, circa 1930, $30,000. (*Collection of James R. and Diane Cook*)

Canada geese, rare standing field decoys, by John Tax of Osakis, Minnesota, circa 1920, $40,000. (*Collection of James R. and Diane Cook*)

Wooduck drake by Herter's Inc. of Waseca, Minnesota, circa 1960, $250. Herter's decoy catalog, circa 1942, $75.

Coot, by unknown maker, used at Leech Lake Hunting Club in Walker, Minnesota, circa 1900. $500 each.

Abe Nelson (center) is attributed with originating the Heron Lake "Horse head" style canvasback decoy. Heron Lake, Minnesota, circa 1910. (*Courtesy of Morton Smith Jr.*)

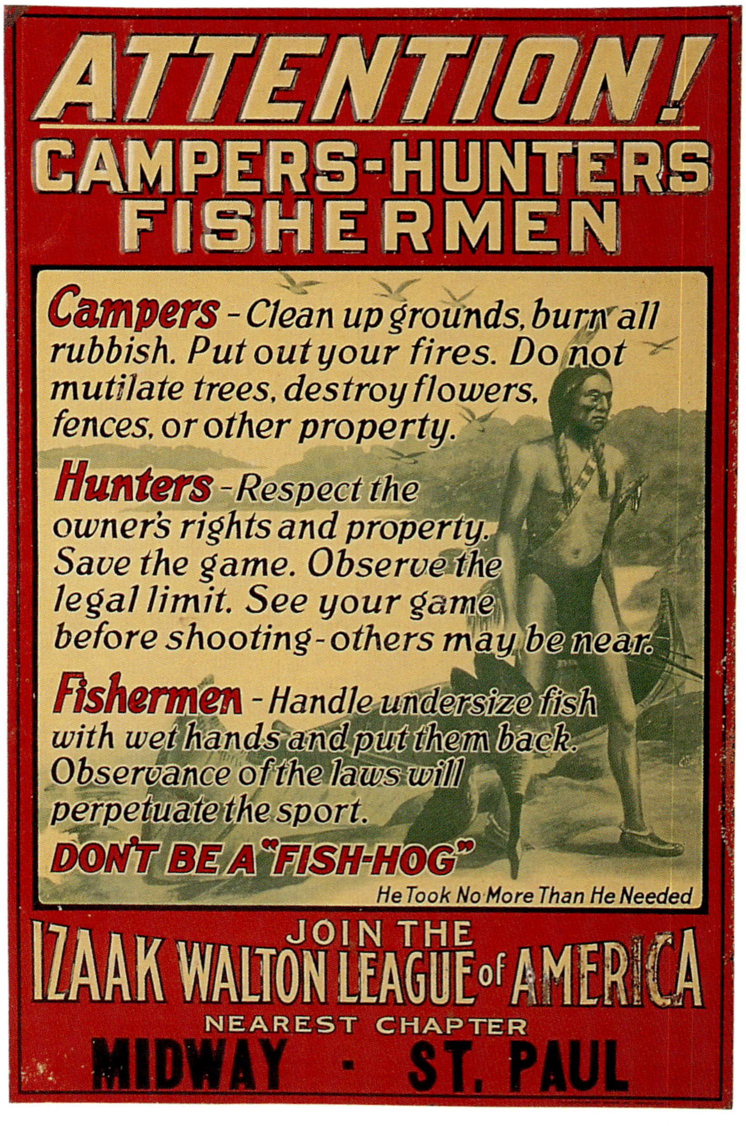

Conservation sign, porcelain, from Izaak Walton League of America, Minneapolis, Minnesota chapter, circa 1965, $75.

Canvasback drakes, classic "horse head cans" used on Heron Lake—"The Chesapeake of the West," circa 1880: top, attributed to Harry Converse of Heron Lake, $1,500; bottom, attributed to Joseph Peterson of Heron Lake, $1,500.

A guide from the Ranch poses with the day's kill, circa 1910. (*Photograph by Morton Smith, Jr.*)

Canvasback drakes used on Heron Lake by Joseph Marr of Sioux Falls, South Dakota: top, immature drake, $1,500; bottom, drake, $1,000.

Canvasbacks from Heron Lake: top, hen by Joseph Marr of Sioux Falls, South Dakota, $2,000; bottom, drake by Harry Converse, $2,000.

Harry Converse (left) frequently guided John D. McMillan (right), vice-president of the Cargill Corp., as he hunted Heron Lake. He was a member of the noted club known simply as "the Ranch," circa 1920. (*Photo courtesy of Morton Smith, Jr.*)

Mallard drakes from the Tuveson Decoy Co. in St. James, Minnesota, circa 1930: top: flying mallard decoy, $750; bottom; standard decoy, $400.

Bluebill pair, working decoys, Marty Hanson, St. Cloud Minnesota, circa 1960, $600.

Mallard pair, Pascagoula-type factory decoys, Pascagoula, Mississippi, circa 1950, $100.

Mallard pair from the Pascagoula Decoy Co. in Pascagoula, Mississippi, circa 1950, $100.

Pintail pair attributed to Charles W. Grubbs of Pascagoula, Mississippi, circa 1940, $200.

Charles Grubbs, noted duck call maker, is credited with originating the Pascagoula type decoy when he moved to Pascagola, Mississippi around 1920.

Blue-winged teal by Paul Lipke of Whiting, Indiana, circa 1940, $3,000. (*Collection of James R. and Diane Cook*)

Mallard hen, sleeper style, by Carl Sattler (1899–1979) of Burlington, Iowa, circa 1930, $2,000. (*Collection of James R. and Diane Cook*)

Canvasback pair, sleepers, by William T. Enright (1913–1979) of Toledo, Ohio, circa 1940, $600.

Redhead drake by John "Jack" Frederick Rider (1881–1967) of Port Clinton, Ohio, circa 1940, $500.

Redhead drake by an unknown maker, from the Blair school, circa 1880, found and used at a hunting club near Sandusky, Ohio, $4,000. (*Collection of Alan and Elaine Haid/ Photograph by Alan Haid*)

Widgeon drake by Jack Musgrove of Des Moines, Iowa, author of *Waterfowl in Iowa*, circa 1940, $2,000.

Benz Lifelike Decoys of Jefferson City, Missouri, circa 1920.

Shoveler drake from J. M. Hays Wood Products Co. in Jefferson, City, Missouri, circa 1925, $500.

Field and Stream—June, 1923

Advertisement for the J. M. Hays Wood Products Co.

Fred Allen (1838–1912) of Mommouth, Illinois.

Redhead drake by Fred Allen, circa 1880, $5,000; and Allen duck calls: metal calls, $400 each, wooden call, $150. (*Collection of Alan and Elaine Haid/Photograph by Alan Haid*)

Mallard pair by Fred Allen, circa 1880, $8,000. (*Collection of Alan and Elaine Haid/Photograph by Alan Haid*)

Pintail drake by Charles Althoff (1859–1942) of Princeton, Illinois, circa 1890, $3, 500. (*Collection of Alan and Elaine Haid/Photograph by Alan Haid*)

Canada goose by George "Homerun Skippy" Barto (1880–1959) of Joliet, Illinois, circa 1940, $4,000. (*Photograph courtesy of Lakeview Museum, Peoria, Illinois*)

Photo taken in 1957 of Verne Cheesman (1897–?) of Mommouth, Illinois, with a pintail drake, circa 1930, $2,000. (*Photo courtesy of Joseph French*)

Shoveler, pair, only known examples, by Frank Cassini (1899–1967) of Galesburg, Illinois. This pair of decoys are featured on the cover of *Decoys and Decoy Carvers of Illinois*. Circa 1930, $40,000. (*Collection of James R. and Diane Cook*)

Sign for the Coleman Club, owned and operated by Fred W. Coleman of Putman County, Illinois, circa 1930. The area is now the Donnelley Wildlife Area managed and owned by the State of Illinois. $250.

Green-winged teal by Fred W. Coleman (1898–1990) of Hennipen, Illinois, circa 1940, $2,500.

Mallard drake in the classic Illinois River sleeper style by Duane Corbin, Joilet, Illinois, circa 1920. $1,200.

Mallard pair, oversized style, by Walter H. "Tube" Dawson (1882–1955) of Putman, Illinois, circa 1920. $1,800.

Robert (1848–1915) and Catherine (1858–1953) Elliston with family in Bureau, Illinois.

Below: Blue-winged teal drake, extremely rare, carved by Robert Elliston and painted by Catherine, circa $35,000.

Blackduck, oversized sleeper style, only known example, by Robert Elliston, circa 1880, $50,000. (*Collection of Alan and Elaine Haid/ Photography by Alan Haid*)

Bluebill drakes by Robert Elliston, painted by Catherine: top, round body style, circa 1880, $12,000; bottom, flat body style, circa 1890, $6,000.

Canvasback drake, flat body style, painted by Catherine, circa 1880, $5,000.

Redhead drake, round body style, by Robert Elliston, painted by Catherine, circa 1880, $12,000.

Canvasback drake, round body style, by Robert Elliston, painted by Catherine, circa 1880, $8,000.

Mallard pair by Robert Elliston, painted by Catherine, circa 1880, $6,000.

Pintail drake by William "Skinny" Evans (1892–1937) of Peru, Illinois, circa 1920, $2,500. (*Collection of James R. and Diane Cook*)

Pintail drake by August P. Ewand (1865–1925) of Peru, Illinois, circa 1890, $800. (*Collection of Alan and Elaine Haid/Photograph by Alan Haid*)

Mallard drake with original box and instructions, paper mâché with movable metal wings from the Flap-o-matic Co. in Chicago Illinois, Patent #2, 747, and 316, Frank J. Benedetto, circa 1950, $400.

Otto Garren (1890–1968) of Canton, Illinois, with mallard hen sleeper, $1,000. (*Photograph circa 1952 by Joseph French*)

Mallard pair by G. Bert Graves of Peoria, Illinois, painted by Catherine Elliston, circa 1920, $8,000.

Pintail drake by G. Bert Graves, painted by Catherine Elliston, circa 1920, $4,000.

Wooduck by Otto Garren of Canton, Illinois, circa 1940, $5,000. (*Collection of James R. Cook*)

G. Bert Graves (1887–1956) of Peoria with his brother-in-law and hunting companion, George Snider (on right) after a day's shoot on the far west side Upper Peoria Lake off the sea wall at Rome, Illinois, where there was once a 3,000-acre bed of sago pond weed and celery grass that attracted great rafts of canvasbacks. Circa 1920.

Canvasback pair by G. Bert Graves, circa 1920, $10,000.

Mallard hen sleeper style, by G. Bert Graves, painted by Catherine Elliston, circa 1920, $15,000.

Mallard drake, mammoth style, by G. Bert Graves, painted by Catherine Elliston, circa 1920, $10,000.

Pintail drake by August Haas (1890–1962) of Peru, Illinois, circa 1920, $15,000.

Hunter's sign for the Fox Valley Archers, circa 1950, $100.

Pintail hen with brood by Harold Haertel of Dundee, Illinois, $4,000. Photo circa 1995 by Kurt Butcher.

Harold Haertel (1904–1996) of Dundee, Illinois, with the late Charles Klopp. Charles Klopp was an early decoy collector from Palatine, Illinois, circa 1960. (*Photograph by Joseph French*)

Western grebe pair by Harold Haertel, $1,200. Photo circa 1995 by Kurt Butcher.

Pintail drake by Henry Holmes (1870–1940) of Bureau, Illinois, circa 1915, $2,000.

Gadwall pair by Harold Haertel of Dundee, Illinois, circa 1960, $6,000. (*Collection of Barbara Sorenson*)

Mallard pair, oversized style, by Henry Holmes of Bureau, Illinois, circa 1915, $5,000.

Mallard drake by Louis P. Kelly (1878–1958) of Peoria, Illinois, circa 1940. $3,000.

Mallard pair by Hiram "Hy" Holtz (1886–1979) of Peoria, Illinois, circa 1940, $8,000.

Blue-winged teal by Stephen Lane (1842–1900) and William Shaw (1849–1927) of Lacon, Illinois, circa 1880, $5,000.

Roy Kamm (1902–?) of Lacon, Illinois, with mallards, $500 each. Photograph circa 1955 by Joseph French

Shown here with his work, Cline McAlpin (1919–1969) of Chicago, Illinois, patterned his decoys after Charles Perdew's work during the 1950s: foreground, pintail pair with sleeper hen, circa 1957, $500 each; background, mallard drake, circa 1957, $500. (*Photo Courtesy of Joseph French*)

Mallard pair with sleeper style hen in miniature by Cline McAlpin, circa 1955. $500 pair

Douglas Moseley (1860–1924) of Princeton, Illinois, was one of the founding members of the Princeton Game and Fish Club in Bureau County. Ironically, although he was president of the Citizen's Bank of Princeton for many years, Moseley will be better remembered as a Illinois River decoy carver. Mallard pair by Douglas Moseley, painted by his wife, Sara Louise Moseley, circa 1880, $6,000.

Oil on composition plate by Sara Louise Moseley of Princeton, Illinois, circa 1890, $200.

Pintail drake by J. Fred Mott, Sr. (1866–1934) of Pekin, Illinois, circa 1920, $400.

Charles Perdew (1874–1963) of Henry, Illinois. Photograph circa 1948 by Dean Sandry.

Redhead drake by Douglas Moseley of Princeton, Illinois, circa 1880, $4,000.

Charles Perdew, circa 1955.

Oil on canvas by Edna Perdew. Although Edna painted many watercolor landscapes, this is one of the few wildlife paintings she executed. Circa 1930, $3,000.

Charles and Edna Perdew (1882–1974). Photograph circa 1955 by Joseph French of Marathon, Florida.

Mallard drake with carved cheeks and raised wings by Charles Perdew, painted by Edna Perdew, circa 1940, $20,000.

Mallard hen, sleepy eye style, carved cheeks, raised wings, by Charles Perdew, painted by Charles Perdew, circa 1940. Most collectors considered this to be the finest decoy Perdew ever carved. It was given with a matching mallard to Saci Sacarro of Spring Valley, Illinois, as repayment for getting saw blades for Perdew during World War II. $50,000.

Mallard drake, carved-wing style, painted by Charles Perdew, circa 1945, $3,000.

Pintail drake by Charles Perdew, painted by Edna Perdew, circa 1940, $5,000.

Mallard drake, painted by Charles Perdew, circa 1940, $2,500

Pintail hen sleeper by Charles Perdew, painted by Edna Perdew, circa 1920, one of two known, $50,000.

Mallard hen sleeper by Charles Perdew, painted by Edna Perdew, circa 1930, $20,000.

Mallard drake, early style, by Charles Perdew, painted by Edna Perdew, circa 1920, $7,000.

Green-winged teal drake, sleeper, rare Perdew, painted by Edna Perdew, circa 1920, $50,000.

Mallard drake, early three-piece style by Perdew, circa 1915, painted by Edna Perdew, $15,000.

Pintail drake by Charles Perdew, painted by Edna Perdew, rare, circa 1920, $15,000.

Canvasback drake by Charles Perdew, painted by Edna Perdew, rare, circa 1920, $20,000.

Ladies brooches by Charles Perdew, circa 1940: pheasant, $750; mallard drake, $300; mallard hen, $750.

Wooduck drake, standing miniature, by Charles Perdew, circa 1930, $1,000.

Mallard drake, standing miniature with outstretched wings, by Charles Perdew, circa 1930, $2,000.

Blue-winged teal, flying in diorama, by Charles Perdew, circa 1920, $3,000.

Mallard pair, three-quarter sized miniatures with standing drake, by Charles Perdew, circa 1940, $4,000.

Mallard pair, flying miniatures in diorama, by Chris B. Powers (1902–1958) of Peru, Illinois, circa 1920, $800.

WM. E. PRATT MFG. CO.

Established 1893—Incorporated 1923

190 North State St.
CHICAGO, ILLINOIS

Works at Joliet, Ill.

FEBRUARY, 1925

MANUFACTURERS OF

Sporting Goods
Malleable Iron Castings

The William E. Pratt Manufacturing Co. was established in 1893 and incorporated in 1923. Prior to 1920 the plant produced malleable iron castings. Sometime after 1920, William E. Pratt (d. 1939) introduced a line of sporting goods including hunting decoys, live decoy halters, and cast iron decoy weights.

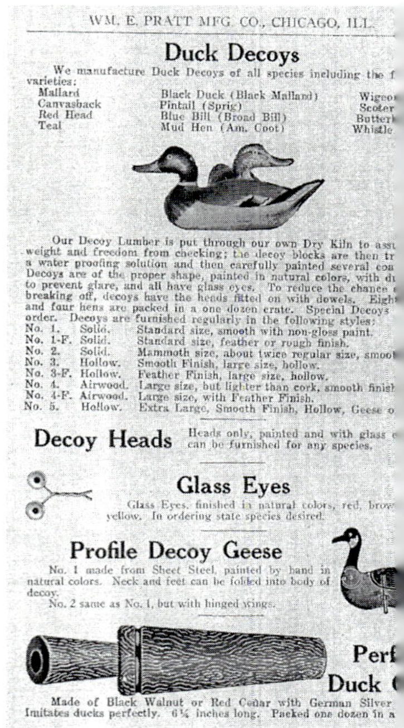

WM. E. PRATT MFG. CO., CHICAGO, ILL.

Duck Decoys

We manufacture Duck Decoys of all species including the f
varieties:

Mallard	Black Duck (Black Mallard)	Wigeo
Canvasback	Pintail (Sprig)	Scoter
Red Head	Blue Bill (Broad Bill)	Butterb
Teal	Mud Hen (Am. Coot)	Whistle

Our Decoy Lumber is put through our own Dry Kiln to assu weight and freedom from checking; the decoy blocks are then tr a water proofing solution and then carefully painted several coa Decoys are of the proper shape, painted in natural colors, with du to prevent glare, and all have glass eyes. To reduce the chance o breaking off, decoys have the heads fitted on with dowels. Eigh and four hens are packed in a one dozen crate. Special Decoys order. Decoys are furnished regularly in the following styles:

No. 1.	Solid.	Standard size, smooth with non-gloss paint.
No. 1-F.	Solid.	Standard size, feather or rough finish.
No. 2.	Solid.	Mammoth size, about twice regular size, smoot
No. 3.	Hollow.	Smooth Finish, large size, hollow.
No. 3-F.	Hollow.	Feather Finish, large size, hollow.
No. 4.	Airwood.	Large size, but lighter than cork, smooth finish
No. 4-F.	Airwood.	Large size, with Feather Finish.
No. 5.	Hollow.	Extra Large, Smooth Finish, Hollow, Geese o

Decoy Heads — Heads only, painted and with glass e can be furnished for any species.

Glass Eyes

Glass Eyes, finished in natural colors, red, brow yellow. In ordering state species desired.

Profile Decoy Geese

No. 1 made from Sheet Steel, painted by hand in natural colors. Neck and feet can be folded into body of decoy.

No. 2 same as No. 1, but with hinged wings.

Perf
Duck

Made of Black Walnut or Red Cedar with German Silver Imitates ducks perfectly. 6¼ inches long. Packed one dozen in a

Mallard pair by Chris B. Powers, circa 1940, $5,000. (*Collection of Alan and Elaine Haid/Photograph by Alan Haid*)

Mallard drake, metal with wooden head and bottom board, by William E. Pratt Manufacturing Co., stenciled inside "patent applied," $300.

Mallard hen, canvas decoy with movable wings, from the J. W. Reynolds Decoy Factory in Chicago, Illinois, circa 1910, $500.

Canada goose by Otto Quesh (1865–1949) of Chicago, Illinois, circa 1940, $2,500. (*Photograph courtesy of Lakeview Museum, Peoria, Illinois*)

Shoveler pair from the Rose Folding Decoy Co. in Chicago, Illinois, circa 1900, $800.

Emile Heilbron, original owner of the Rice Pond Hunting Club grounds in Henry, Illinois, poses around 1910. In the background stands a typical Illinois River shanty, high on stilts to accommodate river fluctuations. Decoys piled at his side were carved by Henry W. Ruggles (1830–1897) of Henry, Illinois.

Charles Schoenheider, Sr., (1854–1944) of Peoria, Illinois, supplemented his income as a carpenter and fed his nine children by hunting for the market.

Canada goose by Charles Schoenheider, Sr. of Peoria, Illinois, circa 1890, $75,000. (*Collection of Alan and Elaine Haid/Photograph of Alan Haid*)

Pintail pair, standing "ice ducks" by Charles Schoenheider, Sr., circa 1880, $75,000. (*Collection of James R. and Diane Cook*)

Photo taken by Charles Schoenhieder family of a rig of field goose decoys he created for the Vorhees family. The decoys were refused by Vorhees and remained in Schoenhieder's garage until collectors started to buy them during the 1960s from his son, Charles Jr.

Blue-winged teal drake by Charles Schoenheider Sr., painted by Charles Franks of Peoria, Illinois, circa 1890, $35,000.

Mallard by Charles Shelstrom (1856–1932) of Princeton, Illinois, circa 1880, $4,000; rule book from the Mallard Club in Bureau County, Illinois, circa 1890, $200.

Mallard hen, standing "ice duck" by Charles Schoenheider, Jr. (1892–1977) of Peoria, Illinois, circa 1950, $2,500.

"Mr X" decoys carved by George Sibley of Chicago, circa 1890: top, widgeon drake, $7,000; bottom, mallard drake, $4,000; original brochure discovered in 1990, which identified this famed decoy carver.

Decoy carver diorama miniature by Wendell B. Sheerman (1920–present) of Streator, Illinois, circa 1967, $300.

Mallard drake standing field decoy, feeding style, by Jack F. Stiles (1902–?) of Savanna, Illinois, circa 1940, $3,000; Cobbe Corn Decoy from the Bedard & Morency Mill Co. in Oak Park, Illinois, circa 1930, $200. *(Collection of James R. and Diane Cook)*

Mallard pair from the Tru-dux Wood Products Co. owned and operated by Alfred E. Ries (d. 1959), Chicago, Illinois, circa 1940, $400.

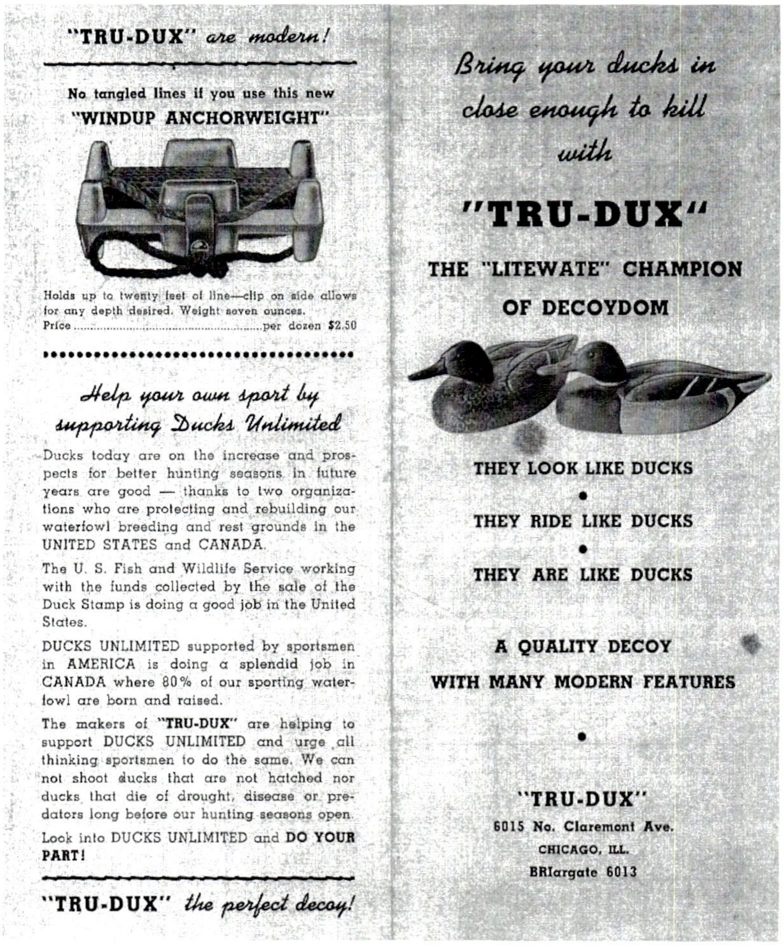

"Tru-Dux, The 'litewate' champion of decoydom."

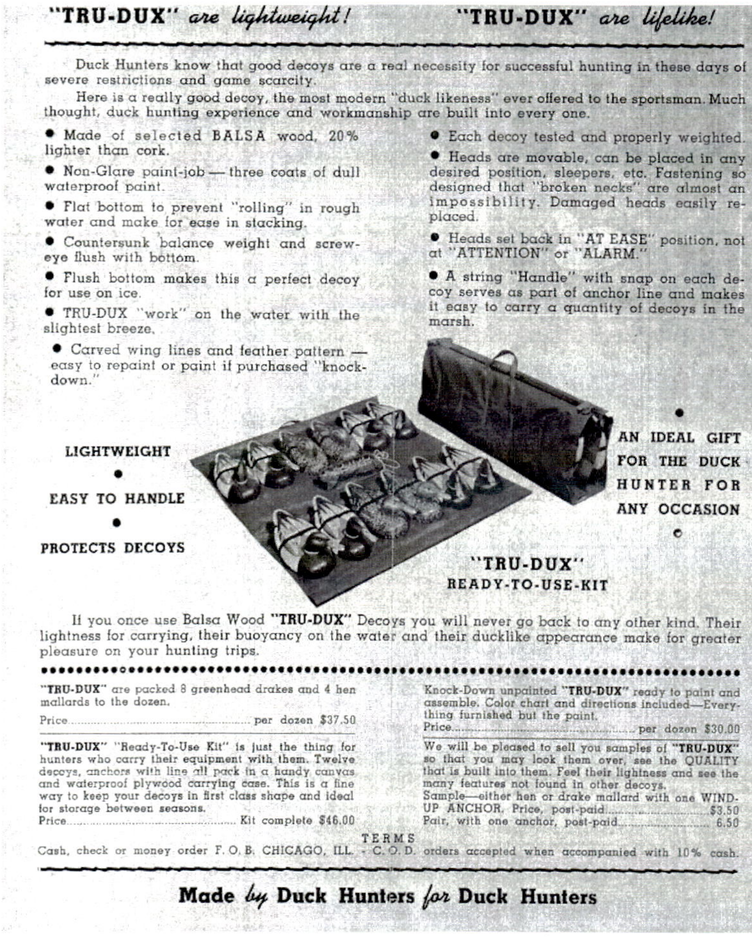

"For sale" sign, painted wood, circa 1950, $75.

Mallard pair by Michael Vallero (1906–19?) of Spring Valley, Illinois, circa 1930, $4,000.

Factory decoys: top, mallard drake, special order, from the Wildfowler Decoy Co. in Old Saybrook, Connecticut, circa 1940, $300; bottom, pintail drake, Tru-Dux, circa 1940, $400.

Charles Walker (1876–1954) of Princeton, Illinois, on the far right with sons and friends, from the left: Clarence "Fats" Anderson, Harold Walker, Bixley Berry, and George Walker. Circa 1925.

Mallard pair, carved-wing style, by Charles Walker, circa 1930, $35,000.

Mallard pair, round body style, by Charles Walker, circa 1940, $30,000

Pintail drake, carved-wing style, by Charles Walker, circa 1930, $25,000.

Canada goose with removable head by Charles Walker circa 1920, extremely rare, $50,000.

Mallard drake, carved-wing style, by Charles Walker, circa 1930, $15,000.

Mallard pair with duckling, miniatures by Charles Walker, signed and dated to his son, Forrest Walker, circa 1937, $8,000.

Robert Week's early decorative decoys were sold exclusively by Ranch House Lodge in Bureau, Illinois. Mallard pair with sleeper-style hen, by Robert Weeks of Bureau, Illinois, circa 1950, $800.

Pintail pair by Hector Whittington of Oglesby, Illinois, circa 1940, $3,000.

Mallard pair by Hector Whittington of Oglesby, Illinois, circa 1930, $3,000.

Canada goose by Hector Whittington (1907–1981) of Oglesby, Illinois, circa 1950, $5,000. (*Photograph courtesy of Lakeview Museum, Peoria, Illinois*)

Perry Wilcoxen (1862–1954) of Liverpool, Illinois, with Canada goose, $1,000; miniature mallard and pintail, $150 each; also full size mallard and pintail, $400 each.

Canvasback drake by Perry Wilcoxen, circa 1920, $600.

Gadwall hen, extremely rare, by an unknown maker, painted by Charles Franks of Peoria, Illinois, circa 1890, $2,500.

Hunters sometimes tried to use decoys other than the birds they were hunting to create a more natural appearance to their decoy set up. This crane decoy was one of two known to have been used at the Crane Lake Gun Club in Bath, Illinois. The decoy, maker unknown, is carved of pine with a detachable head. The walnut bill and legs were inset as were multiple copper tail feathers. $35,000.

The Wizard Company in St. Louis, Missouri , patented their "Duck-In" decoys. Canvas "Tip-Up" Decoy with "Duck-In" mushroom anchor is worth $35 today.

Ringbill drake by Mark McCool Whipple (1884–1961) of Louisiana, $1,200. (*Collection of Alan and Elaine Haid/Photography by Alan Haid*)

Advertisement from the Bayco Decoy Co. in New Orleans, Louisiana.

Pintail drake by Sidney Foret (1902–1975) of Bayou LaFourche, Louisiana, circa 1940, $400. (*Collection of Alan and Elaine Haid/Photography by Alan Haid*)

Blue-winged teal drake by Mitchel LaFrance (1882–1979) of Phoenix, Louisiana, circa $2,000. (*Collection of Alan and Elaine Haid/ Photography by Alan Haid*)

Mallard hen, sleeper, by Tanasia St. Germain (1885–1957) of Chalmette, Louisiana, circa 1930, $2,500. (*Collection of Alan and Elaine Haid/Photography by Alan Haid*)

Shoveler hen by Laurent Verdin (1909–1991) of Houma-Bayou Terrebonne, Louisiana, circa 1940, $500. (*Collection of Alan and Elaine Haid/Photography by Alan Haid*)

Blue-winged teal hen by Xavier Bourg (1901–1984) of LaRose, Louisiana, circa 1930, $1,000. (*Collection of Alan and Elaine Haid/Photography by Alan Haid*)

Decoys of the Central and Pacific Flyways

South Dakota farmers found good shooting on the potholes created by the spring thaw, circa 1910. (*Courtesy of Robert Summerfield*)

Few quality wooden decoys were produced in the Central flyway, mainly because there were few waterfowlers and little need for decoys. The prairies of the western states were fertile grounds for waterfowl. Canvasbacks in particular used this area as a breeding ground. As birds migrate out of the western prairies of Saskatchewan, they follow the Missouri River southward in such numbers that primitive stuffed canvas Canada goose decoys drew Canada geese to a hunters as easily as the finest wooden goose decoy and simple white rags would draw in all the snow geese a hunter wanted in the rice fields of Texas.

Waterfowl migrating along the Pacific Coast frequented the Puget Sound region of Washington moving on to the marshy watersheds of the Columbia River in Oregon and then to the Sacramento and San Joaquin rivers in California. Early market hunters supplied the commission brokers of San Francisco with snow geese, black brant, trumpeter swans, Canada geese, widgeon, pintail, mallards, canvasback, blue bills, and teal as well as sea ducks and shorebirds. Since most of the decoys were carved for individuals or a single gunning club, it seems there were no master carvers who produced large numbers of decoys. Although many of the carvers patterned their decoys after the factory decoy makers like the Mason Decoy Company, Dodge Decoy Factory, or Wildfowl decoys, there were several notable carvers from the Pacific Flyway. Californians created unique "picklehead" decoys with gracefully carved and painted duck heads on the ends of stakes that were stuck in the mud among the tall pickleweed of the California marshes.

No matter what region a decoy was produced in, they represent a interesting functional art form and are easily classified as folk art. As collectibles they demand high prices and have a strong following among specialized decoy collectors as well as folk art collectors.

Market hunter after a day's shooting on the prairie of South Dakota, circa 1900. (*Courtesy of Robert Summerfield*)

Canada geese made of canvas stuffed with straw, by John Albert Lundgren (1880–1964) of Aztell, Nebraska, circa 1930, $750 each.

Canada goose by an unknown maker from Platte, Nebraska, circa 1930, $400.

A hunter can never resist a chance to brag to his buddies back home when he has a good shoot. Circa 1920.

Canada geese, molded rubber blow-up decoys with hard rubber legs by the Rex Manufacturing Co. in Morrill, Nebraska, circa 1950, $150 each.

Mallard drakes from Armstrong Featherweight Decoys, Inc. in Houston, Texas, circa 1938–1945, $100 each.

When Charles Grubbs, a noted duck maker from Illinois, moved to Texas, he marketed this unique grass hunting suit in a catalog, which also offered his decoys and game bird calls. Note the metal silhouette goose decoys. Several companies produced this type of decoy, most notably the Danz Decoy Co. in St. Paul, Minnesota. The Danz Decoy was patented in 1883. Photo circa 1900, by T.W. Ingersoll.

Having one's photo taken with the day's kill was popular even in the 1880s. Studio photograph, circa 1900.

Unique stick-up head decoys were used in the pickleweed stubble around lakes and sloughes of the Rich Island Club in San Joaquin Valley in central California. In stein: "Pickleweed" head decoys by various unknown makers, circa 1940, $200 each; foreground; "Artichoke" or "Grapefruit" head decoy by Gene Copp (circa 1880–1950) of Oakland, California, circa 1945, $250. (*Photograph courtesy of Barbara Sorenson*)

Decoys by Horace "Hie" Crandall (1892–1969) of Westwood, California, circa 1930: left, pintail pair, $4,000; right, mallard pair, drake sleeper style, $3,000. (*Photograph courtesy of Barbara Sorenson*)

Green-winged teal pair by Horace "Hie" Crandall of Westwood, California, circa 1930, $4,000. (*Photograph courtesy Barbara Sorenson*)

Pintail drakes: top one by Richard "Fresh Air Dick" Jansen (1872–1951) of Sonoma Creek, California, circa 1930, $1,200; bottom one by Amiel "Ame" Garibaldi (1908–?) of Sacramento, California, circa 1940, $800. (*Photograph courtesy of Barbara Sorenson*)

Pintail drake by John Luedtke (1901–1957) of Stockton, California, circa 1945, $800. (*Photograph courtesy of Barbara Sorenson*)

Black brant decoys by George William McLellan (1897–1987) of Eureka, California, circa 1930: top, hollow redwood floater, $1,500; bottom, flying brant, one of nine, $8,000. (*Photograph courtesy of Barbara Sorenson*)

Mallard hen, preening style, by F. Edward Synder (1928–present) of Rio Vista, California, circa 1941–1951, $600. (*Photograph courtesy of Barbara Sorenson*)

Pintail drake, feeding style, by John Tornberg (1902–1971) of San Francisco, California, circa 1948, $3,000. (*Photograph courtesy of Barbara Sorenson*)

Pintail drake, standing field decoy, by an unknown maker from the Suisun Marsh area of central California, from the estate of Olie Olsen, circa 1930, $7,500. (*Photograph courtesy of Barbara Sorenson*)

Pintail hen by Frank Bay (1896–1980) of Astoria, Oregon, circa 1940, $400. (*Photograph courtesy of Barbara Sorenson*)

Decoys by Charles Bergman (1856–1946) of Astoria, Oregon: swan, $4,000; canvasback drake, $3,000; green-winged teal pair, $7,000. (*Photograph courtesy of Barbara Sorenson*)

Green-winged teal drake jewelry box by Charles Bergman of Astoria, Oregon, $1,500. (*Photograph courtesy of Barbara Sorenson*)

Canada goose by Jerry Mastin (1880–1959) of Portland, Oregon, circa 1937, $4,000. (*Photograph courtesy of Barbara Sorenson*)

Top: mallard drake by James Andrew Titus, Sr. (1879–1956) of Astoria, Oregon, circa 1935, $600. Bottom: pintail drake by Charles A. Pice (1890–1958) of Astoria, Oregon, circa 1940, $600. (*Photograph courtesy of Barbara Sorenson*)

Johnson's Folding Goose Decoys from the Wm. R. Johnson Co., Inc. in Seattle, Washington, waxed paper silhouettes, packaged one dozen in imprinted canvas drawstring bag, circa 1950, $150 per dozen with bag.

Miscellaneous Decoys

The mourning dove is a migratory bird which is very fertile. Hens can produced as many as three clutches in a single breeding season. The United States Department of Conservation has found that since the dove has a high natural mortality rate, almost eighty percent, controlled hunting has little effect on their population. Many a hunter has found that the mourning dove, with its speedy and erratic flight patterns, offers challenging sport shooting and a succulent meal. Doves like to perch nearby before they enter a field to feed or land on the muddy shores of a water place. This is why dove decoys are very effective. Most are designed to balance on a tree limb or wire, the dove's favorite perching sites.

The common crow has long tormented the farmer, earning a reputation as a despicable predator. When agricultural development spread throughout continental North America during the 1900s, the common crow followed the growth in farmland and flourished. Huge roosts began to show up in many states and the nest-robbing crow became a major threat to farmers and game birds alike. Governmental agencies and private conservation groups initiated aggressive campaigns to eradicate the crow. Some states actually dynamited roosts, and others offered bounties for crows.

Hunters found the crow to be challenging prey. Although the crow is a wary bird, he was easily decoyed and responded well to a game bird call. Once a hunter mastered the art of crow calling, he could spend hours shooting at live targets that offered a variety of angles and plenty of fast-moving action all year round. At the height of the campaign against crows, several companies and commercial decoy carvers supplied crow decoys, owl decoys, and crow calls.

Doves, wooden, raised carved wing, black pin eyes, by Reme Ange Roussel, Jr. (1911–present) circa 1950, $500 each. Roussel is considered the father of Louisiana dove decoys.

Doves, hollow pine, unknown maker, Texas, circa 1925, $3,000 pair

Doves, cardboard silhouettes from the Real D-coy, C. L. B. Co. in Houston, Texas, circa 1950, $40 each.

Doves, left to right: white dove, rare novelty bird from the Carry-Lite Co. of Milwaukee, Wisconsin, circa 1940, $75; hard plastic dove from the TrenDecoy Co. in Whitehouse, Florida, circa 1960, $40; regular dove from the Carry-Lite Co., circa 1940, $40; and dove from the Animal Trap Co. of America in Lititz, Pennsylvania, circa 1940, $40.

P.S. Olt Co. also produced a line of cardboard silhouette dove decoys similar to their crow decoys that were sold individually or by the dozen, circa 1950, $300 per dozen in box.

Chapter 4

Game Bird Calls

A group of Wisconsin hunters relax after an afternoon crow shoot with a few dead crows and their owl decoy, carved by Mandt Homme. Left to right: John Sundry, Mandt Homme, Enoch Reindahl, Harold Omrud, and Howard Halverson, circa 1940. (*Photograph by Enoch Reindahl, Stoughton, Wisconsin*)

While shorebirds were legally hunted, there was little need for any type of calling. Huge flocks of shorebirds were easily lured with decoys even after the waterfowlers fired several volleys into a flock. Yet shorebirds did respond to bird whistles, so calls were used, often by the guides who assisted hunters. Most snipe whistles were made of thin sheet metal, tin, brass, or German silver, which were fashioned into hollow disks in either a full or semi-circular shape. Even commercially produced snipe whistles appear to be handmade. Small simple bone and wooden whistles also worked well for shorebird hunting. As one would expect, most snipe whistles were produced and used on the Atlantic flyway.

The first duck call simply held a metal reed between a double tone board. These were hard on the caller's mouth, thus earning the name "tongue pincher" duck calls. This style of call effectively reproduced the sound of diving ducks. When waterfowling became popular in the Midwest, the tongue pincher call lacked the versatility to call mallards, the mainstay of Midwestern hunting. No one is certain when or where the first modern duck call was produced. It is generally accepted that Charles Grubbs, Joseph Victor Glodo, or Fred Allen are likely candidates for this honor. The modern duck call encased the reed and a single-grooved tone board within a barrel creating a sound chamber. The resulting instrument can sing as sweetly as any mallard hen when used properly. The art of the duck call is the craftsmanship found in the barrel designs and embellishments, from the simple cane calls of the Louisiana bayous to the elaborate relief carvings executed by carvers like Charles Perdew. Most duck calls were fashioned out of wood, but metals, bakelite, hard rubber, and eventually plastics were also used.

The common crow call combined the features of the tongue pincher duck call with the modern duck call, by reducing the length of the tongue pincher's double tone boards and adding a barrel-shaped tone chamber. Most crow calls—whether they made of wood, hard rubber, or plastic—utilized this type of design, which creates the loud, harsh caw associated with the common crow.

Wild turkey hunters rely heavily upon calling during the spring hunting seasons. Toms are especially active during the mating season and are always susceptible to any imagined threat to their harem by other toms or the possible addition of a breeding hen. To this end the turkey call is usually used to recreate yelps and chirps, seldom gobbles. The most successful method of hunting turkeys is to call them into firing range with as little movement as possible, because these birds have keen eyesight and hearing. Even the slightest hint of activity will make an entire flock of turkeys disappear in an instant. There are three collectible types of turkey calls: the slate striker, the box call, and the yelper.

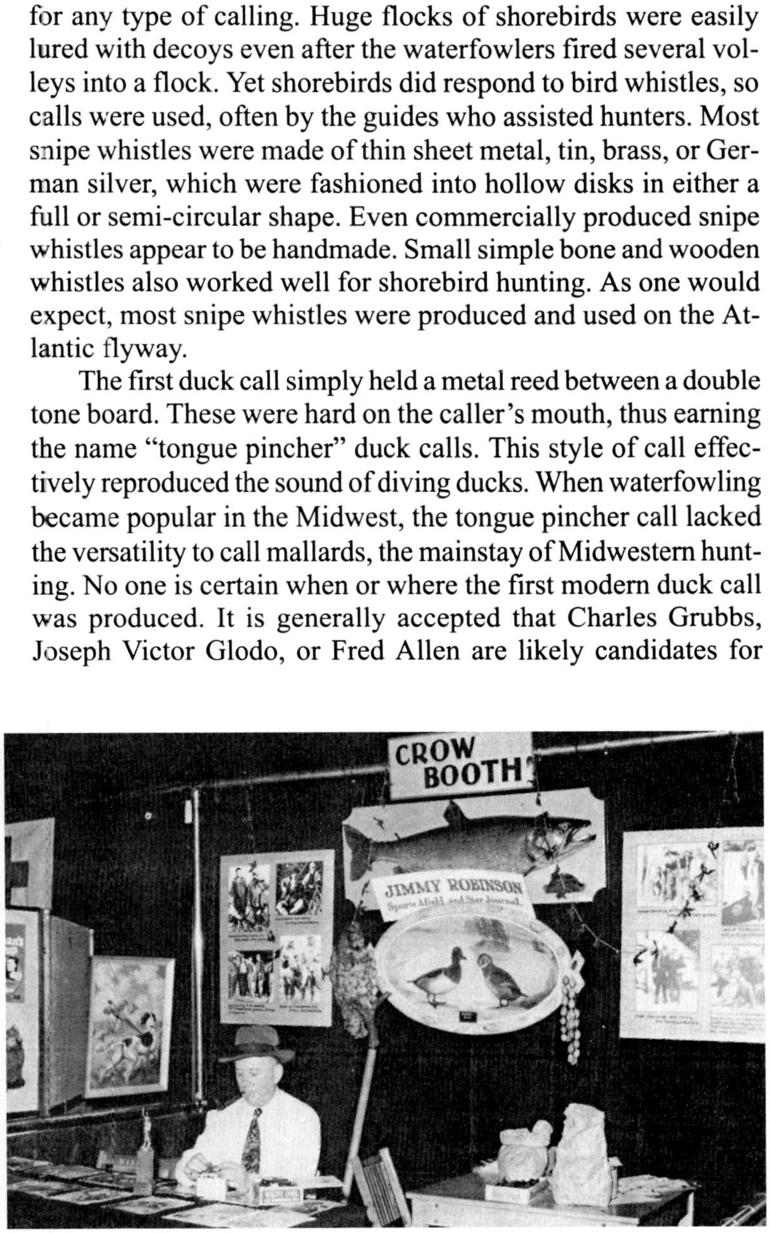

During the 1940s, a massive publicity campaign was in full swing promoting the total destruction of the common crow because the nest-robbing crow was seen as a major threat to the game bird populations. Bounties were paid by federal, state, and local governments. Conservation organizations sponsored crow shoots and game dinners featuring grommet crow dishes to encourage crow shooting as enjoyable way to sharpen one's shooting skills and help protect waterfowl and game birds. Sporting personalities like Jimmy "Mr. Minnesota" Robinson helped promote the cause by running crow shooting contests for *Sports Afield* and *The Minneapolis Star Tribune* at local sportsmen's shows. "Every hunter should kill 10 crows and we would soon balance this egg-robber." — Jimmie Robinson, circa 1940.

Hollow crow by Charles Quimby (1875–1940) of Spring Valley, Illinois, circa 1925, $1,200; and crow call by Charles Quimby, $750.

Crow by Wm. E. Pratt Manufacturing Co. of Joliet, Illinois, circa 1930, $400.

Crow calls: Jim Crow call in box by J & M Manufacturing in Oshkosh, Wisconsin, circa 1930, $250; and Pull-Em crow call in box from Olivero's Manufacturing in Houston, Texas, circa 1940, $125.

Crow, folding masonite board silhouette, by C. S. Adams of Evanston, Illinois, produced by Ultra Products, Wilmette, Illinois, circa 1950, $150.

No. D-7 Victor Owl

Crows can't resist attacking this true-to-life reproduction of a great horned owl. Molded fiber. Large fierce-glaring glass eyes.

Overall size: 16¼" high x 6½"
Packed: ⅓ doz.—6 lbs.

No. D-8 Victor Crow and Owl Set

Perfect shooting set—two crows and one horned owl. Great gift idea for hunters.

Packed: 1 set—5½ lbs.

No. D-6 Victor Crow

Attract crows into gunning range with these realistic molded fiber decoys. Wire legs for setting in the field and a convenient opening for attaching to tree limbs.

Overall size: 15¾" x 5"
Packed: ½ doz.—4½ lbs.

NEW!

No. D-21 Shell Box

Convenient shell and utility box for hunters, skeet and trap shooters. Carries up to four boxes of shotgun shells and gun accessories. Non-rusting plastic—no metal parts to corrode. Seamless bottom and strong self hinge. Ideal for use in wet boats and blinds.

Size: 12½" x 6½" x 5" high.
Packed: 1 doz.—14 lbs.

No. 40 Old Pal Folding Seat

For hunting, fishing, shooting or attending spectator sports. So compact it can be carried in jacket pocket or tackle box. Plated steel frame and support chains. Heavy double-stitched Army duck seat holds up to 250 lbs.

Open: 14¼" x 7" x 13½" high; closed: 10" x 7" x 1½".
Packed: 1 doz.—23 lbs.

Victor Accessories for Decoys

No. 1 Decoy Anchor

Unreels lines automatically as tide rises.

Packed: 1 doz.—13 lbs.

No. 2 Decoy Anchor

Unreels lines automatically as tide rises.

Packed: 1 doz.—25 lbs.

No. 3 Mushroom Anchor

Steady and dependable.

Packed: 1 doz.—7 lbs.

No. 1
No. 2
No. 3

ANIMAL TRAP COMPANY OF AMERICA / Lititz, Pa. Niagara Falls, Canada

Printed in U.S.A.

INO-15M-366

Flyer illustrating Victor Crow and Owl decoys, Animal Trap Co. of America, circa 1950.

Because the horned owl is a natural enemy of the crow, owl decoys were used to lure crows. When faced with their nemesis, the horned owl, crows will work themselves into a frenzy, diving and swooping at the owl. In their excitement, they become unaware of the hunter even when shots are fired. Owl decoys: front, molded by Carry-Lite Decoys from Milwaukee, Wisconsin, circa 1950, $100; left, General Fibre Co. of St. Louis, Missouri, circa 1950, $100; back, Neumann & Bennetts, Plasti-Products, Klamath Falls, Oregon, circa 1940, $150.

Mandt Homme (left) and friend, Howard Halverson, pose with Homme's owl decoy, circa 1935.(*Courtesy of Mrs. Mandt Homme*)

Great horned owl by Mandt Homme of MacFarland, Wisconsin, the only known example, circa 1935, $10,000. (*Collection of Mrs. Mandt Homme*)

Great Horned Owl, canvas stuffed with wool and cork, glass eyes, and real beak, extremely rare, unlimited production, circa 1940, $750; crow by Herter's Inc., Waseca, Minnesota, Model Perfect, white cedar, carved feather detail, circa 1940, $800. (*Collection of Ron Adamson*)

Crow, Model Perfect featherweight with spring mount, balsa wood, Herter's Inc., circa 1945, $150

Great horned owl, Model Perfect featherweight with clutch crow, Herter's Inc. Waseca, Minnesota, circa 1945, $1,500.

Great horned owl decoy by John Hyatt of Pekin, Illinois, made for the P. S. Olt Co., circa 1935, marketed with Olt's cardboard crow decoys and E-1 crow call, $2,500.

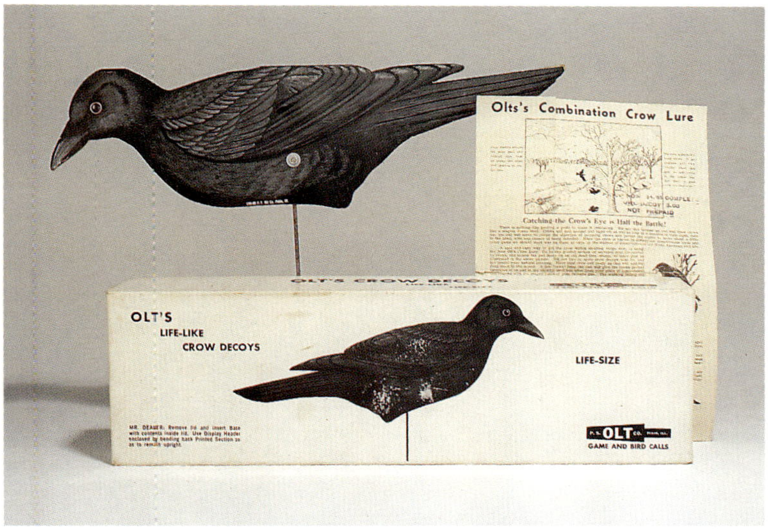

Crow, cardboard silhouette, packaged one dozen in a box, by P.S. Olt Co., circa 1930, $300 per dozen in box.

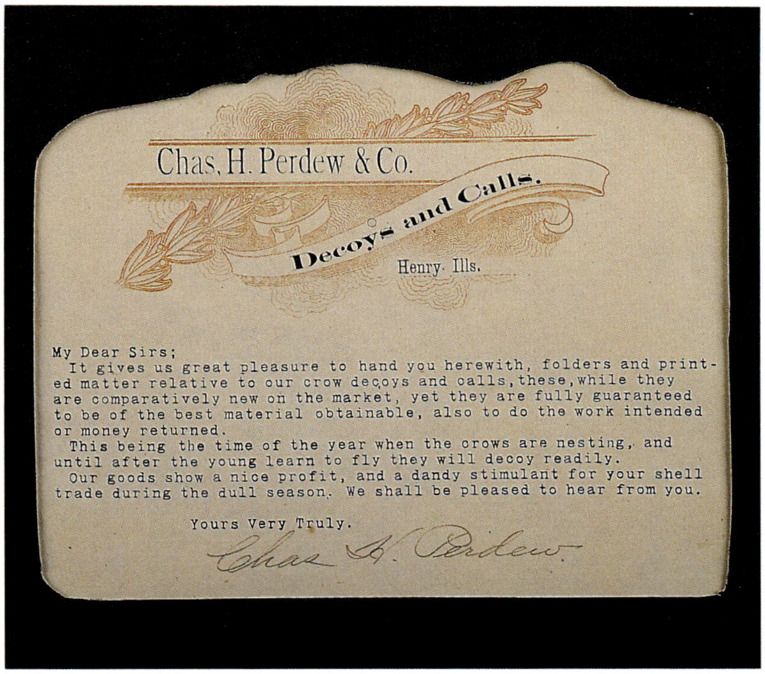

Chas. H. Perdew & Co.

Decoys and Calls.

Henry. Ills.

My Dear Sirs;
It gives us great pleasure to hand you herewith, folders and printed matter relative to our crow decoys and calls, these, while they are comparatively new on the market, yet they are fully guaranteed to be of the best material obtainable, also to do the work intended or money returned.
This being the time of the year when the crows are nesting, and until after the young learn to fly they will decoy readily.
Our goods show a nice profit, and a dandy stimulant for your shell trade during the dull season. We shall be pleased to hear from you.

Yours Very Truly.

Chas H. Perdew

Original letter from Charles Perdew to prospective dealers discussing the merits of his calls and decoys.

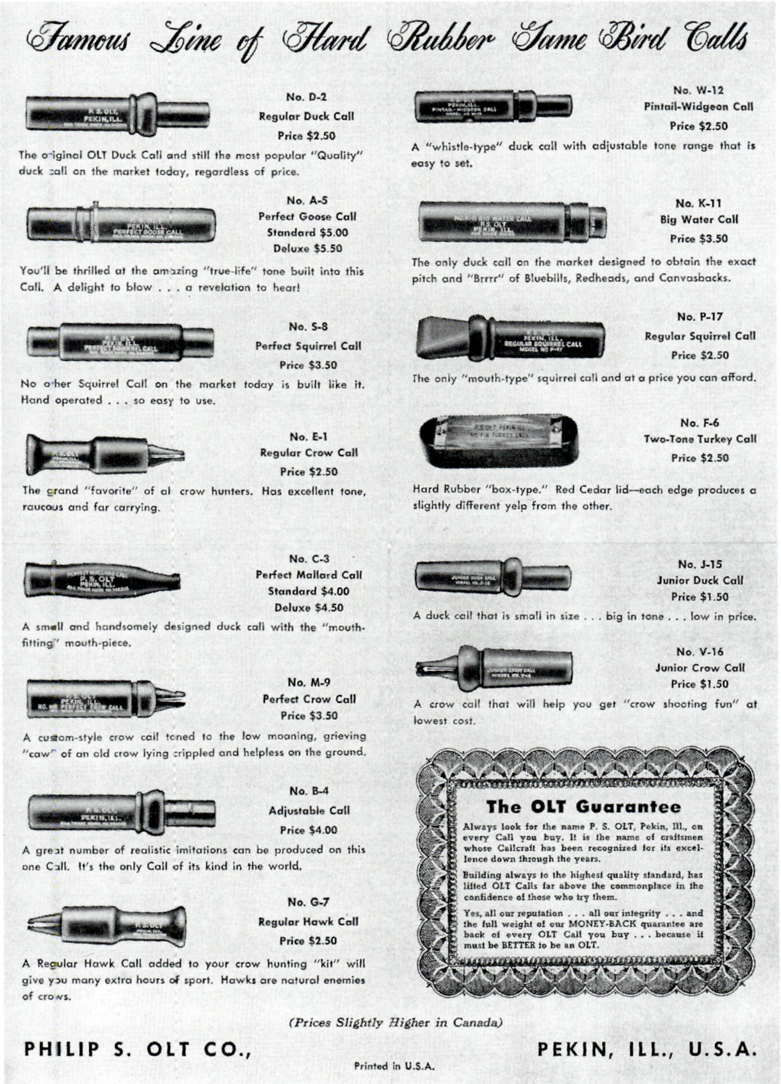

Famous Line of Hard Rubber Game Bird Calls

No. D-2
Regular Duck Call
Price $2.50
The original OLT Duck Call and still the most popular "Quality" duck call on the market today, regardless of price.

No. A-5
Perfect Goose Call
Standard $5.00
Deluxe $5.50
You'll be thrilled at the amazing "true-life" tone built into this Call. A delight to blow . . . a revelation to hear!

No. S-8
Perfect Squirrel Call
Price $3.50
No other Squirrel Call on the market today is built like it. Hand operated . . . so easy to use.

No. E-1
Regular Crow Call
Price $2.50
The grand "favorite" of all crow hunters. Has excellent tone, raucous and far carrying.

No. C-3
Perfect Mallard Call
Standard $4.00
Deluxe $4.50
A small and handsomely designed duck call with the "mouth-fitting" mouth-piece.

No. M-9
Perfect Crow Call
Price $3.50
A custom-style crow call toned to the low moaning, grieving "caw" of an old crow lying crippled and helpless on the ground.

No. B-4
Adjustable Call
Price $4.00
A great number of realistic imitations can be produced on this one Call. It's the only Call of its kind in the world.

No. G-7
Regular Hawk Call
Price $2.50
A Regular Hawk Call added to your crow hunting "kit" will give you many extra hours of sport. Hawks are natural enemies of crows.

No. W-12
Pintail-Widgeon Call
Price $2.50
A "whistle-type" duck call with adjustable tone range that is easy to set.

No. K-11
Big Water Call
Price $3.50
The only duck call on the market designed to obtain the exact pitch and "Brrrr" of Bluebills, Redheads, and Canvasbacks.

No. P-17
Regular Squirrel Call
Price $2.50
The only "mouth-type" squirrel call and at a price you can afford.

No. F-6
Two-Tone Turkey Call
Price $2.50
Hard Rubber "box-type." Red Cedar lid—each edge produces a slightly different yelp from the other.

No. J-15
Junior Duck Call
Price $1.50
A duck call that is small in size . . . big in tone . . . low in price.

No. V-16
Junior Crow Call
Price $1.50
A crow call that will help you get "crow shooting fun" at lowest cost.

The OLT Guarantee
Always look for the name P. S. OLT, Pekin, Ill., on every Call you buy. It is the name of craftsmen whose Callcraft has been recognized for its excellence down through the years.
Building always to the highest quality standard, has lifted OLT Calls far above the commonplace in the confidence of those who try them.
Yes, all our reputation . . . all our integrity . . . and the full weight of our MONEY-BACK guarantee are back of every OLT Call you buy . . . because it must be BETTER to be an OLT.

(Prices Slightly Higher in Canada)

PHILIP S. OLT CO., **PEKIN, ILL., U.S.A.**

Printed in U.S.A.

Flyer for P.S. Olt game bird calls, circa 1960.

Original display box found in a hardware store in southern Illinois. Perdew shipped his calls throughout the country. The crow calls were wrapped in an instruction sheet (pictured). Red cedar duck call, $500; red cedar crow call, $300.

Variations of early Perdew crow calls; measuring 3.5 inches, very rare, circa 1930, $500 each. Far right: crow call with rare "Mfg. by Chas. Perdew, Sr." stamp, $750.

Common red cedar crow call by Charles Perdew, instruction sheet, stamped "Patented Applied Nov. 1909," produced circa 1909–1960, $200.

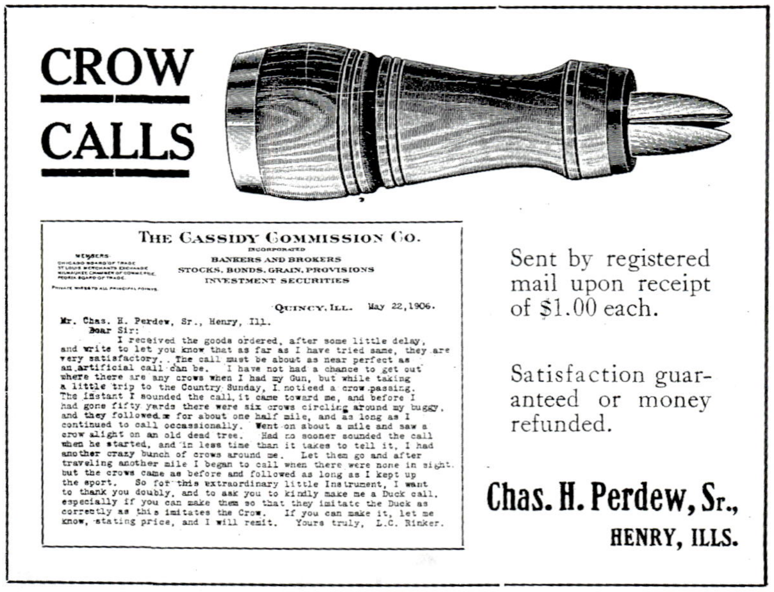

Advertisement for Perdew red cedar crow call, circa 1907.

Charles Perdew of Henry, Illinois, produced probably the best selling crow decoys during the heyday of sport crow shooting. Left, smooth un-flocked decoy, circa 1940, $750; right, early flocked crow with turned head, circa 1930, $900; *The Crow Shooter's Handbook*, Nickolas Karas, 1963, $10.

Variations of common red cedar Perdew crow calls with original brochure advertising Perdew's crow decoys and calls, $200-250 each.

Crow calls with original instruction sheet by Charles Perdew. Left, fancy carved call with crows in tree by nest with eggs, circa 1930, $6,000; right, common red cedar crow call, one of the best sounding crow calls ever produced, production probably exceeded 5,000 calls, $200.

Charles Perdew's creative genius is embodied in this mechanical crow decoy. Hidden within its hollow body are gears to raise the decoy's metal wings and cause the mouth to open, showing the crow's tongue. The entire decoy is flocked. Circa 1930, $15,000.

Crows by Charles Perdew: left, early hollow crow, circa 1925, $1,500; right, fancy crow, raised carved wings, flocked, circa 1930, $4,000.

Fancy crow call, Charles Perdew, three views show in-the-round carved scene of a hunter hidden beneath a tree working his Perdew owl decoy as crows sit in the branches above, circa 1945, $7,500.

Variations of fancy carved crow calls by Charles Perdew, each call has a slightly different scene and personalized initials, $5,000-7,000 each.

Game bird calls by Charles Quimby (1875–1940) of Spring Valley, Illinois, circa 1925. Quimby was a founding member of the West End Gun Club in Putman County, Illinois. Duck call, red cedar, $1,000; crow call, red cedar, $750.

Game bird calls by Fred Allen of Mommouth, Illinois, shown with Allen advertising handbill, circa 1880: left; duck call with raised lip, $200; duck call, $125; crow call, $100.

Nickel-plated metal duck calls by Fred A. Allen of Mommouth, Illinois, circa 1880, $400 each.

Wooden shell duck call from Fred A. Allen Sportsmen's Specialty Co., circa 1880, one dozen in original box, $125 each; box, extremely rare, $300.

Illinois River duck calls by Richard Burnes (1865–circa 1927), Pekin, Illinois, circa 1900. Burnes was one of the first makers of hard rubber calls. The middle call was his personal call, $750. Other calls with bands, $500 each.

Relief-carved fancy duck calls: left, walnut call with two flying ducks by Dale Crooks of Louisiana, circa 1950, $400; right, walnut checkered background with flying duck by Edward "Doll" Emerick (1923–1985) of Rushville, Illinois, circa 1945, $1,000.

Duck calls by William Clifford of Chicago, Illinois, circa 1940. Paneled calls were formed by laminating various woods together before the barrel was turned on a lathe. $1,500 each. (*Collection of Gary Reiker*)

Illinois River duck calls, circa 1880, from Putman County: left, fancy hand-carved duck call with vine and leaf design by George Cunningham (1842–1923) of Hennipen, $7,000; right, large checkered duck call by Delbert S. "Dell" Woods (1860–1933), the first Putman County game warden and caretaker of Hennipen Shooting Club, $3,000; rule book from Hennipen Gun Club, circa 1890, $100; shooting pass from Hennipen Shooting Club, circa 1886, $75.

Charles Harris Ditto (1865–1935) of Keithsburg, Illinois. This man's fame as an Illinois River duck, goose, and crow call producer overshadowed his accomplishments as a champion trapshooter, even though he once held the U.S. Amateur Championship in 1908 as well as numerous other championships.

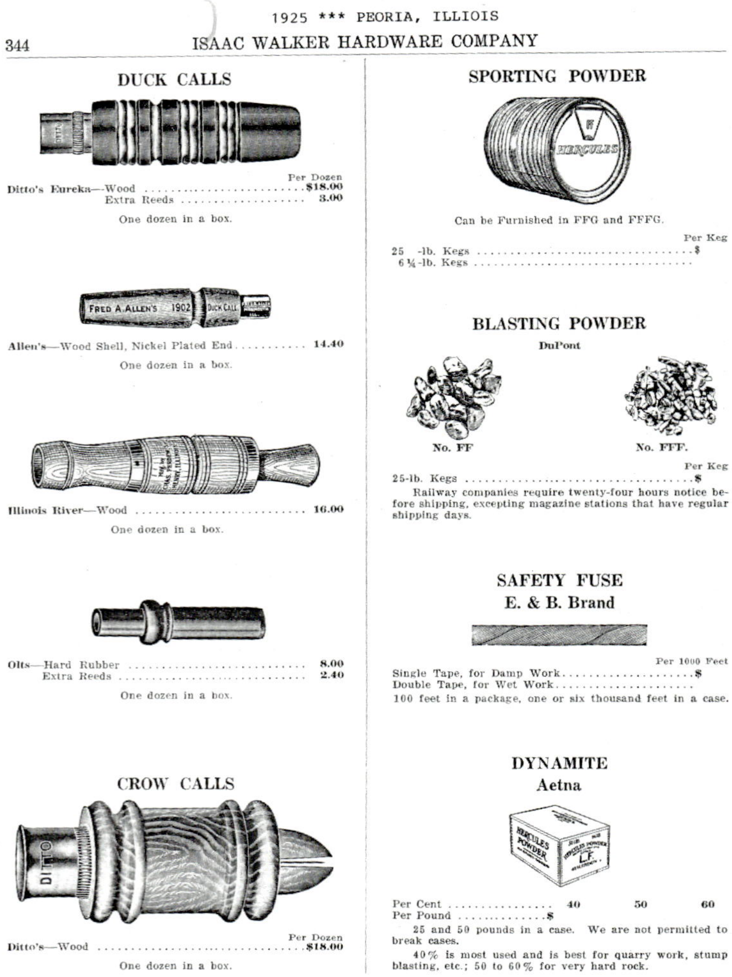

1925 *** PEORIA, ILLIOIS

344 ISAAC WALKER HARDWARE COMPANY

DUCK CALLS

	Per Dozen
Ditto's Eureka—Wood	$18.00
Extra Reeds	3.00

One dozen in a box.

Allen's—Wood Shell, Nickel Plated End	14.40

One dozen in a box.

Illinois River—Wood	16.00

One dozen in a box.

Olts—Hard Rubber	8.00
Extra Reeds	2.40

One dozen in a box.

CROW CALLS

	Per Dozen
Ditto's—Wood	$18.00

One dozen in a box.

SPORTING POWDER

Can be Furnished in FFG and FFFG.

	Per Keg
25 -lb. Kegs	$
6 ¼-lb. Kegs	

BLASTING POWDER

DuPont

No. FF　　No. FFF.

	Per Keg
25-lb. Kegs	$

Railway companies require twenty-four hours notice before shipping, excepting magazine stations that have regular shipping days.

SAFETY FUSE

E. & B. Brand

	Per 1000 Feet
Single Tape, for Damp Work	$
Double Tape, for Wet Work	

100 feet in a package, one or six thousand feet in a case.

DYNAMITE

Aetna

Per Cent	40	50	60
Per Pound	$		

25 and 50 pounds in a case. We are not permitted to break cases.

40% is most used and is best for quarry work, stump blasting, etc.; 50 to 60% for very hard rock.

Catalog entries from Isaac Walker Hardware Co. of Peoria, circa 1925, showing Ditto, Allen, Perdew, and P.S. Olt duck calls.

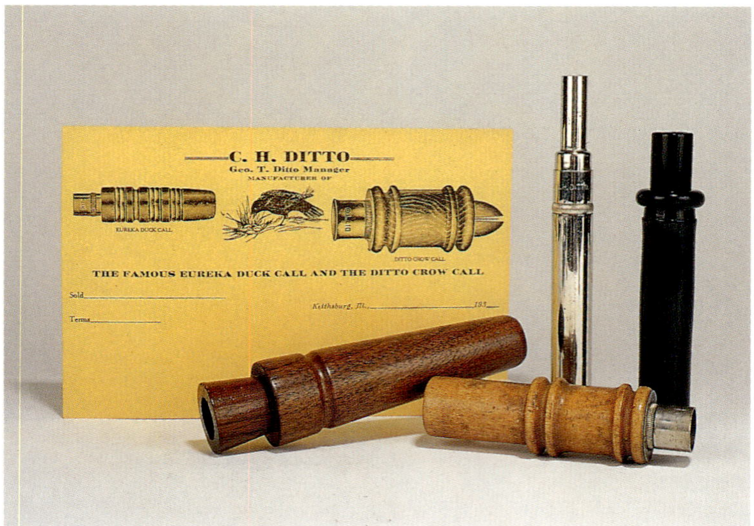

Duck calls with original order form from Charles H. Ditto: special order duck call made for Ditto's brother-in-law, circa 1890, $700; Eureka duck call, standard No. 1 production call, wooden barrel, metal reed, circa 1910, $250; all-metal combination duck and goose call, extremely rare, circa 1900, $800; hard rubber blackduck call, patent later sold to P.S. Olt, $350.

Selectone Wild Mallard Duck Calls with boxes and literature, by Walter "Wally" Drennen (1902–1980) of Depue, Illinois, circa 1940, $250 each.

Walnut duck calls, banded, by Frank O. "Cotton" Eckard (1898–1965), caretaker of the Senachwine Duck Club in Putman, Illinois, circa 1920, $1,000 each; original rule book from the Senachwine Duck Club, $100.

Tongue-pincher duck call, walnut with bone bell, Elam Fischer, Detroit, Michigan, considered the first commercial American duck call maker, only two known calls stamped "Elam Fischer Detroit, $1,500.

Detail shot of Fischer tongue pincher showing patent date.

Harry's Ear Toned Duck Call in original box by Harry Edwards of Minneapolis, Minnesota, circa 1940, $350.

Goose call store display, Clarence "Patin" Faulk, Lake Charles, Louisana, circa 1960, $300.

Fuller's goose and crane call with box and instruction sheet (distributed by Ward-Anderson-Southard Co.); metal call by David S. Fuller (1859–?) of Chicago, Illinois, circa 1920, $250 each.

Goose hunting sign, painted wood, double sided, circa 1940, $500.

Charles Grubbs (1848–1933) of Senachwine Lake, Chicago, Illinois; Pascagoula, Mississippi, and Houston, Texas, was an all around sportsman. He was instrumental in the formation of Hennipen Shooting Club and accredited with the original design of the "Pascagoula" factory decoy. His duck calls are among the oldest and finest ever produced.

Duck call by Joseph Victor Glodo, Jr. (1845-1910), Jackson County, Illinois and Reelfoot Lake, Tennessee, can be traced directly to the original owner, Jack Hogg, Reelfoot Lake, Tennessee who traded the call to Ken Anderson, Wisconsin Rapids, Wisconsin for a pressure cooker for Mrs. Hogg in 1956. Glodo is considered to be the father of modern duck call, circa 1880, $10,000.

Cover from Grubbs catalog.

Duck calls by Charles Grubbs, left to right: Perfection duck call, circa 1870, $400; Perfect duck call, circa 1890, $700; Perfection duck call, circa 1880, $500; Perfection duck call, circa 1880, $500.

Fancy walnut duck calls with brass bands made by Charles Grubbs for his good friend and hunting companion, George Sibley, circa 1890, $4,000 each. Sibley's business cards advertising his hunting decoy factory, circa 1890, $100.

Variations of Grubb's Standard duck call sold by Montgomery Ward, Sears Roebuck, and various sporting goods distributors, circa 1880, $200 each.

Duck calls by George Herter of Herter's in Waseca, Minnesota, circa 1940: left, early model with box, brass tag, rare, $1,000; right, special edition "Jimmie Robinson" call, $1,200; widgeon call box, Herter's Inc. Duck Calling Manual, $25.

Sign, address plaque, Jimmy Robinson, St. Louis Park, Minnesota.

Jimmie Robinson of St. Louis Park, Minnesota, *The Minnesota Star Tribune's* outdoor writer known as "Mr. Minnesota."

Arkansas style duck calls, left to right: walnut checkered duck call by Perry Hooker of Memphis, Tennessee, circa 1920, $3,000; walnut checkered raised paneled duck call by Claude Stone of Hornersville, Arkansas, circa 1920, $5,000; walnut checkered duck call with Bakelite mouth guard by Robert Kelso (1891–?) of Alexandria, Louisana, circa 1920, $4,000; and an unknown Bowles-style paneled checkered walnut duck call, possibly a very early, unmarked A. M. Bowles, Little Rock, Arkansas, circa 1920, $5,000.

The New Beckhart Duck Call in original box by Kenwood brothers John and Sidney of Jonesboro, Arkansas, distributed by the Novelty Sales Co., Memphis, Tennessee, circa 1930, $1,000 each.

Extra fancy duck call, carved duck head with shot shell in mouth by C.L.V. Kinney and William F. Harlow of Newark, Ohio, circa 1890. Leather is stretched over the wooden duck head, "Kinney & Harlow" is stamped into the brass casing of the shotshell. Extremely rare limited production call, $7,000.

Duck calls, left to right: finely checkered duck call by an unknown Tennessee maker, circa 1900, $1,000; checkered duck call by Frank Dougherty (1872–1942) of Bean Lake, Missouri, circa 1890, $5,000; classic reelfoot style duck call by G. D. Kinny of Hughes Arkansas, circa 1900, $1,000; and Illinois River duck call by Charles Quimby (1875–1940) of Spring Valley, Illinois, circa 1930, $1,000.

Mascot call with instruction literature by August R. Kuhlemeier, patented in 1903, manufactured by Multi Novelty Co. of Chicago, Illinois, circa 1900, $1,000.

Tru-tone duck calls by Lawrence Casper Larson, Sr. (1888–1947) of Oak Park, Illinois, circa 1930; standing calls, Blue Ribbon call, burl walnut, $350 each; foreground, special order Blue Ribbon duck call, curly maple, circa 1935, $400, and original store display board, $750. (*Collection of Gary Rieker*)

SeDUCKtive female duck call in box from H. E. McMahon Sportsmen Specialties Co. in Delafield, Wisconsin, circa 1940, $400 each.

Goose call with brochure by Ken Martin (1922–present) of Lemont, Illinois, Horse Shoe Lake Model, circa 1950, $200.

Flapping bill duck call from the Natural Duck Call Manufacturing Co., Francis J. Muehlstein, St. Paul, Minnesota, patented 1932, available with glass eyes or tack eyes, early calls are stamped patent applied, $300.

Elam Fischer-style tongue pincher duck call with original box, rosewood with nickel plate bell and band, Union Hardware Manufacturing, Torrinton, Connecticut, circa 1900, $125.

Variations B-4 adjustable duck calls with order form and box, hard rubber by Philip Sanford Olt (1870–1950), P.S. Olt Co., Pekin, Illinois: left, $200; right (standing), $200; foreground, earliest style with brass band, $600.

Truetone duck call with original carrying bag and instruction pamphlet, circa 1940, Lawrence C. Larson, Sr., Oak Park, Illinois, $125.

Reelfoot Lake-style duck calls by John "Sandy" Alexander Morrow (1880–?) of Michigan, circa 1935, $700.

Charles Perdew of Henry, Illinois, was undeniably the most prolific of the master game bird call makers. Decoratively carved calls were his specialty. This matched duck and crow call set was made for John L. Peer, circa 1952: Crow call, $6,000; duck call, $5,000.

Carved duck calls by Charles Perdew with carved "Crown" stoppers are considered Perdew's top of the line calls, circa 1925–1930, $7,000 each.

Special order set of Perdew carved calls made for the Postulka family, Granville, Illinois, included a smaller call designed to fit a woman's hand and personalized to Sandra Postulka, who hunted with her father, Joseph J., and brother, Joseph A. Postulka, circa 1952, $4,500 each.

Companion duck calls made by Charles Perdew for Chet Caswell, who hunted Rice Pond near Chillicothe, Illinois, initials C.J.C., circa 1935: left, fancy carved duck call with initials carved into a raised banner, $5,000; right, St. Francis River-style walnut duck call, $3,000.

Carved duck and crow call set by Charles Perdew, one of three known matched sets, made for Robert E. McFarland, Chicago, Illinois, circa 1935, $4,000 each.

Poster for the Von Lengerke & Antoine Sporting Goods sponsored duck calling contest, circa 1945, $150.

Von Lengerke & Antoine offered duck calling classes taught by Fred Kucaba, noted duck caller and hunter from the Illinois River area.

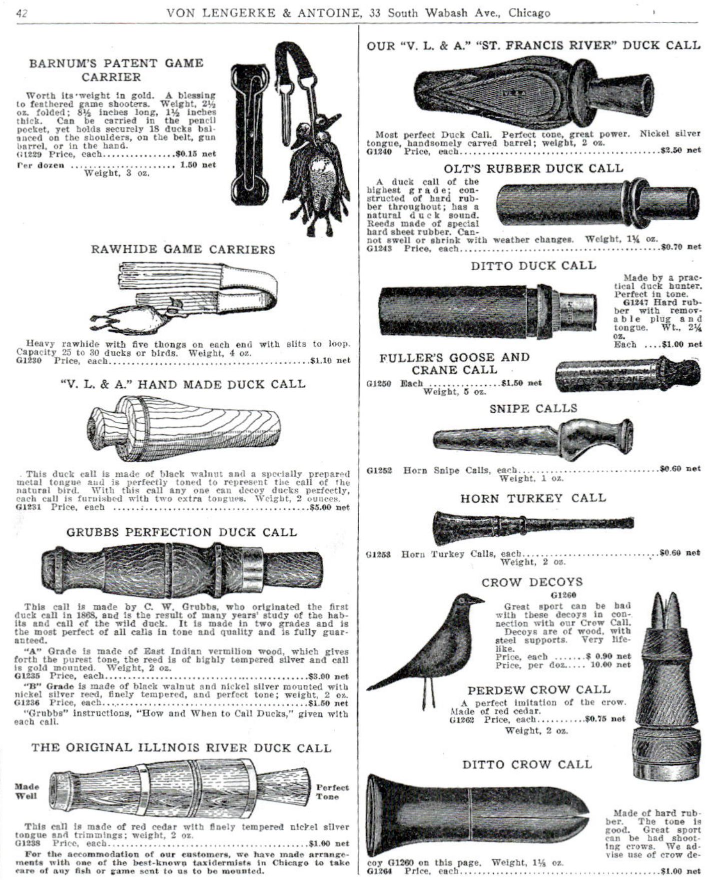

42 VON LENGERKE & ANTOINE, 33 South Wabash Ave., Chicago

BARNUM'S PATENT GAME CARRIER

Worth its weight in gold. A blessing to feathered game shooters. Weight, 2½ oz. folded; 8½ inches long, 1½ inches thick. Can be carried in the pencil pocket, yet holds securely 18 ducks balanced on the shoulders, on the belt, gun barrel, or in the hand.
G1229 Price, each................$0.15 net
Per dozen .... 1.50 net
Weight, 3 oz.

RAWHIDE GAME CARRIERS

Heavy rawhide with five thongs on each end with slits to loop. Capacity 25 to 30 ducks or birds. Weight, 4 oz.
G1230 Price, each..........................$1.10 net

"V. L. & A." HAND MADE DUCK CALL

This duck call is made of black walnut and a specially prepared metal tongue and is perfectly toned to represent the call of the natural bird. With this call any one can decoy ducks perfectly, each call is furnished with two extra tongues. Weight, 2 ounces.
G1231 Price, each ....$5.00 net

GRUBBS PERFECTION DUCK CALL

This call is made by C. W. Grubbs, who originated the first duck call in 1868, and is the result of many years' study of the habits and call of the wild duck. It is made in two grades and is the most perfect of all calls in tone and quality and is fully guaranteed.

"A" Grade is made of East Indian vermilion wood, which gives forth the purest tone, the reed is of highly tempered silver and call is gold mounted. Weight, 2 oz.
G1235 Price, each..........................$3.00 net

"B" Grade is made of black walnut and nickel silver mounted with nickel silver reed, finely tempered, and perfect tone; weight, 2 oz.
G1236 Price, each..........................$1.50 net

"Grubbs" instructions, "How and When to Call Ducks," given with each call.

THE ORIGINAL ILLINOIS RIVER DUCK CALL

Made Well — Perfect Tone

This call is made of red cedar with finely tempered nickel silver tongue and trimmings; weight, 2 oz.
G1238 Price, each..........................$1.00 net

For the accommodation of our customers, we have made arrangements with one of the best-known taxidermists in Chicago to take care of any fish or game sent to us to be mounted.

OUR "V. L. & A." "ST. FRANCIS RIVER" DUCK CALL

Most perfect Duck Call. Perfect tone, great power. Nickel silver tongue, handsomely carved barrel; weight, 2 oz.
G1240 Price, each..........................$2.50 net

OLT'S RUBBER DUCK CALL

A duck call of the highest grade; constructed of hard rubber throughout; has a natural duck sound. Reeds made of special hard sheet rubber. Cannot swell or shrink with weather changes. Weight, 1¼ oz.
G1243 Price, each..........................$0.70 net

DITTO DUCK CALL

Made by a practical duck hunter. Perfect in tone.
G1247 Hard rubber with removable plug and tongue. Wt., 2¼ oz.
Each ....$1.00 net

FULLER'S GOOSE AND CRANE CALL

G1250 Each ....$1.50 net
Weight, 5 oz.

SNIPE CALLS

G1252 Horn Snipe Calls, each..........................$0.60 net
Weight, 1 oz.

HORN TURKEY CALL

G1253 Horn Turkey Calls, each..........................$0.60 net
Weight, 2 oz.

CROW DECOYS

G1260

Great sport can be had with these decoys in connection with our Crow Call. Decoys are of wood, with steel supports. Very lifelike.
Price, each ....$ 0.90 net
Price, per doz..... 10.00 net

PERDEW CROW CALL

A perfect imitation of the crow. Made of red cedar.
G1262 Price, each..........$0.75 net
Weight, 2 oz.

DITTO CROW CALL

Made of hard rubber. The tone is good. Great sport can be had shooting crows. We advise use of crow decoy G1260 on this page. Weight, 1⅛ oz.
G1264 Price, each..........................$1.00 net

Page from V. L. & A fall/winter 1929 catalog showing various Illinois River game bird calls.

Fred Kucaba (1889–1968) of Chicago, Illinois, learned to call mallards hunting the Calumet/Deep River marshes near Hobart, Indiana, as a young man. In later years he hunted the flooded Illinois River bottoms near Hennipen, Illinois.

St Francis River duck call, walnut, checkered with V. L.& A. initials and original labeled box. Charles Perdew was marketed by V.L. & A. (Von Lengerke, & Antoine) Sporting Goods, Chicago, Illinois, circa 1923–1948, $2,000.

Variations of St. Francis River (V.L. & A.) duck call, walnut, checkered with personalized initials, Charles Perdew, circa 1930s, $1,500 each.

Variations of rare three-banded Illinois River red cedar duck calls by Charles Perdew, circa 1900–1920, $1,000 each.

Variations of St. Francis River (V.L. & A.) calls by Charles Perdew, circa 1923–1945: far left, special order call with decorative German silver band, $2,500; other calls, $1,000.

Variations of standard Illinois River red cedar duck calls by Charles Perdew, circa 1900–1940, stamped "Chas. Perdew Patent Applied Nov. 1909." Calls stamped "Manufactured by Chas. Perdew" are much rarer. Earliest to later calls, left to right, $500 each.

St. Francis River-style duck calls by unknown makers, marketed by V.L. & A. Sporting Goods, circa 1910, prior to Charles Perdew's association with V.L. & A. Note that the initials run in the opposite order than Perdew's. $1,500 each.

Variations on standard red cedar duck calls by Charles Perdew, circa 1935–1945, $300 each.

A typical Charles Perdew carved duck call with raised checkered panels, circa 1950, $3,000.

Duck calls by Haddon Perdew (1910–present) of Henry, Illinois, circa 1970–1980: left to Right, St. Francis River-style red cedar duck call, $500; St. Francis style, decorative silver band, with initials, $500; Illinois River style, cocobols wood, $400; classic Illinois River red cedar Perdew style call, $300. (*Collection of Gary Reiker*)

Duck calls by Oscar Quam of Minneapolis, Minnesota, circa 1930: left, early octagonal barrel with duck head medallion, $350; center, octagonal barrel with large decal, $300; right, round barrel with original tube container, circa 1924, $400.

Duck calls by Oscar Quam of Minneapolis, Minnesota, circa 1930, with literature and "Doctor of Quackery" certificate: front, special oversized call worn by Quam at sports shows, $2,000; back; early octagonal barrel call, stamped, no label, circa 1924, $250.

Duck call with decal by Ervin Redshaw (1897–1974) of Granville, Illinois, circa 1930, $500; and Buster Thompson business card, famous duck hunter and guide on Lake Senachwine in Putman County, Illinois, circa 1930.

Duck calls by Slim Brothers of Chillicothe, Illinois, circa 1880, embossed bakelite, available in brown and black, $1,000 each.

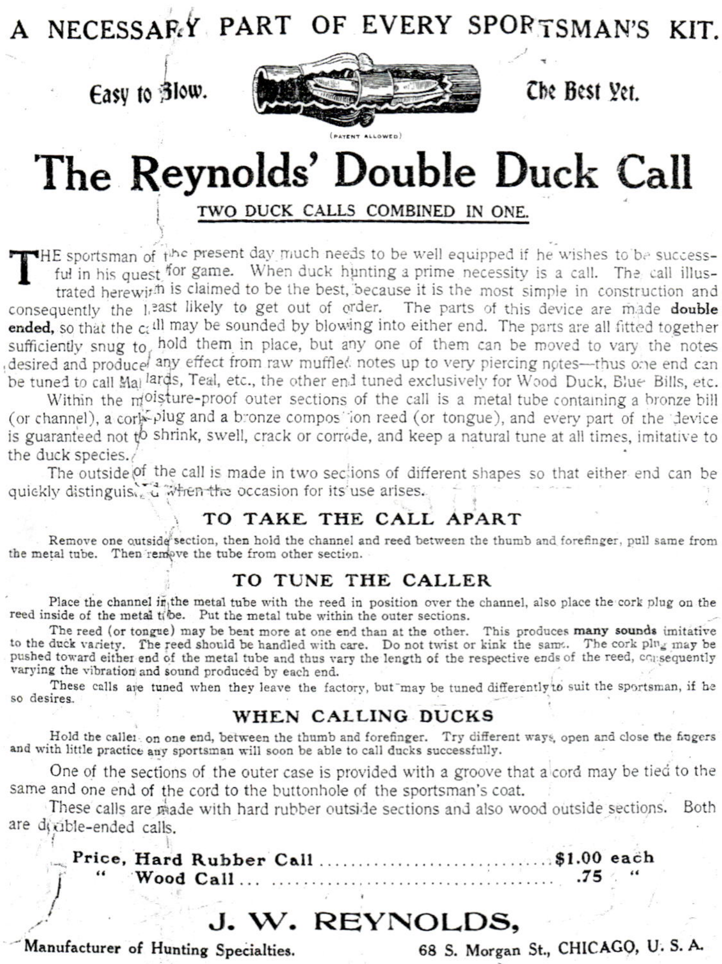

A NECESSARY PART OF EVERY SPORTSMAN'S KIT.

Easy to Blow. The Best Yet.

(PATENT ALLOWED)

The Reynolds' Double Duck Call

TWO DUCK CALLS COMBINED IN ONE.

THE sportsman of the present day much needs to be well equipped if he wishes to be successful in his quest for game. When duck hunting a prime necessity is a call. The call illustrated herewith is claimed to be the best, because it is the most simple in construction and consequently the least likely to get out of order. The parts of this device are made **double ended,** so that the call may be sounded by blowing into either end. The parts are all fitted together sufficiently snug to hold them in place, but any one of them can be moved to vary the notes desired and produce any effect from raw muffled notes up to very piercing notes—thus one end can be tuned to call Mallards, Teal, etc., the other end tuned exclusively for Wood Duck, Blue Bills, etc.

Within the moisture-proof outer sections of the call is a metal tube containing a bronze bill (or channel), a cork plug and a bronze composition reed (or tongue), and every part of the device is guaranteed not to shrink, swell, crack or corrode, and keep a natural tune at all times, imitative to the duck species.

The outside of the call is made in two sections of different shapes so that either end can be quickly distinguished when the occasion for its use arises.

TO TAKE THE CALL APART

Remove one outside section, then hold the channel and reed between the thumb and forefinger, pull same from the metal tube. Then remove the tube from other section.

TO TUNE THE CALLER

Place the channel in the metal tube with the reed in position over the channel, also place the cork plug on the reed inside of the metal tube. Put the metal tube within the outer sections.

The reed (or tongue) may be bent more at one end than at the other. This produces **many sounds** imitative to the duck variety. The reed should be handled with care. Do not twist or kink the same. The cork plug may be pushed toward either end of the metal tube and thus vary the length of the respective ends of the reed, consequently varying the vibration and sound produced by each end.

These calls are tuned when they leave the factory, but may be tuned differently to suit the sportsman, if he so desires.

WHEN CALLING DUCKS

Hold the caller on one end, between the thumb and forefinger. Try different ways, open and close the fingers and with little practice any sportsman will soon be able to call ducks successfully.

One of the sections of the outer case is provided with a groove that a cord may be tied to the same and one end of the cord to the buttonhole of the sportsman's coat.

These calls are made with hard rubber outside sections and also wood outside sections. Both are double-ended calls.

Price, Hard Rubber Call .... $1.00 each
" Wood Call .... .75 "

J. W. REYNOLDS,

Manufacturer of Hunting Specialties. 68 S. Morgan St., CHICAGO, U. S. A.

Advertisement for extremely rare Double Duck Call, patent received by J. W. Reynolds (1872–1949) of Forest Park, Illinois, first known call to use cast metal toneboard, which allowed the caller to blow from either end of the call, circa 1900; duck call, $500.

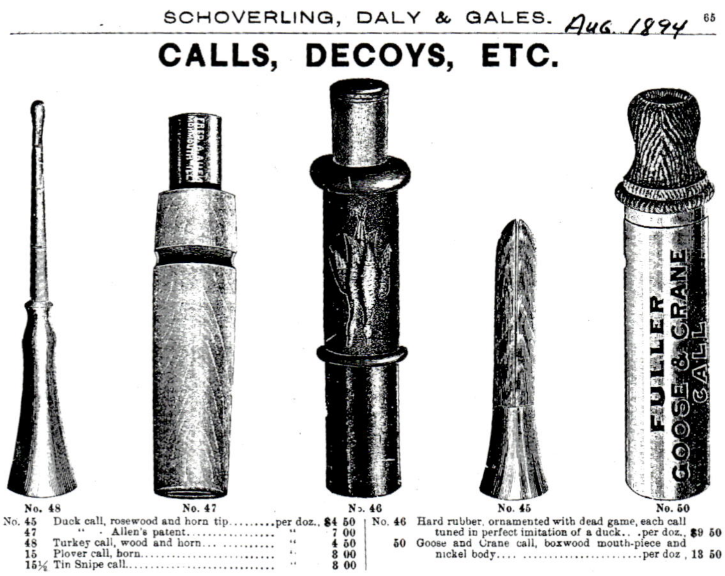

SCHOVERLING, DALY & GALES. Aug. 1894 65

CALLS, DECOYS, ETC.

No. 48 No. 47 No. 46 No. 45 No. 50

FULLER GOOSE & CRANE CALL

No. 45 Duck call, rosewood and horn tip.........per doz., $4 50
47 " Allen's patent........ " 7 00
48 Turkey call, wood and horn........ " 4 50
15 Plover call, horn........ " 8 00
15½ Tin Snipe call........ " 8 00

No. 46 Hard rubber, ornamented with dead game, each call tuned in perfect imitation of a duck.. .per doz., $9 50
50 Goose and Crane call, boxwood mouth-piece and nickel body.... ....per doz., 13 50

Schoverling, Daly & Gales Sporting Goods catalog, circa 1894, ad for duck calls.

Calls by Ralf True of Minneapolis, Minnesota, circa 1940: left, goose call, $200; right, duck call, $300.

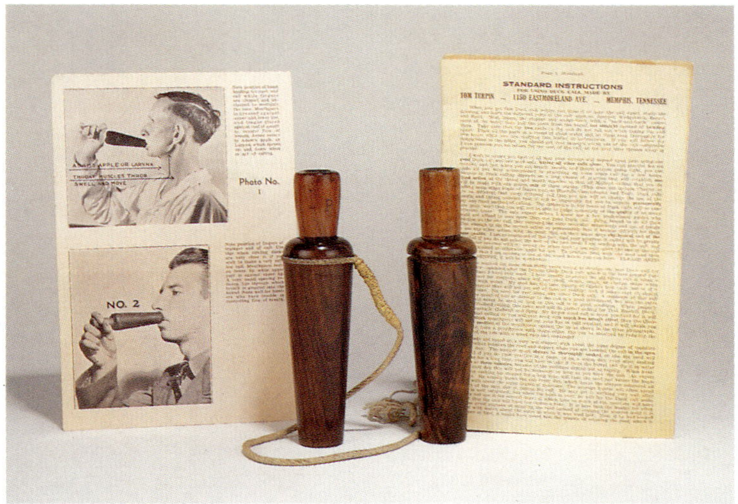

Duck calls with instruction sheets and original manuals by Tom Turpin of Reelfoot, Tennessee, circa 1930: left, burl walnut call, $750; right, three flying ducks stamp model, $750.

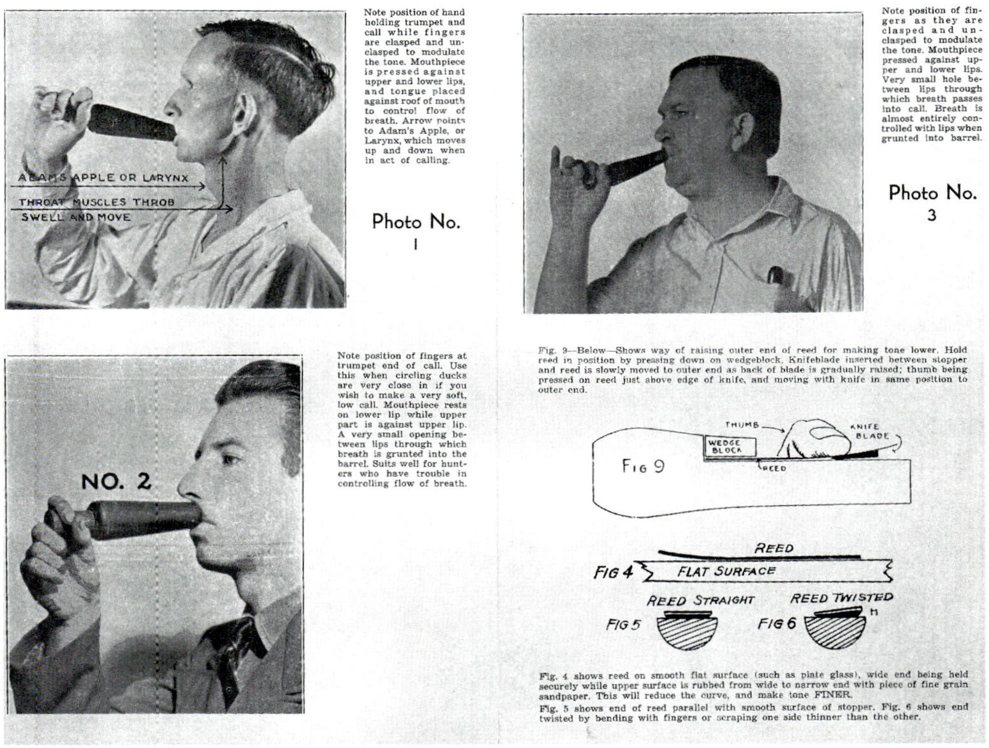

Note position of hand holding trumpet and call while fingers are clasped and unclasped to modulate the tone. Mouthpiece is pressed against upper and lower lips, and tongue placed against roof of mouth to control flow of breath. Arrow points to Adam's Apple, or Larynx, which moves up and down when in act of calling.

Photo No. 1

Note position of fingers as they are clasped and unclasped to modulate the tone. Mouthpiece pressed against upper and lower lips. Very small hole between lips through which breath passes into call. Breath is almost entirely controlled with lips when grunted into barrel.

Photo No. 3

Note position of fingers at trumpet end of call. Use this when circling ducks are very close in if you wish to make a very soft, low call. Mouthpiece rests on lower lip while upper part is against upper lip. A very small opening between lips through which breath is grunted into the barrel. Suits well for hunters who have trouble in controlling flow of breath.

Fig. 9—Below—Shows way of raising outer end of reed for making tone lower. Hold reed in position by pressing down on wedgeblock. Knifeblade inserted between stopper and reed is slowly moved to outer end as back of blade is gradually raised; thumb being pressed on reed just above edge of knife, and moving with knife in same position to outer end.

Fig. 4 shows reed on smooth flat surface (such as plate glass), wide end being held securely while upper surface is rubbed from wide to narrow end with piece of fine grain sandpaper. This will reduce the curve, and make tone FINER.

Fig. 5 shows end of reed parallel with smooth surface of stopper. Fig. 6 shows end twisted by bending with fingers or scraping one side thinner than the other.

Instructions for blowing a duck call featuring Ralf True (upper left photo) and his duck call.

Duck calls by Tom Turpin, circa 1940: left, novelty duck call used as store display and at sports shows, $1,000; right, walnut burl duck call, $750.

J. T. Berkhart (1864–1922) market hunted and guided on Big Lake, the Missouri/Arkansas waterfowling center. Pictured with sportsmen from St. Louis, Berkhart on the far right is considered the father of the Big Lake duck call style. (*Photograph courtesy Jim Goodrich*)

Brass game call, extremely rare, early combination duck and goose call, stamped "H. W. White, Yankton, Dakota Territory," circa 1880, $4,000.

Duck call of ebony with ivory insets and a stopper carved like a die, one of a kind fancy call by an unknown maker from Tennessee, circa 1940, $2,000.

Checkered duck calls, left to right: walnut, by an unknown Tennessee maker, circa 1890, $1,000; raised-panel duck call personalized with initials "H.H.T." by Joe Willingham of Pine Bluff, Arkansas, circa 1920, $2,000; unusually fat, finely checkered duck call by an unknown Tennessee maker, circa 1920, $2,000; and raised panel duck call by J. T. Beckhart of Swiftwater, Arkansas, Stamped "J. T. Beckhart" across top of barrel, circa 1910, $3,500.

Duck call, walnut with etched design, brass rings, by an unknown Illinois River maker, circa 1900, $1,000.

Unknown Arkansas-style duck calls, circa 1930: left, $250; right with checkering, $400.

Unknown Illinois River-style duck calls: left, hand-turned duck call, circa 1900, $1,000; center, duck call, circa 1900, $500; right, "Old Bill's Call," marketed by V.L. & A. Chicago, Illinois, circa 1910, $1,200; and duck hunting brochure, circa 1920, from Beardstown, Illinois.

Tennessee-style duck calls, makers unknown, circa 1940, $300 each.

Turkey box call by Henry C. Gibbson (1848–?) of Dardanelle, Arkansas, patented 1897, considered the first commercial turkey box call maker and the most collectible of all turkey calls, marked "Simmons Hardware Co., St. Louis, Missouri," circa 1900, $1,500. (*Collection of Howard Harlan*)

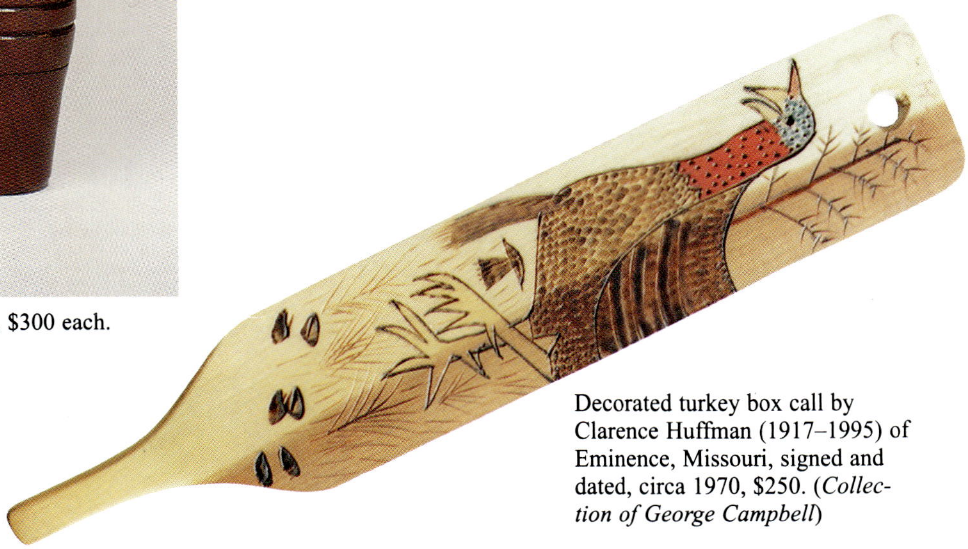

Decorated turkey box call by Clarence Huffman (1917–1995) of Eminence, Missouri, signed and dated, circa 1970, $250. (*Collection of George Campbell*)

Turkey call in box, slate box call, Allen Jerkins, M. L. Lynch Co., Liberty, Missouri, circa 1970, $200. (*Collection of Howard Harlan*)

Turkey box call, Tru-Tone, by Roger Latham of Gibsonia, Pennsylvania, circa 1940, $200. (*Collection of Howard Harlan*)

Turkey box call by Michael, L. Lynch (1896–1974) of Birmingham, Alabama, World Champion Turkey Call, circa 1950, $125. (*Collection of Howard Harlan*)

"Fence post" turkey calls: foreground, paddle box turkey call, red and white cedar, by D. Dan Searcy of Eminence, Missouri, circa 1970, $400; background, large cedar fence post turkey call by Walter Winterbottom (1912–1991) of Eminence, Missouri, circa 1975, $400. (*Collection of George Campbell*)

Turkey "crank" calls by John "Pete" Pulley of Centerville, Missouri, franchised to P.S. Olt and marketed as CT-220 Crank turkey call, circa 1975: left, Crank Wild Turkey Call, signed John Pulley, circa 1975, $150; EZ Tom #2 Turkey Call, circa 1950, $150. (*Collection of George Campbell*)

Fence post turkey call by Walter Winterbottom of Eminence, Missouri, $400. (*Collection of George Campbell*)

Turkey calls: left, friction call by W.J. Walker of Sagamore, Pennsylvania, patent #2, 643, 483, $250; right; paddle box call with Stihl Chain Saw Co. name plate attached, by John Pulley of Centerville, Missouri, circa 1970, $300. (*Collection of George Campbell*)

Slate-box type turkey call by an unknown maker from Arkansas or Missouri, circa 1920, $200. (*Collection of Howard Harlan*)

Turkey paddle box call by an unknown maker, found in Beebe, Missouri, $150. (*Collection of George Campbell*)

Unknown turkey calls, Arkansas box and slate style, $150 each. (*Collection of Howard Harlan*)

Turkey box call by an unknown Arkansas maker, circa 1890, $200. (*Collection of Howard Harlan*)

Turkey calls, bone yelper calls from the Bridgeport Gun and Implement Co. in New York, circa 1890, $100 each. (*Collection of Howard Harlan*)

Turkey yelper call, quill style, by Vedna Ottis Johnson, Jr. (1918–1990) of Gould Arkansas, patent #3, 419, 996, circa 1970, $300. (*Collection of George Campbell*)

Turkey yelper call, quill style, by Vedna O. Johnson, Jr., circa 1940, $400. (*Collection of George Campbell*)

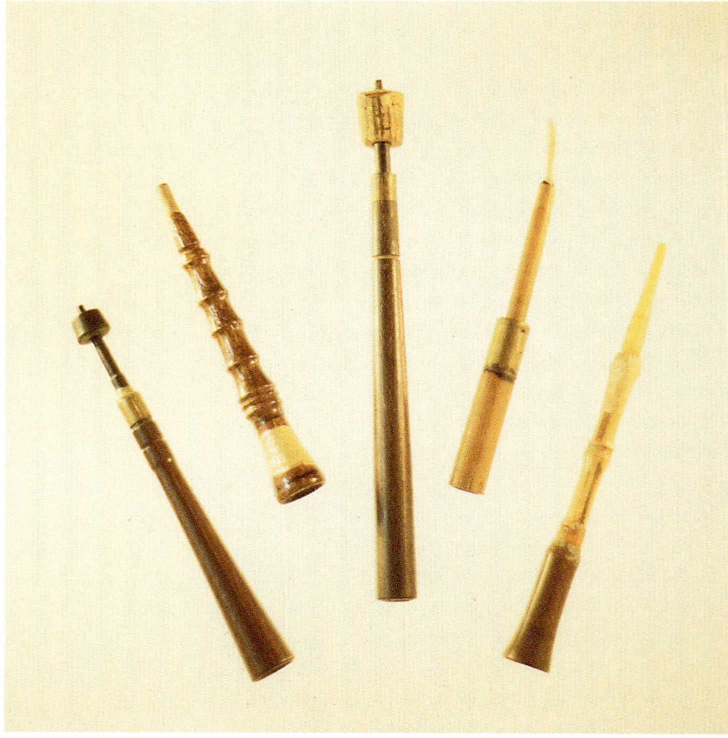

Yelper turkey calls, left to right: cocobols wood with bone mouthpiece and cork gauge by Tom Turpin, circa 1920, $500; unknown Tennessee-style call, circa 1930, $500; Tom Turpin cane and bone call, circa 1930, $750; unknown, cane and bone call, circa 1930, $500; and unknown Arkansas, cane and bone call with wooden bell, $500. (*Collection of Howard Harlan*)

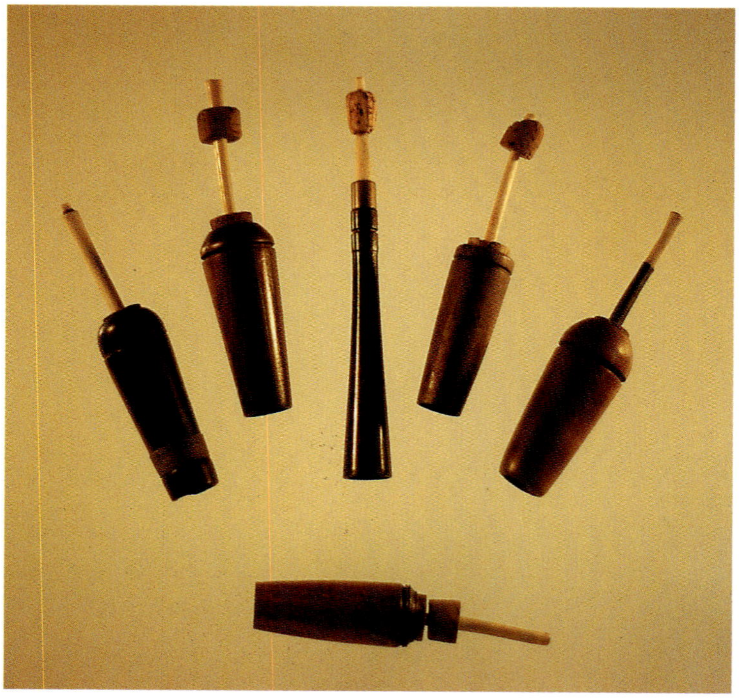

Various turkey calls by Tom Turpin, extremely rare: center call, #3 yelper; others, tree yelper calls, circa 1930, $750-1,000 each. (*Collection of Howard Harlan*)

Various unknown commercially produced bone yelper turkey calls, circa 1900–1920. Mostly sold by the better sporting good stores such as V.L.& A, and Abercrombie and Fitch, $200 each. (*Collection of Howard Harlan*)

Snipe whistle, sterling silver, carved and engraved bowl with turquoise setting, maker unknown, circa 1880, $1,000. Marbled Godwit decorative carving by Elmer Crowell, East Harwich, Massachusetts. $2,000. (*Collection of Alan and Elaine Haid/Photography by Alan Haid*)

Second view of snipe whistle.

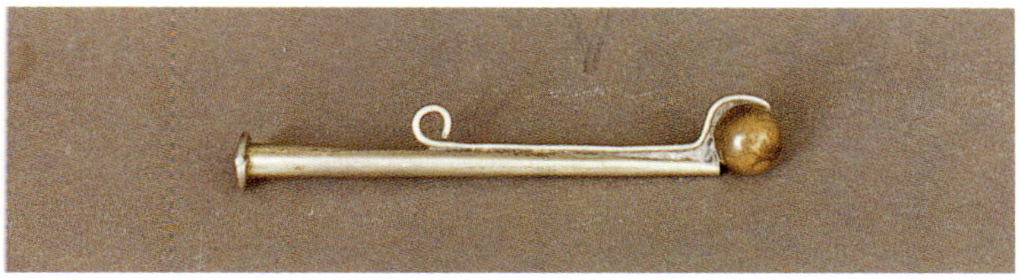

Snipe whistle, rare "ball" type whistle, stamped "A F" for Abercrombie & Fitch Co., New York, New York, circa 1900, $700. (*Collection of Alan and Elaine Haid/Photography by Alan Haid*)

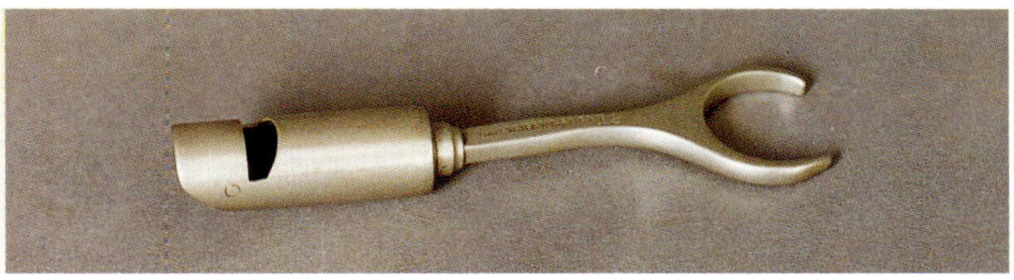

Snipe whistle, stamped "G. & J. W. Hawksley," and 12-gauge shell extractor, circa 1900, $700. (*Collection of Alan and Elaine Haid/Photography by Alan Haid*)

Eureka snipe whistle from National Sportsman, Inc., stamped, circa 1900, $400. (*Collection of Alan and Elaine Haid/Photography by Alan Haid*)

Snipe whistles, two different styles produced by Willard Manufacturing Co. in Melrose, Massachusetts, circa 1900, $500 each. (*Collection of Alan and Elaine Haid/Photography by Alan Haid*)

Various styles of snipe whistles, makers unknown, circa 1900, $100 each.(*Collection of Alan and Elaine Haid/Photography by Alan Haid*)

Snipe whistles, stamped "Kirkwood Bros., Boston, Massachusetts," circa 1900, $500 each. (*Collection of Alan and Elaine Haid/Photography by Alan Haid*)

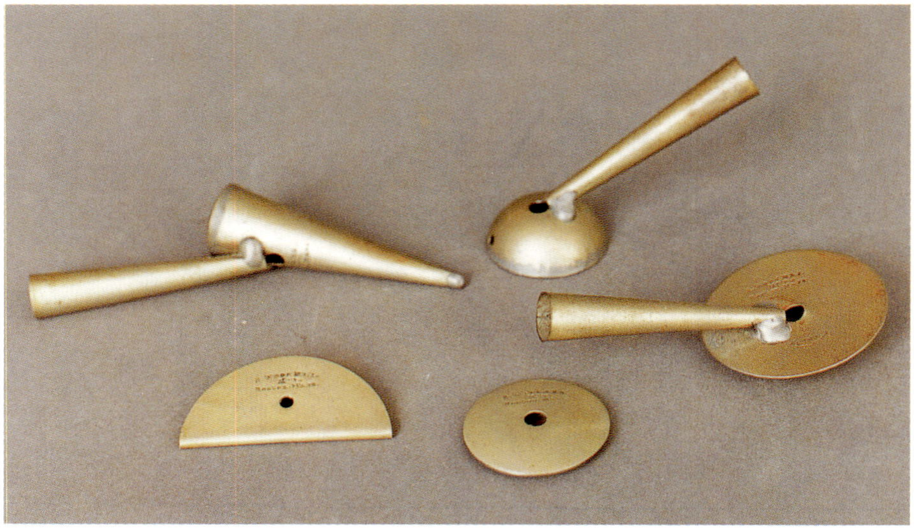

Various styles of snipe whistles, all stamped "R. Woodman manufacturer, Boston, Massachusetts," circa 1900, $500 each.(*Collection of Alan and Elaine Haid/Photography by Alan Haid*)

Various styles of snipe whistles, makers unknown, circa 1900, $100 each. (*Collection of Alan and Elaine Haid/Photography by Alan Haid*)

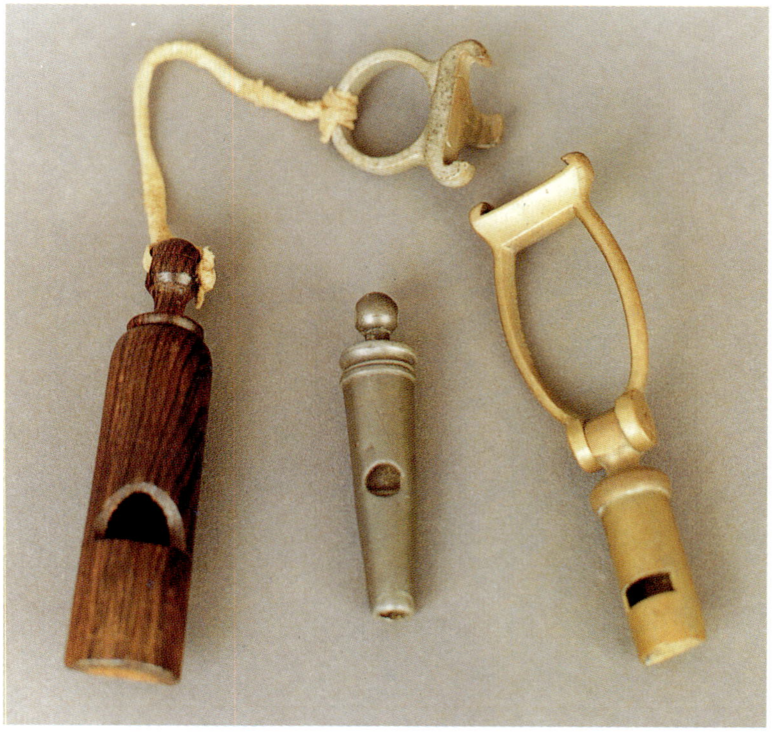

Various styles of snipe whistles, with shell extractors, makers unknown, circa 1900, $150 each. (*Collection of Alan and Elaine Haid/Photography by Alan Haid*)

Chapter 5

Advertising

In our age of mass media, it is hard to relate to the problems companies had presenting their products to the general public prior to radio and television. Most companies relied heavily upon graphic arts to attract customers. Many of the country's finest wildlife artists were commissioned to create beautifully illustrated posters, calendars, die-cut cardboard displays, pin-back buttons, shell boxes, and gunpowder tins to catch the consumer's eye. These items represent one of the strongest fields of sporting collectibles. As with all collectibles, rarity and condition are the determining factors in evaluating gun company advertising.

Small companies, even local hardware and sporting goods stores, used this form of advertising. The shops would hand-load pre-primed casings and market them under a private label. While the first graphics, usually simple one- to two-color designs with elaborate lettering are desirable because of their age, later full-color graphics are more appealing to the average collector. The value of posters and calendars featuring artwork by Alexander Pope, Richard Bishop, or Lynn Bogue Hunt reflect the popularity of the artists. Calendars that show signs of use—for example, pages removed from calendars—lose some of their collector value, but cutting advertising graphics to fit a frame makes the piece almost worthless. Additionally, size may effect the value of advertising collectibles. For instance, many of the larger die-cut cardboard advertising pieces that were distributed to store owners to promote various product lines have limited appeal among collectors because they are hard to display, thus smaller versions used as counter displays are usually more valuable.

Shotgun shells were first marketed as empty casings packaged twenty five or one hundred in a two-piece cardboard box with thumb notches on opposite sides of a top-lifting lid. An illustrated paper label was normally wrapped around the entire box and glued in place to act as a seal. Boxes with the label intact should not be opened. Later one-piece shell boxes are becoming more collectible. In both cases, the colorful graphics determine the value of a box. Some collectors specialize in boxes with hunting scenes, dogs, shooting scenes, wild game, or game birds on the labels. The most collectible boxes are private-label shotgun shells marketed by small companies and hardware stores that hand-loaded shotgun shells, and specially designed, limited-supply Christmas boxes distributed by the major ammunition companies.

As machinery was developed to mass produce loaded shotgun shells, large ammunitions companies absorbed most of the small distributors. Manufacturing giants like Winchester Repeating Arms used more aggressive marketing techniques to introduce their new product lines to the general public. Their newly developed firearms and ammunitions could make a marksman out of any man. To create potential customers, manufacturers had to get their products into the hands of the average man. Sharpshooters were hired to travel throughout the country to give shooting demonstrations and entertain fair goers. Shooting galleries were set up so people could try out the new guns firsthand. Competitions were sponsored

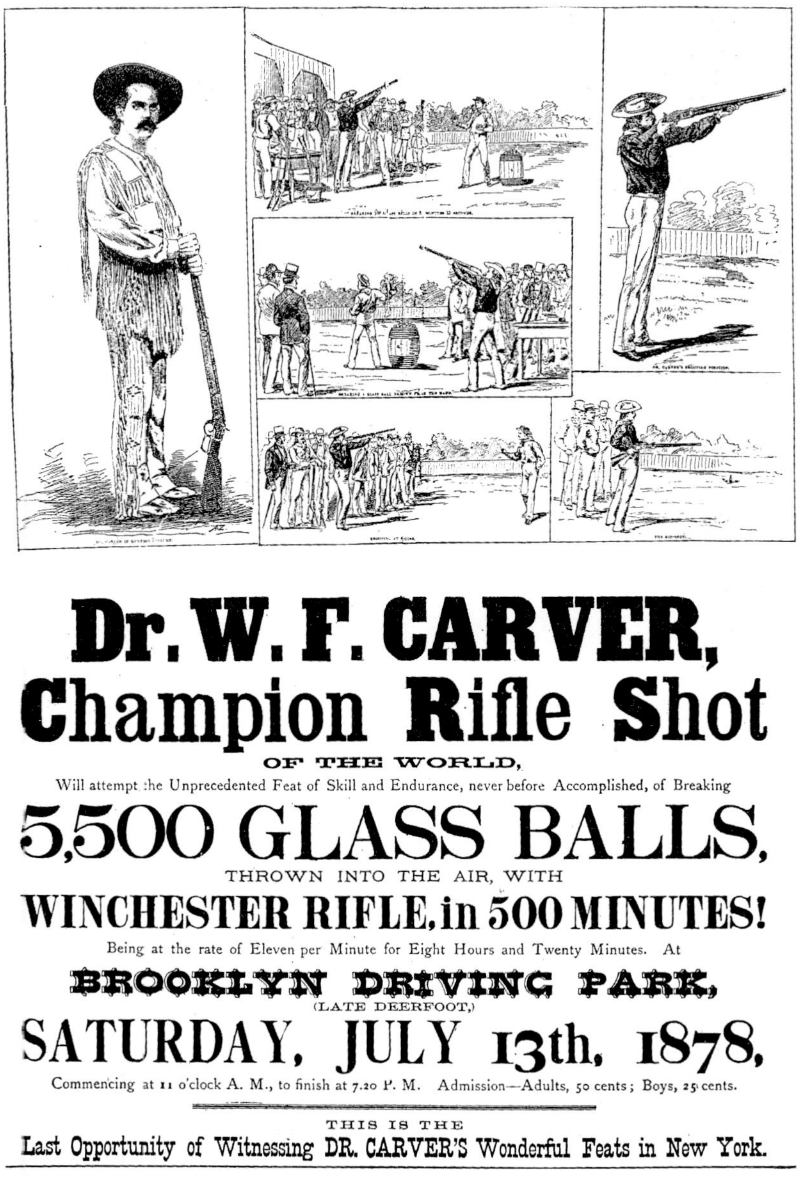

Sharpshooters were highly respected personalities in the days before television and radio. W. F. "Doc" Carver (1840–1927) was one of the world's greatest rifle shots during the 1880s. Associated with noted western folk heroes, Wild Bill Hickok, Buffalo Bill, Buffalo Jones, and Texas Jack, he shared billing for the Buffalo Bill and Dr. Carver's Wild West Show, circa 1892.

where local shooters could vie for handsome trophies and try to out gun the company marksmen in shooting glass, and later clay, targets. Advertising pin backs and stickpins decorated with miniature artwork that corresponded with the company's advertising campaign were popular giveaways at all these events.

Not all collectible sporting buttons were produced by firearms and ammunition companies. Some states used pin backs as a licensing form for hunters, fishermen, and trappers. Collectors also value the various badges and embroidered patches that game wardens and guides wore. Ducks Unlimited, an international conservation organization initiated by concerned waterfowlers in 1937 to protect the migratory bird populations, sold buttons decorated with wildlife art at their first fund-raisers. These pin backs became popular collectibles, and the Ducks Unlimited organization expanded their fund raising offerings to include numerous special-edition collectibles such as prints, decoys, shotguns, liquor decanters, etc. One of the rarest Ducks Unlimited collectibles is a simple tin bank from their Duck-a-Nickle campaign, valued at $500.

Fox Gun Co., Super Fox catalog, $150; Fox Gun Co., gun pocket catalog, $75; Western Ammunition catalog, $25. (*Collection of Lee Schultz*)

Assorted glass target balls which were hand-blown into molds. Individual balls were filled with feathers or wood shavings so the shooter could see if he hit the target. Circa 1880–1900, $100-150 each.

Card Trap, patent 1882, glass target thrower, $2,000. (*Collection of Ron Willoughby*)

Various fur trading company envelopes, $25-50 each. (*Collection of Lee Schultz*)

Savage Arms and Ammunition catalogs, circa 1930: Indian Chief catalog, $75; bottom left, Sporting Arms catalog, $40; and bottom right, arms and ammunition catalog, $50. (*Collection of Lee Schultz*)

Berth glass target ball, cobalt blue, fishnet pattern, N B Glass Works, circa 1880, $125.

Stock & Morris Trap patent 1879, glass target thrower, $3,500. (*Collection of Ron Willoughby*)

The Wm. R. Burkhard Co. of Minneapolis, Minnesota, letterhead and envelope, circa 1916, $35. (*Collection of Lee Schultz*)

Assorted glass target balls, circa 1880–1900, $100-150 each. (*Collection of Ron Willoughby*)

Mole Double Trap, glass target thrower, patent 1882, $3,500. (*Collection of Ron Willoughby*)

Parker Gun Co. letterhead and envelope, rare, circa 1918, $200. (*Collection of Lee Schultz*)

Wooden live pigeon trap, spring release for live pigeon shoots, circa 1880, $500.

Presentation award, china pitcher, 24 inches, extremely rare, L. C. Smith Gun Co., $2,000.

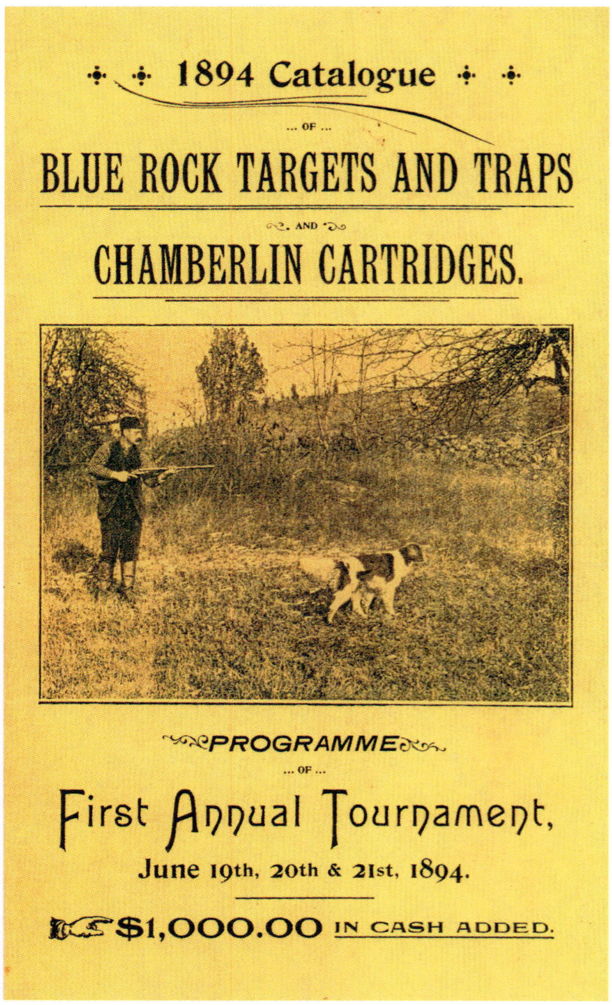

Chamberlain Cartridge Co. sponsored shooting tournament catalog, 1894, $250.

Presentation shooting award, china vase, 12 inches, extremely rare, Hunter Arms Co., L.C. Smith Guns, $2,000. (*Collection of Lee Schultz*)

Professional trap shooters squad from Iowa falls, Iowa, 1909, left to right: Fred Gilbert, the "Wizard of Spirit Lake (Iowa)"; William Heer, "Silent Bill"; George Maxwell; Charles Spencer, and Maxwell Hensler. (*Courtesy of Morton Smith Jr.*)

John "Newt" Rule (1870–1949) of Beardstown, Illinois, decoy carver, duck call maker, waterfowling guide, also operated a shooting gallery at local fairs, circa 1900. (*Photograph courtesy of Mrs. R. Donaldson*)

Jim Dickey, champion marksman from Minneapolis, Minnesota, circa 1900. (*Courtesy of Morton Smith, Jr.*)

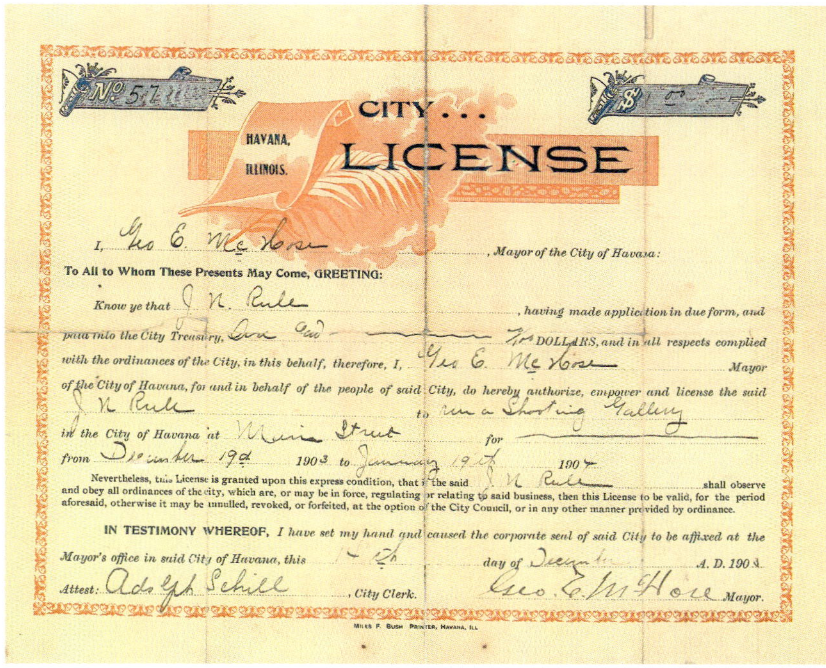

HAVANA, ILLINOIS.

CITY . . . LICENSE

I, Geo E. McHose, Mayor of the City of Havana:

To All to Whom These Presents May Come, GREETING:

Know ye that J. N. Rule, *having made application in due form, and paid into the City Treasury,* One Hund ——— Dollars, *and in all respects complied with the ordinances of the City, in this behalf, therefore, I,* Geo E. McHose *Mayor of the City of Havana, for and in behalf of the people of said City, do hereby authorize, empower and license the said* J N Rule *to* run a Shooting Gallery *in the City of Havana at* Main Street *for* ——— *from* December 19th *1903 to* January 19th *1904*

Nevertheless, this License is granted upon this express condition, that if the said J N Rule shall observe and obey all ordinances of the city, which are, or may be in force, regulating or relating to said business, then this License to be valid, for the period aforesaid, otherwise it may be annulled, revoked, or forfeited, at the option of the City Council, or in any other manner provided by ordinance.

IN TESTIMONY WHEREOF, *I have set my hand and caused the corporate seal of said City to be affixed at the Mayor's office in said City of Havana, this* 14th *day of* December *A. D. 1903.*

Attest: Adolph Schill, *City Clerk.* Geo. E. McHose *Mayor.*

MILES F. BUSH PRINTER, HAVANA, ILL.

City license for Rule's shooting gallery from Havana, Illinois, dated 1903, $100. (*Photograph courtesy of Mrs. R. Donaldson*)

Men organized local shooting clubs where they regularly competed among themselves to sharpen their shooting skills. Riverview Rod & Gun Club, Chicago, Illinois, circa 1920.

Uncle Sam rifle shot portrait "drawn" in sheet metal with 150-200 quickly fired 22-caliber rifle shots as part of his shooting exhibition, sponsored by Remington-Peters Arms Co., William Johnson, circa 1930, $2,000. (*Photograph courtesy of Norma Johnson*)

William Johnson (1900–1987) of Scandinavia, Wisconsin, worked as a sharpshooter for Peter Cartridge and Remington-Peter Arms Co., around 1929–1965. (*Photograph courtesy of Norma Johnson*)

William Johnson performing a trick shooting exhibition for U.S. Army, 4th Ferrying Group, Memphis, Tennessee, circa 1944. (*Photograph courtesy of Norma Johnson*)

Miscellaneous trap and skeet shooting award patches, circa 1930–50, $35-50 each.

Miscellaneous advertising patches, $100-150 each; wallets, $75-100 each, and trick shot slugs, $5-10 each.

Oil on canvas, original cover art by Evan Keith Soward, classic Lynn Bogue Hunt style, circa 1950, $500.

Oil on canvas, original cover art by Evan Keith Soward, circa 1950, $500.

Hunting & Fishing, Vol. 28, Number 10, November, 1951, $10.

Poster, American Powder Mills, Walker Lithographers, Boston, 13 x 21 inches, top and bottom bands, $3,000.

Poster, American Powder Mills, 13 x 20 inches, top and bottom bands, $3,000.

Poster, American Powder Mills, 14 x 24 inches, top and bottom bands, $2,000.

Poster, Colt Patent Fire Arms Manufacturing Co., Frank Schoonover, 20 x 33 inches, top and bottom bands, $1,000.

Assorted pin backs: DuPont, Crow, $150; DuPont quail & woodcock, $50-75; DuPont dynamite, $85; DuPont setters, $50-75; DuPont red, $35-50; Western Ammunition, $30; circa 1930-40.

Self-framing tin, 1903, E. I. DuPont de Nemours & Co., Edmond H. Osthaus, $1,000.

Poster, 1904, E.I. DuPont de Nemours & Co., Edmond H. Osthaus, 20 x 30 inches, top and bottom bands, $2,000.

Poster, 1909, E.I. DuPont de Nemours & Co., 20 x 25 inches, top and bottom, $1,500.

Poster, 1909, E. I. DuPont de Nemours & Co., Worth Brehm, American Litho Co., top and bottom bands, $400.

Poster, 1909, E. I. DuPont de Nemours & Co., 20 x 25 inches, top and bottom bands, $1,500.

LYNN BOGUE HUNT
BROADBILLS-"HERE THEY COME!"
HAVE YOUR SHELLS LOADED WITH
INFALLIBLE
SMOKELESS SHOTGUN POWDER
ABSOLUTELY WATERPROOF
BEST FOR ALL KINDS OF SHOOTING
HANDLED BY ALL FIRST CLASS DEALERS

USE
DU PONT
SMOKELESS POWDER
FOR
WILD FOWL SHOOTING.
"A DOUBLE WITH DU PONT SMOKELESS"

DU PONT
DU PONT
SMOKELESS
SHOTGUN POWDER
LYNN BOGUE HUNT
THE STANDARD OF THE WORLD

SHOOT
BALLISTITE
DENSE
Smokeless Shotgun Powder
DU PONT

Opposite page:
Top left: Poster, 1912, E. I. DuPont de Nemours & Co., *Broadbills, Here They Come*, Lynn Bogue Hunt, 18 x 27 inches, top and bottom bands, $1,000.

Bottom left: Poster 1913, E.I. DuPont de Nemours & Co., Lynn Bogue Hunt, Sachett & Wilheims Co., 21 x 30 inches, top and bottom bands, $500.

Top right: Poster, E. I. DuPont de Nemours & Co., G. Muss Arnolt, $2,000.

Bottom right: Poster, E.I. DuPont de Nemours & Co., Charles DeFeo,19 x 30 inches, top and bottom bands, $2,500.

Poster, Hercules Powder Co., 15 x 24 inches, top and bottom bands, $1,000.

Opposite page:
Poster, King's Powder Co., Strobridge Co., Cincinnati, 17 x 24 inches, no bands, $4,000.

Poster, Harrington & Richardson Arms Co., $2,000. (*Collection of Lee Schultz*)

Although advertising depicting women hunters is very rare, many women enjoy waterfowling. Mrs. Morton Smith poses with her pusher on Heron Lake, Minnesota, circa 1920. (*Photograph courtesy of Morton Smith, Jr.*)

Poster, Hopkins & Allen Co., 17 x 25 inches, no bands, $3,000.

QUICK SHOT.
GUNPOWDER

Poster, 1908, Laflin & Rand Powder Co., American Lithograph Co., $4,000.

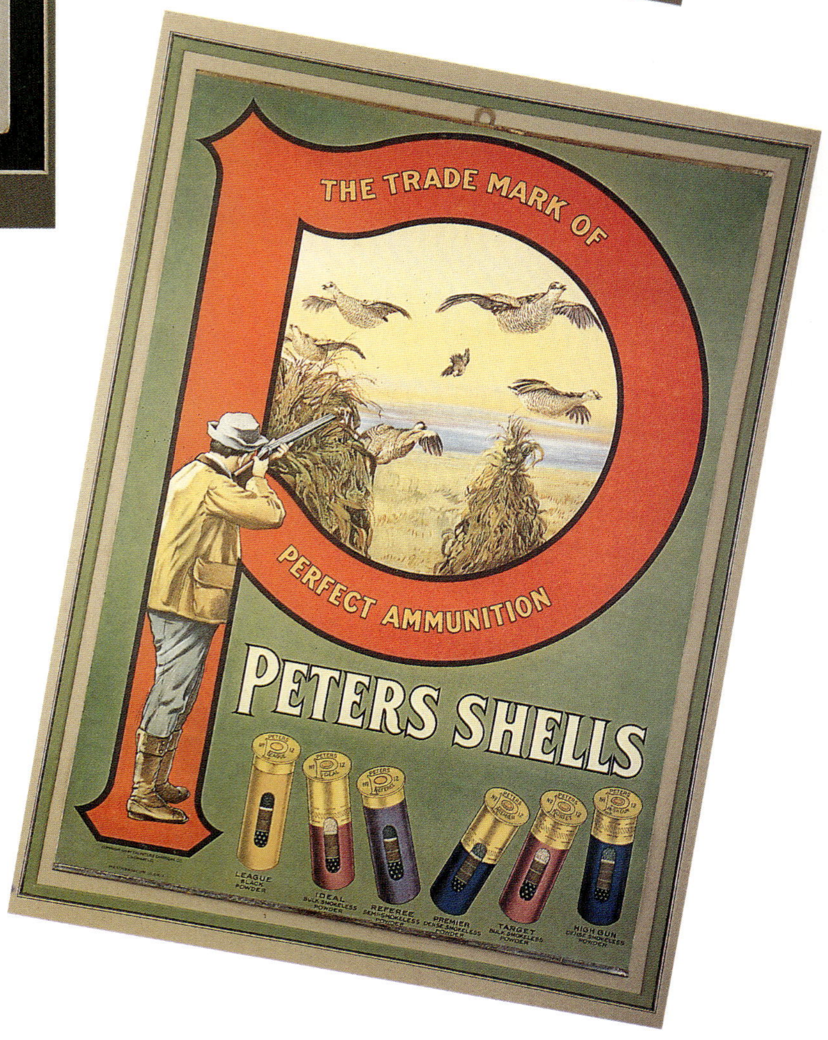

Top right: Poster, 1908, Marlin Fire Arms Co., by G. Muss Arnolt, 15 x 24 inches, top and bottom bands, $1,500.

Bottom right: Poster, 1911, Peters Cartridge Co., Strobridge Litho Co., Cincinnati, 15 x 21 inches, top and bottom bands, $500.

Poster, Peters Cartridge Co., by G. Muss Arnolt, 20 x 30 inches, top and bottom bands, $2,000.

Poster, Peters Cartridge Co., $1,200.

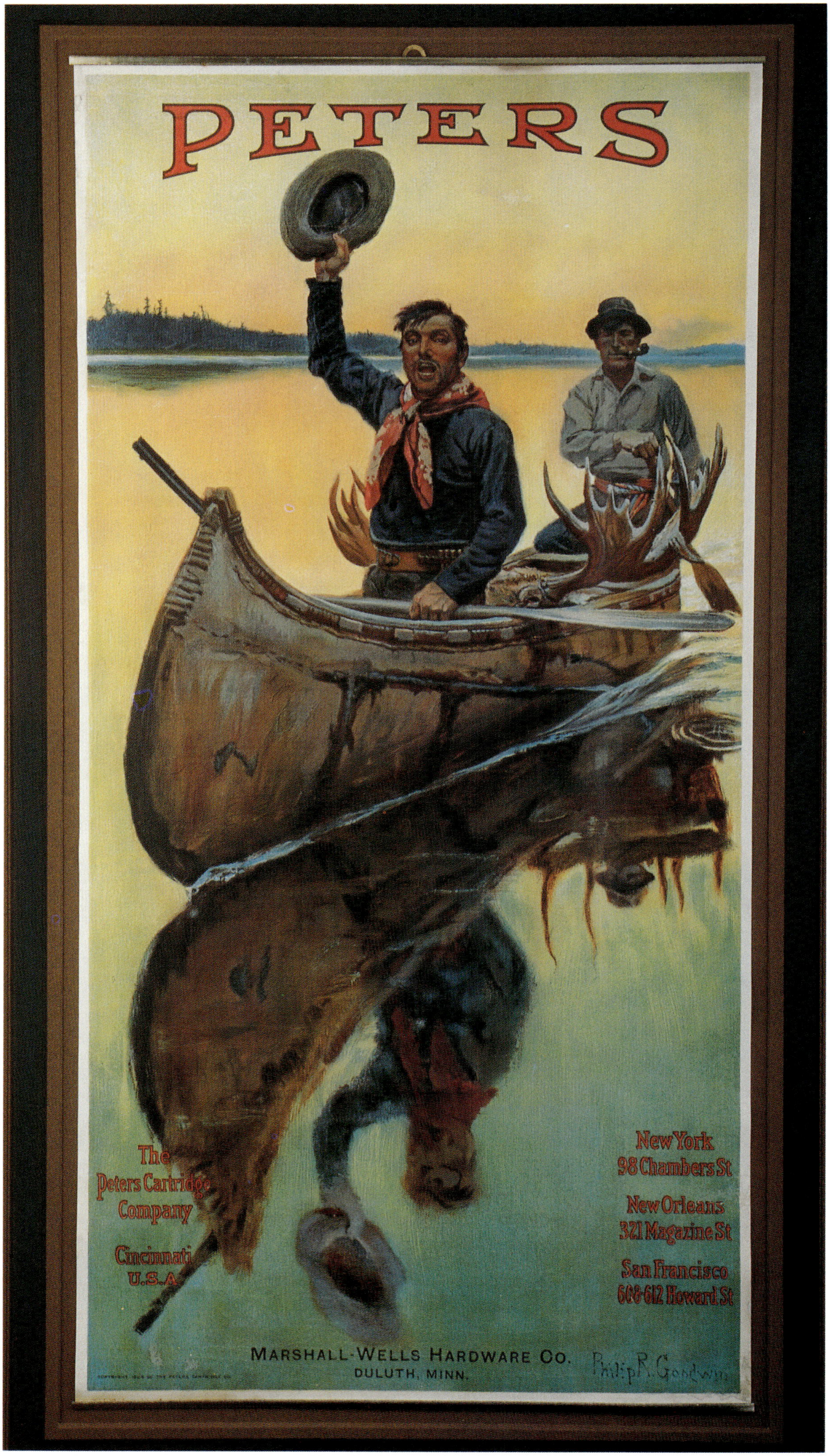

Poster, Peters Cartridge Co., 13 x 21 inches, top and bottom, $1,500.

Poster, Peters Cartridge Co., $400. (*Collection of Ron Wiloughby*)

Store display, die-cut cardboard, Peters Cartridge Co., $600. (*Collection of Ron Willoughby*)

Miscellaneous Remington Arms Co. catalogs; $25-50 each. (*Collection of Lee Schultz*)

Poster, 1923, Remington Arms Co., 18 x 26 inches, top and bottom bands, $350.

Poster, 1906, Savage-Stevens Arms Corp., Kaufman & Strauss, 15 x 20 inches, top and bottom bands, $2,000.

Advertising button, Stevens Shotguns, Stevens Arm Co., rare, circa 1920, $200.

Assorted pin backs; John Lowell Arms Company, $35 each; White Flyer, $100; Winchester Repeating Arms, $35-50 each; Colt Firearms Company, $75; Dominion Powder Company watch fob, $35; Dominion Powder Company, stick pin, $25; Western Stick pin, $25, Daisy Air Rifle, $75; DuPont quail, $50 each, Western Ammunition, $35 each; Iver Johnson Arms & Cycle Company, $50-75 each; Stevens Arms Company, $50 each; Hunter Arms Company, $50 each; National Sportsman Sporting Goods, $50; Annie Oakley, $500; Sporting Life Magazine, $75, Austin Ammunition Company, $200; Baker & Batavia Guns, $50; circa 1930-40.

Miscellaneous gun company and sporting goods catalogs, circa 1930–40, $100-150 each.

Poster, Union Metallic Cartridge Co., American Lithographic Co., 13 x 26 inches, 1901, $400; calendar, 1903, Hazard Powder Co., Smokeless Powder—The Trophy Winner, 18 x 25 inches, top and bottom bands; calendar, 1900 (store calendar), Laflin & Rand Powder Co., moose in oval, 13 x 22 inches, top and bottom bands, $800.

Store display, Remington-United Metallic Cartridge Co., cardboard, $300.

Store display, Remington-United Metallic Cartridge Co., printed on cardboard, $300.

Store display, die-cut cardboard, Union Metallic Cartridge Co., $500. (*Collection of Ron Willoughby*)

Poster, 1907, Union Metallic Cartridge Co., Lynn Bogue Hunt, 12 x 34 inches, top and bottom bands, $700.

Poster, 1908, Union Metallic Cartridge Co., 15 x 29 inches, top and bottom bands, $800.

Store display, die-cut, Union Metallic Cartridge Co., New Club quail, cardboard, $400.

Poster, 1927, United States Cartridge Co., mallards in flight, $4,000.

Oil on wood, unsigned, amateur artists often copied popular gun company artwork, circa 1930, $400.

Poster, United States Cartridge Co., hawk hitting green-winged teal, 20 x 30 inches, top and bottom bands, $4,000.

Poster, 1926, United States Cartridge Co., Joe Burgess, 20 x 31 inches, top and bottom, $800.

Poster, 1921, Western Ammunition, H. C. Edwards, 17 x 30 inches, top and bottom bands, $600.

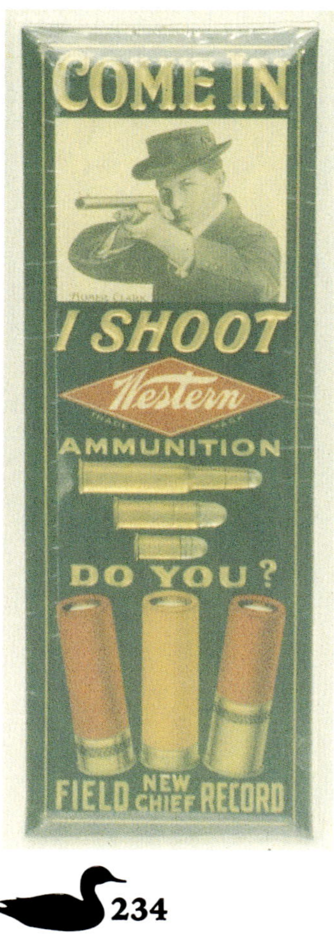

Door push, enameled, Western Cartridge Co., $2,500. (*Collection of Ron Willoughby*)

Poster, 1907, *The Winning Combination* (Geese), 16 x 29 inches, top and bottom bands, $1,500.

Poster, 1909, *.401 Caliber Self-loading Rifle.* Winchester Repeating Arms Co., 15 x 30 inches, top and bottom bands, $2,000.

Poster, 1909, Winchester Repeating Arms Co.; Edward Knobles, 15 x 30 inches, top and bottom bands, $2,500.

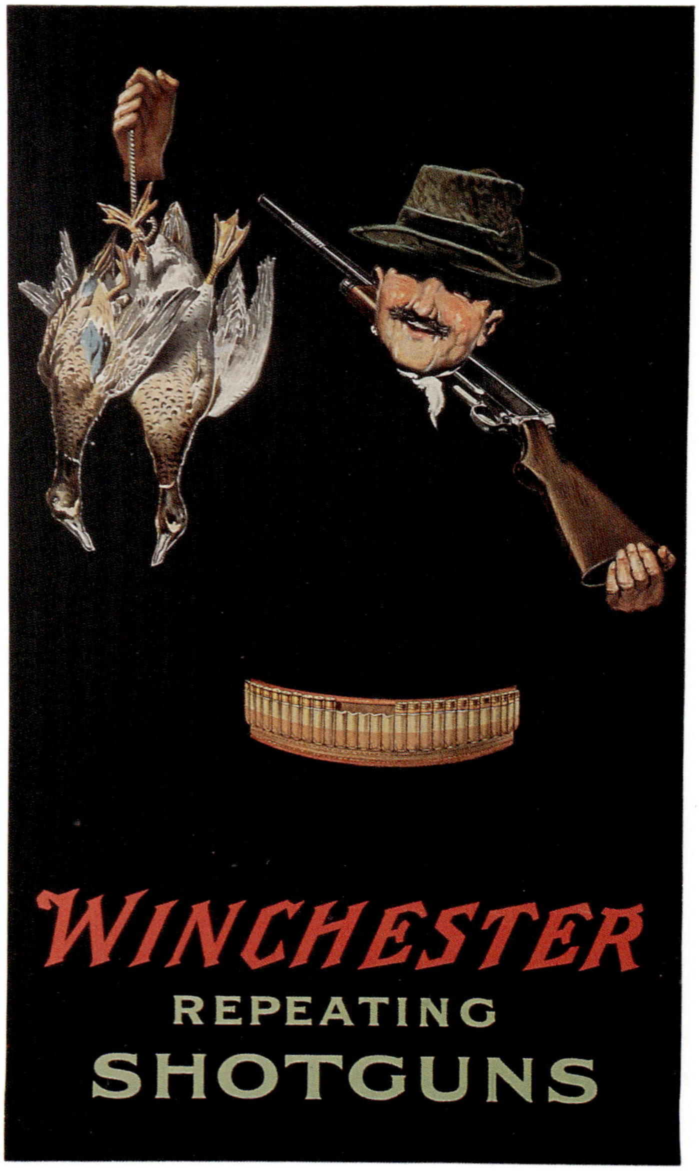

Poster, Winchester Repeating Arms Co., American Litho; 12 x 20 inches, printed on cardboard, $800.

Poster, 1910, Winchester Repeating Arms Co., N. C. Wyeth, American Color Type Co., N.Y., 19 x 30 inches, top and bottom bands, $800.

Poster, Winchester Repeating Arms Co., Forbes Co., Boston; 16 x 26 inches, top and bottom bands; $1,500.

Poster, tin, Winchester Repeating Arms Co., Alexander Pope, $4,000.

Poster, Winchester Repeating Arms Co., water spaniel with redhead; 15 x 27 inches; top and bottom bands; $1,000.

Poster, Repeating Shotguns, 16 x 30 inches, $600.

Oil on canvas, signed "E. L.", amateur artist's rendition of Winchester Repeating Arms Co. poster for 20-gauge shotguns, circa 1930, $500.

Calendar, 1901, E.I. DuPont de Nemours & Co., 12 x 24 inches, top and bottom bands; calendar, 1904, Marlin Fire Arms Co., 14 x 30 inches, $700; and calendar, 1903, E.I. DuPont de Nemours & Co., Forbes Co., Boston, 14 x 29 inches, top and bottom bands, $750.

Tin, 1903, E.I. DuPont de Nemours & Co. Companies often used the same artwork in several different mediums, $1,500.

Oil on canvas, G. Muss Arnolt, original art commission by E.I. DuPont de Nemours & Co., circa 1900, $5,000.

Calendar, 1904, E.I. DuPont de Nemours & Co., Edmond H. Osthaus, $2,000.

Calendar, 1906, E.I. DuPont de Nemours & Co., Forbes Co., Boston, 15 x 30 inches, top and bottom bands, $3,500.

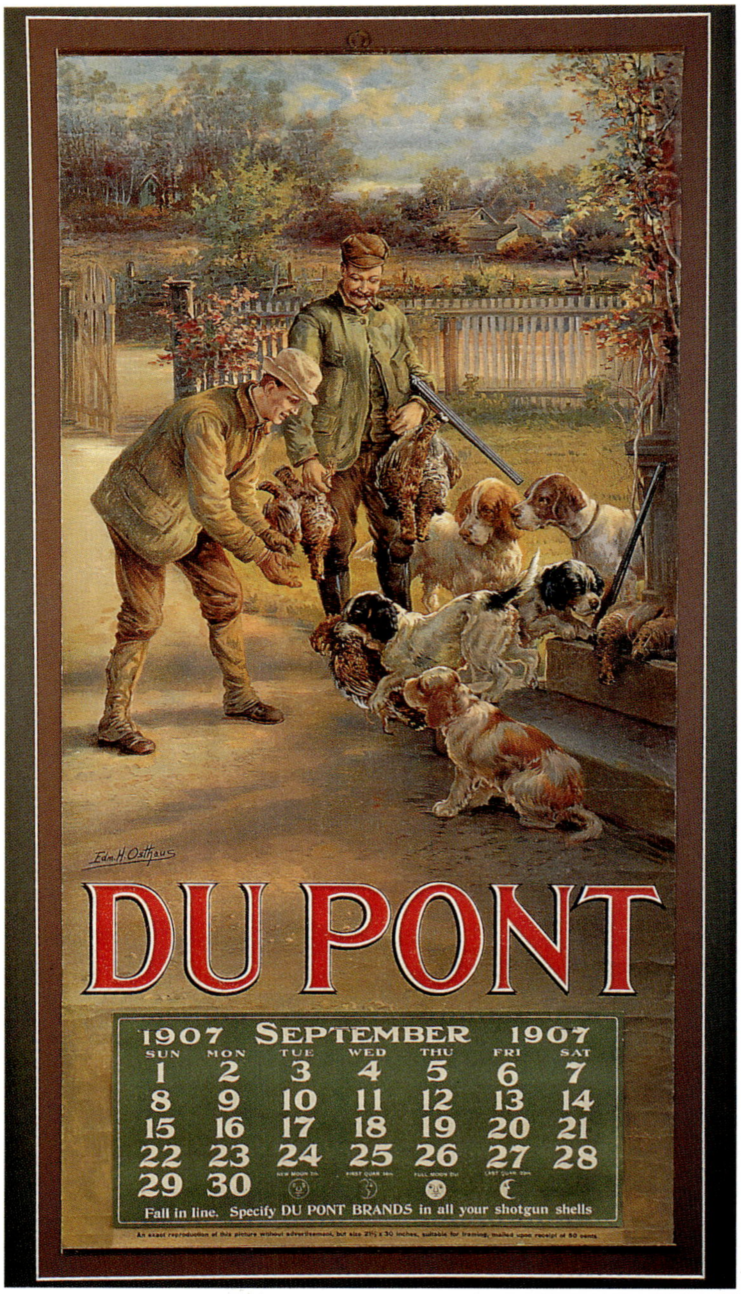

Calendar, 1907, E. I. DuPont de Nemours & Co., Frank H. Osthaus, 15 x 29 inches, top and bottom bands, $500.

Calendar, 1911, E.I. DuPont de Nemours & Co., Edmond H. Osthaus, 15 x 27 inches, top band, $400.

Advertising letterhead envelopes: Laflin & Rand Smokeless Powder, $50; Hazard Gunpowder Co., $50; and Winchester Repeating Arms, $35. (*Collection of Lee Schultz*)

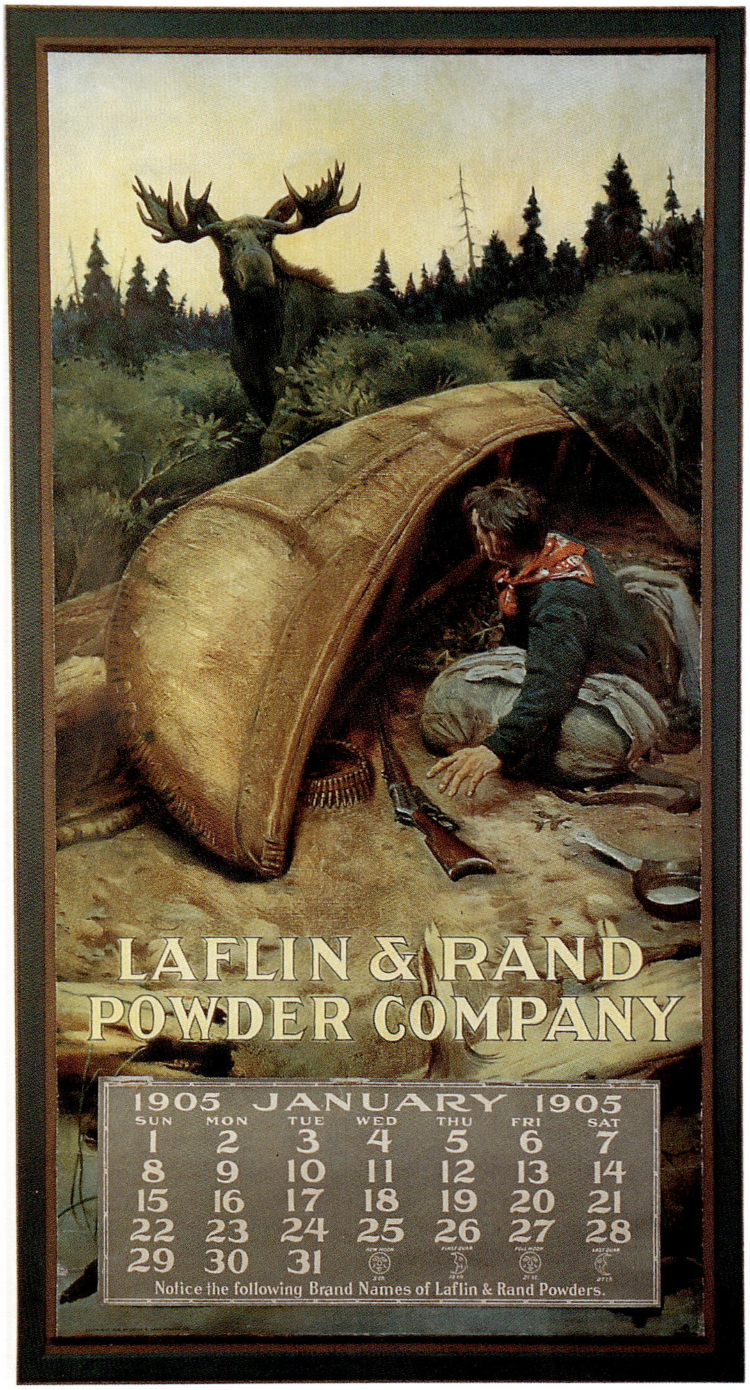

Calendar, 1905, Laflin & Rand Powder Co., $2,000.

Store calendar, J. D. Martin (tavern), Bureau, Illinois, Embossed cardboard, dead mount, circa 1911, $100.

Pre-printed calendar, twelve different pages, Charles Perdew, Henry, Illinois, circa 1947, $200.

Calendar, 1907, Peters Cartridge Co., Strobridge Litho Co., Cincinnati, 14 x 27 inches, top and bottom bands, $1,000.

Pre-printed, twelve different pages, Charles Perdew, Henry, Illinois, circa 1948, $200.

Calendar, 1908, Peters Cartridge Co., Strobridge, Cincinnati, 14 x 27 inches, top and bottom bands, $2,500.

Calendar, 1914, Peters Cartridge Co., Lynn Bogue Hunt, 14 x 27 inches, top and bottom bands, $1,000.

Calendar, 1917, Peters Cartridge Co., G. Muss Arnolt, 14 x 27 inches, top band, $400.

Calendar, 1916, Peters Cartridge Co., Frank Stick, 15 x 20 inches, top and bottom bands, $1,000.

Left: Calendar, 1927, Peters Cartridge Co., G. Muss Arnolt, 15 x 26 inches, top band, $350.

Right: Calendar, 1929, Peters Cartridge Co., Lynn Bogue Hunt, 15 x 28 inches, top band, $750.

Below: Calendar, 1912, Remington-United Metallic Cartridge Co., Philip R. Goodwin, 20 x 15 inches, top and bottom bands, $800.

Calendar, 1919, Remington-United Metallic Cartridge Co., Lynn Bogue Hunt, American Litho Co., 15 x 31 inches, top band, $1,500.

Calendar, 1921, Remington-United Metallic Cartridge Co., American Litho Co., New York, 15 x 29 inches, top band, $900.

Calendar, 1917, Selby Smelting & Lead Co., $1,000.

Calendar, 1893, Union Metallic Cartridge Co., The Strobridge Litho Co., Cincinnati, 14 x 28 inches, top and bottom bands, $3,000.

Calendar, 1901, Union Metallic Cartridge Co., American Litho Co., 13 x 26 inches, top and bottom bands, $1,200.

Top left: Calendar, 1916, United States Cartridge Co., Alexander Pope, American Art Works, Cochochoton, Ohio, 18 x 28 inches, top and bottom bands, $1,000.

Top right: Two-year calendar, 1919, United States Cartridge Co., 13 x 28 inches, top and bottom, $1,000.

Bottom left: Calendar, 1925, United States Cartridge Co., H. C. Edwards, 16 x 35 inches, top and bottom bands, $2,500.

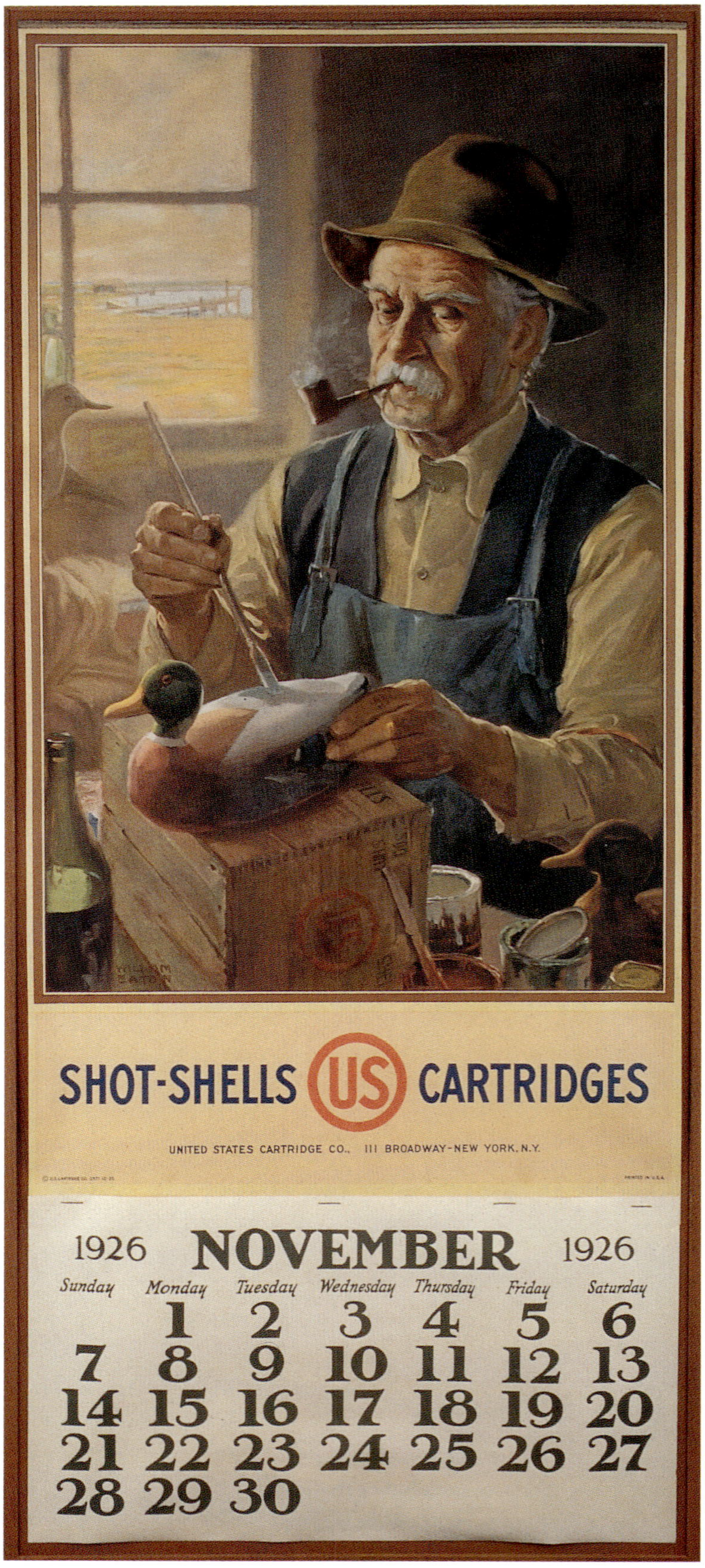

Calendar, 1926, United States Cartridge Co., William Eaton, 15 x 34 inches, top band, $800.

Calendar, 1924, Western Ammunition, A. Russell, 15 x 31 inches, top band, $200.

Calendar, 1928, Western Ammunition, Lynn Bogue Hunt, 14 x 28 inches, top band, $350.

Miscellaneous Winchester Repeating Arms pocket catalogs; $25-35 each. (*Collection of Lee Schultz*)

Left: Calendar, 1912, Winchester Repeating Arms Co., N. C. Wyeth, 15 x 30 inches, top and bottom bands, $2,000.

Above: Calendar, 1924, Winchester Repeating Arms Co., G. Ryder, 14 x 28 inches, top and bottom bands, $1,200.

Calendar, 1929, Winchester Repeating Arms Co., Lynn Bogue Hunt, 15 x 26 inches, top band, $1,000.

Store calendar, 1924, Winchester Repeating Arms Co., 10 x 21 inches, no bands, $300.

Store calendar, 1928, Winchester Repeating Arms Co., 12 x 20 inches, no bands, $300.

Store calendar, 1929, Winchester Repeating Arms Co., 10 x 20 inches, top and bottom bands, $300.

Store display, die-cut cardboard, Winchester Repeating Arms Co., $1,000. (*Collection of Ron Willoughby*)

Store display, die-cut cardboard, Winchester Repeating Arms Co., $1,250. (*Collection of Ron Willoughby*)

Store display, die-cut cardboard, Winchester Repeating Arms Co., $1,500. (*Collection of Ron Willoughby*)

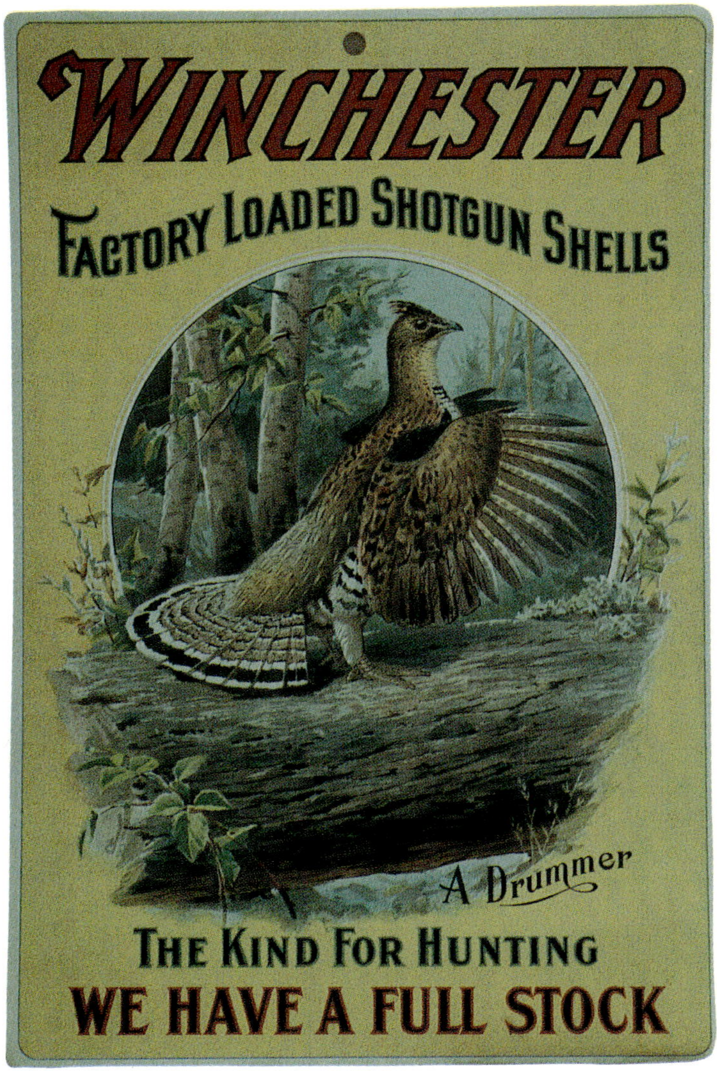

Paper crate insert, Winchester Repeating Arms Co., $1,000. (*Collection of Ron Willoughby*)

Store display, die-cut cardboard, Winchester Repeating Arms Co., $1,500. (*Collection of Ron Willoughby*)

Store display, die-cut cardboard, Winchester Repeating Arms Co., $1,000. (*Collection of Ron Willoughby*)

Store display, cardboard, Winchester Repeating Arms Co., $500. (*Collection of Tim Melcher*)

Store display, die-cut cardboard, Winchester Repeating Arms Co., $800. (*Collection of Ron Willoughby*)

Store display, die-cut cardboard, Winchester Repeating Arms Co., $600. (*Collection of Ron Willoughby*)

Toy on card, pewter, Winchester Repeating Arms Co., give-away, $400. (*Collection of Jerry Castagna*)

Chapter 6
Shell Boxes

Christmas Box, United States Cartridge Co., Defiance Shot Shells, 100 count, $3000. (*Collection of Ron Willoughby/ Photography by Ron Willoughby*)

Christmas Box, Peters Cartridge Co., Quick Shot, 100-count shot shell box, circa 1920, $3,500. (*Collection of Ron Willoughby/ Photography by Ron Willoughby*)

Christmas box, United Metallic Cartridge Co., New Club, 100-count shot shell box, circa 1920, $2,500. (*Collection of Ron Willoughby/ Photography by Ron Willoughby*)

Christmas box, Union Metallic Cartridge, Club, 100 count, $3,000. (*Collection of Ron Willoughby/ Photography by Ron Willoughby*)

Christmas Box, Winchester Repeating Arms Co., Star Paper Shot Shells, only known example, extremely rare, $8,000. (*Collection of James McCleery, MD*)

Top and side views of Christmas box from Winchester Repeating Arms Co., extremely rare, top and side views, Rival, 100-count new-primed empty shot shells, circa 1905, $4,000.

American Jack Rabbit, one-piece shell box, manufactured in Chicago, Illinois, extremely rare, $1,500.

Advertising button, Mrs. Ad Topperwein, Dead Shot Powder, circa 1920, $100.

Dead Shot advertising items from American Powder Mills: envelopes, S100 each; watch fobs, $200-300 each; shot shell box insert, $100; advertising button, $75-100 each; and countertop felt, $300. (*Collection of Rick Simmons*)

American Powder Mills, Red Devil Shot Shells, two-piece box, 16 gauge, $1,000. (*Collection of Ron Willoughby/Photography by Ron Willoughby*)

Shotgun shell box paper insert, $100.

Countertop felt, Dead Shot Smokeless, $400.

End view of American Powder Mills, Red Devil shot shell box. (*Collection of Ron Willoughby/Photography by Ron Willoughby*)

American Powder Mills, Red Devil Shot Shells, one-piece box, 12 gauge, $1,000. (*Collection of Ron Willoughby/ Photography by Ron Willoughby*)

Advertising button, Crack Shot dogs, Austin Cartridge Co., circa 1920, $200.

Austin Cartridge Co., Crack-Shot Shells, 12 gauge, $1,000. (Collection of Ron Willoughby). Photography Ron Willoughby.

Austin Cartridge Loads, Austin Cartridge Co., Crack Shot variation, monotone graphics, extremely rare, $2,500.

Austin Cartridge Co., Austin Cartridges Load #454, 12 gauge, circa 1900, extremely rare, $1,200.

Austin Cartridge Co., Cleveland, Ohio, Crack-Shot Shell, 10 gauge, circa 1900, $1,000. (*Collection of Ron Willoughby/Photography by Ron Willoughby*)

Austin Cartridge Co., Bang Shells, $1,500. (*Collection of Ron Willoughby/ Photography by Ron Willoughby*)

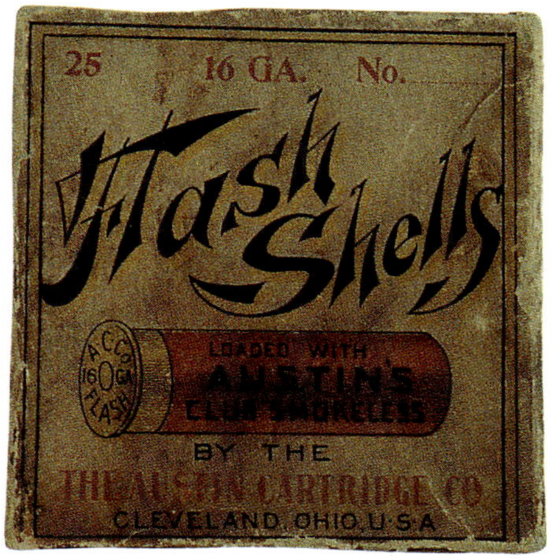

Austin Cartridge Co., Flash Shells, $1,500. (*Collection of Ron Willoughby/Photography by Ron Willoughby*)

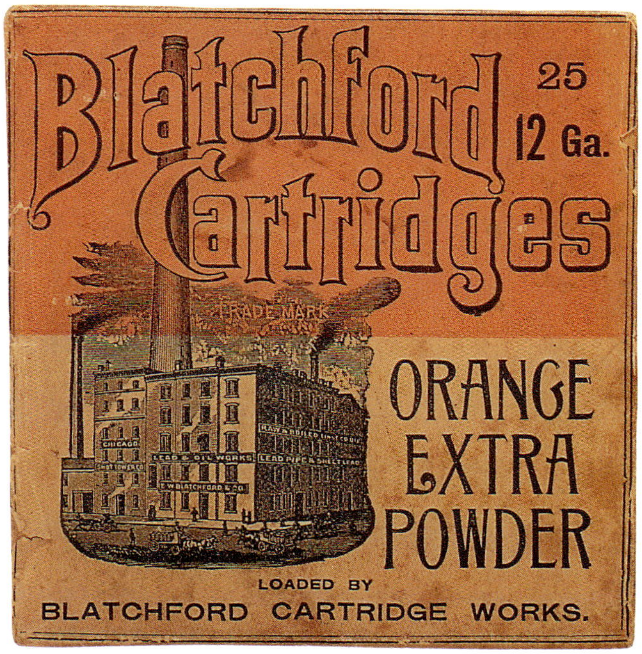

Blatchford Cartridge Works, Chicago, Illinois, Blatchford Cartridges, 12 gauge, rare, circa 1900, $2,000.

Native Sons Shot Gun Cartridges, California Powder Works, Santa Cruz, California, 12 gauge, extremely rare, $2,000.

California Powder Works, Diana Cartridges, extremely rare, $4,500. (*Collection of Ron Willoughby/Photography by Ron Willoughby*)

California Powder Works, Perfection Shotgun Cartridges, circa 1920, $500.

Copy of 1894 catalog, recommendations from shooting celebrities showing shot shell boxes. No known examples of these boxes exist.

COL. J. T. ANTHONY, Charlotte, N. C.

"Chamberlin Tournaments started the tremendous interest in the sport of target shooting, and a revival of them is a grand thing."

"Chamberlin Cartridges have always been strictly first-class in every respect, and I have always found them most excellent for Blue Rock or Field Shooting."

D. M. PORTERFIELD, Vicksburg, Miss.

—23—

C. W. BUDD, Des Moines, Iowa.

"I have used thousands of Chamberlin Nitro Powder Cartridges, and have always found them very reliable. Just wait a minute and see me 'snuff 'em out.'"

"I have managed a great many tournaments, and have always found that I could throw more Blue Rocks with less trouble, and give the shooters better satisfaction, with Expert Traps and Electric Pulls than with any other outfit."

JOHN PARKER, Detroit, Mich.

—21—

Copy from 1894 catalog.

Chamberlain Cartridge Co., Cleveland, Ohio, Winchester Shells, 12 gauge, circa 1890, $2,000.

Chamberlain Cartridge Co., Redhead Cartridges, $2,000. (*Collection of Ron Willoughby/Photography by Ron Willoughby*)

Chamberlain Cartridge Co., extremely rare, Squirrel Cartridges, circa 1890, $3,500.

Creedmore Cartridge Co., Barberton, Ohio, Mandan Shot Shells, 100 count empty shells, $700. (*Collection of Ron Willoughby/Photography by Ron Willoughby*)

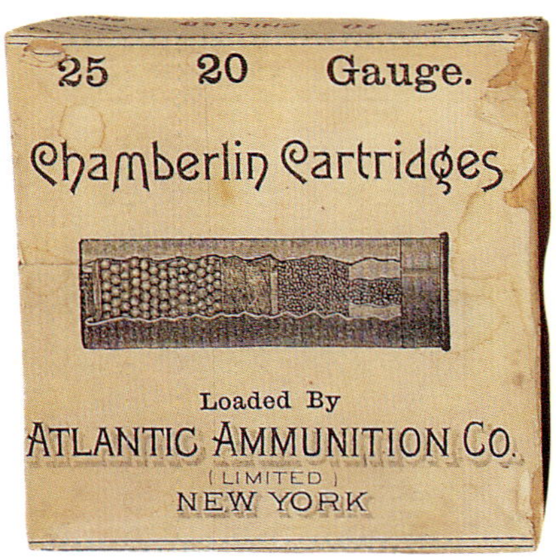

Left: Chamberlain Cartridges, Atlantic Ammunitions Co., New York, New York, 20 gauge, full sealed, $450. Right: Hand-loaded Trap and Game Cartridges, D. Kirkwood, Boston, Massachusetts, circa 1900, $500.

Left to right: Clinton Cartridge Co., Chicago, Illinois, Pointer Shot Shells, circa 1920, $750; Meriden Fire Arms Co., Meriden, Connecticut, Pointer Loaded Shells, circa 1920, $800; and Pointer Loaded Shells, most common, circa 1925, $500.

Cussins & Fearn Co., American Standard Loads, Columbus, Ohio, $1,200.

Federal Cartridge Corp., Minneapolis, Minnesota, Monark Shot Shell boxes, two piece, circa 1940: Trap Load, 12 gauge, $250; Shot Shells, 16 gauge, $125.

Left: Hibbard, Spencer & Bartlett Co., Chicago, Illinois, Ideal shot shell box, 12 gauge, $650. Right: Shelby Smelting Works, San Francisco, California, Shelby Shotgun Loads, $750.

Left to right: Hi-Velocity, Duck and Trap Load, made in Australia, $200; Sears & Roebuck Inc., Xtra Range shot shell, 12 gauge, $200; Western Cartridge Co., St. Louis, Field shot shells, $175.

Store display, Holiday Shotgun Shells, one piece boxes, circa 1950, $500.

One-piece shot shell boxes, left to right: Holiday Target Load, 20 gauge, $75; Western Auto Stores, Revelation Shot Shells, $50; Catton Thirsk, North Yorkshire, England, Thirsk Gunrooms, $75.

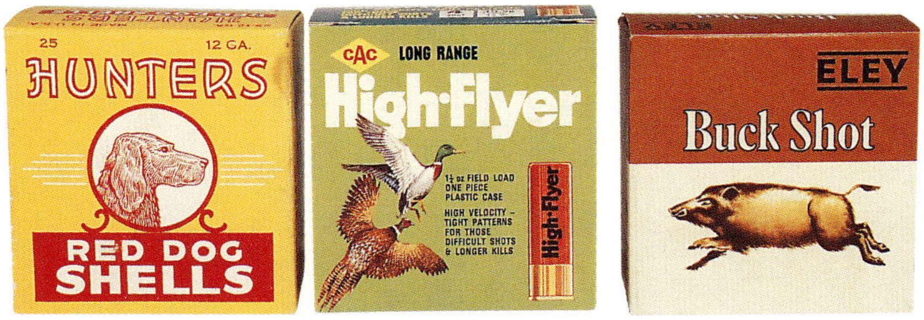

One piece shot shell boxes, left to right: Hunter's Red Dog Shells, $75; CAC High Flyer shot shells, $45; Eley Buck Shot, $35.

Mallard Shot shell boxes distributed by Sears & Reobuck Co., Chicago, Illinois, circa 1920: left, Mallard Loaded Shells, 20 gauge, $250; right, Mallard Loaded Shot Shell, 12 gauge, $500. (*Collection of Lee Schultz*)

Mallard Shot shell boxes distributed by Sears & Roebuck Co., Chicago, Illinois, circa 1920: left, Mallard Loaded Shells, 12 gauge, $400; right, Mallard Sport Loads, 12 gauge, $300.

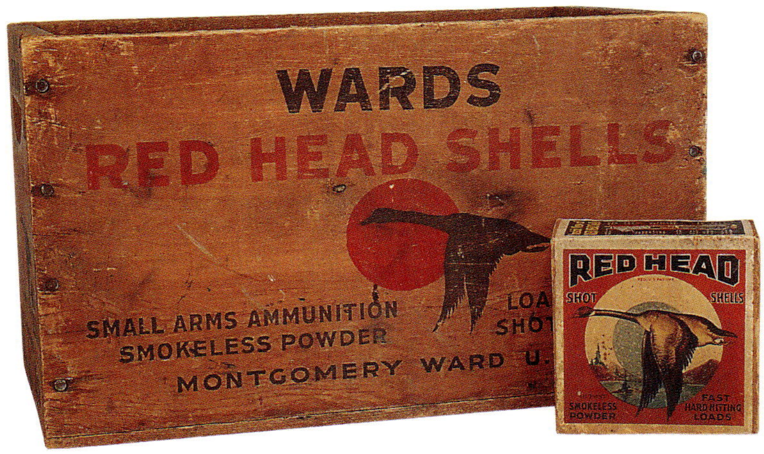

Left: Montgomery Wards, Chicago, Illinois, wooden shipping crate, Red Head Shot Shells, $125. Right: Red Head Shot Shell, one-piece box, $250, circa 1935.

Liberty Shells, Liberty Cartridge Co., Chicago Illinois, $1,000.

Gun show display put on by Bill Johnson of Scandinavia, Wisconsin, sharpshooter for Peters Cartridge Co., circa 1930.

Peters Cartridge Co., advertising envelopes, circa 1910–30, $25-50 each; pocket catalog, $50; advertising buttons and stick pins, $50-75 each. (*Collection of Rick Simmson*)

Peters Cartridge Co., Quick Shot Loaded Shells, 10 gauge, circa 1920, $2,000.

Peters Cartridge Co., advertising envelope, $100, pocket catalog, $50; assorted advertising buttons, $75-100. (*Collection of Rick Simmson*)

Peters Cartridge Co., Quick Shot Crimped Cartridges, 10 gauge, circa 1910, $1,500.

Peters Cartridge Co., Cincinnati, Ohio, Popular Shot shell box, 10 gauge, circa 1910, one of the rarest Peters boxes, $2,000.

On the Mouse River Where Hunters Count Their Shells by the Case, glass plate photograph. Shown is George Sibley on the far left, a noted decoy carver from Chicago, Illinois on a hunting expedition in McHenry County, North Dakota, where J. Clark Salyer National Refuge now exists (northeast of Minot). Note: Peters Cartridge Co. Ideal and Target shot shell crates, circa 1900. (*Photograph by Sumner Matteson/Collection of the Milwaukee Public Museum*)

Peters Cartridge Co. variations in target shot shells, left to right: Target Paper Shot Shells, $350; Target "Spreader Load" Shot Paper Shells, $400; and Target Paper Shot Shells, $300.

Peters Cartridge Co., variations in League Shot shell boxes: left, League Rabbit, rare, $1,200; right, League Head Stamps, $700.

Peters Cartridge Co., variations of High Velocity shot shell boxes, left to right: Redhead drake, 12 gauge, $750; Bluebill drake, 12 gauge, $250; and Blue-winged teal hen, 12 gauge, $300.

Peters Cartridge Co., full, sealed, Rustless Trap Load shot shells, $700.

Peters Cartridge Co., rare New Victor shot shell box, $1,000.

Peters Cartridge Co., Target Lubkote, Handicap Load, full, sealed, circa 1935, only produced for few months, $2,500.

Peters Cartridge Co., left to right: Peters Referee semi-smokeless, $400; Peters Referee, $450; Peters Popular Cartridges, 10 gauge, $2,000.

Peters Cartridge Co., left to right: High Gun Paper Shot Shells, $750; Ideal Shells, $500; and Premier Shot Shells, full, sealed, $700.

Left: Peters Cartridge Co. High Velocity shipping crate, $150. Top: Peters Target Shot Shells, $400. Bottom: Peters League Shot Shells, $500. (*Collection of Lee Schultz*)

Center: Peters Cartridge Co. wooden shipping crate, $250. Left: Peters Skeet Load, $300. Right: Peters League Shot Shells, rare, $700.

Left: Die-cut cardboard display, Remington Arms Co., Kleanbore Game Load shot shells, circa 1920, $300. Top box: Nitro Club Grouse Load, $300. Bottom: Nitro Express Buck Shot, $200. (*Collection of Lee Schultz*)

Right: Die-cut cardboard display, Remington U.M.C., circa 1920, $400; Remington U.M.C. Kleanbore Arrow shot shell box, 20 gauge, $200.

American Eagle shipping crate for small caliber cartridges, $75; and Remington Arms Co. shipping crate, dovetailed, Game Loads, Heavy Duty Duck Load, 12 gauge, $100.

Remington and U.M.C.-Remington advertising pins, $40-50. (Collection of Rick Simmons)

Remington Arms Co., Nitro Club Duck Load, 12 gauge, circa 1920, $250.

Advertising button for U.M.C.-Remington Arms Co., Auto-load gun, circa 1920, $50.

Top view of previous picture.

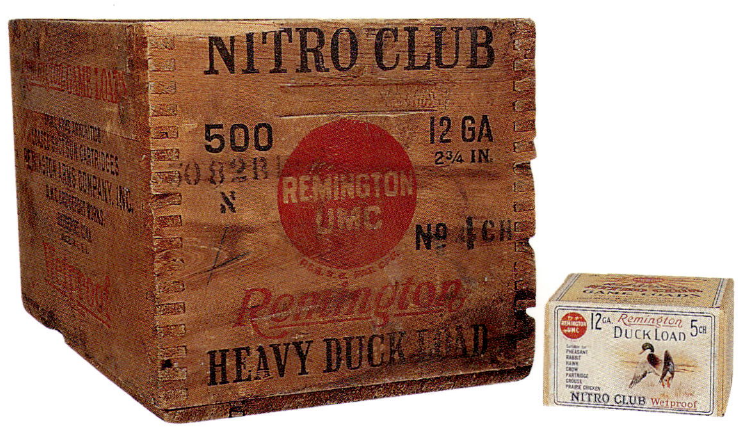

Remington U.M.C. wooden dovetailed shipping crate, Nitro Club Heavy Duty Duck Loads, circa 1920, $75; and Remington U.M.C. Nitro Club Duck Load shot shell box, 12 gauge, circa 1920, $250.

Enameled trade sign, Remington U.M.C. Arrow & Nitro Club Shells, circa 1920, $800.

Variations in Remington U.M.C. Nitro Club shot shell boxes, 12 gauge, circa 1920, left to right: U.M.C. Nitro Club mallard, $300; Remington U.M.C. Nitro Club small mallard, $200; and Remington U.M.C. Nitro Club Kleanbore mallard, $250.

Remington U.M.C. Nitro Club Scatter Load, 16 gauge, circa 1920, $200; and U.M.C. Nitro Club shot shell box, 12 gauge, circa 1920, $400.

Remington countertop display case, 22-caliber rifle shells, circa 1940, $150.

Pennant felt, Robin Hood Ammunition, Stanton, Vermont, extremely rare, $4,000.

Robin Hood Powder Co., Stanton, Vermont shell boxes, circa 1900: top, Eclipse Shells, 12 gauge, $1,500; bottom, Robin Hood green box, 10 gauge, $700; and company bill of sale, $100.

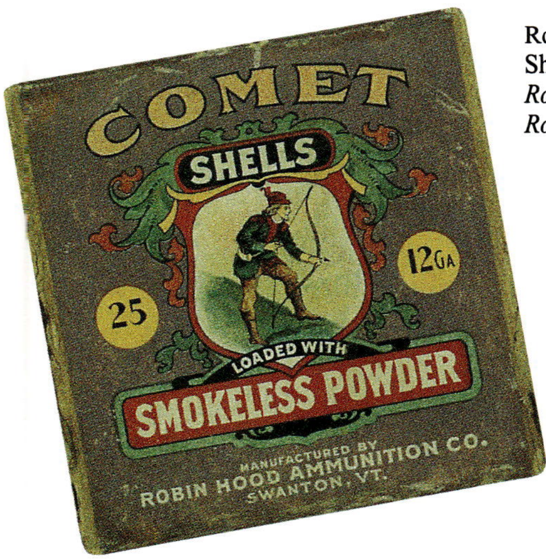

Robin Hood Powder Co., Comet Shells, $1,000. (*Collection of Ron Willoughby/Photography Ron by Willoughby*)

Robin Hood Ammunition Co., Indian Black Powder Shells, $1,500. (*Collection of Ron Willoughby/Photography Ron by Willoughby*)

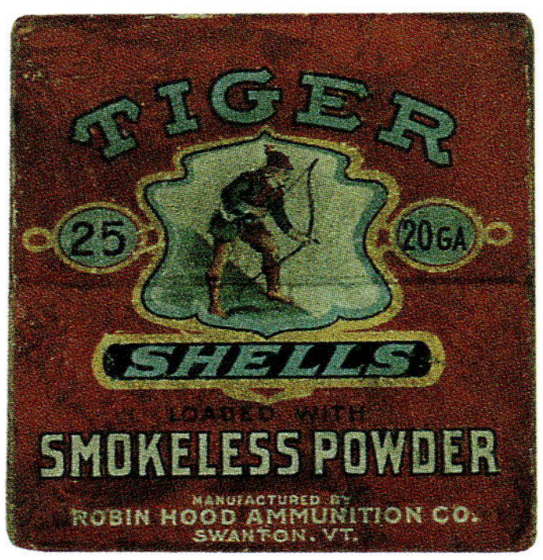

Robin Hood Powder Co., Tiger Shot Shell, 20 gauge, circa 1900, $1,250. (*Collection of Ron Willoughby/ Photography Ron by Willoughby*)

Robin Hood Ammunition Co., Capital Shells, $700. (*Collection of Ron Willoughby/Photography Ron by Willoughby*)

Southern Cartridge Co., Savannah, Georgia, Dixie Black Powder Shot Shells, $2,000. (*Collection of Ron Willoughby/ Photography Ron by Willoughby*)

Standard Cartridge Co., Chicago, Illinois, Standard Cartridge Load #714, 10 gauge, circa 1890, $1,000.

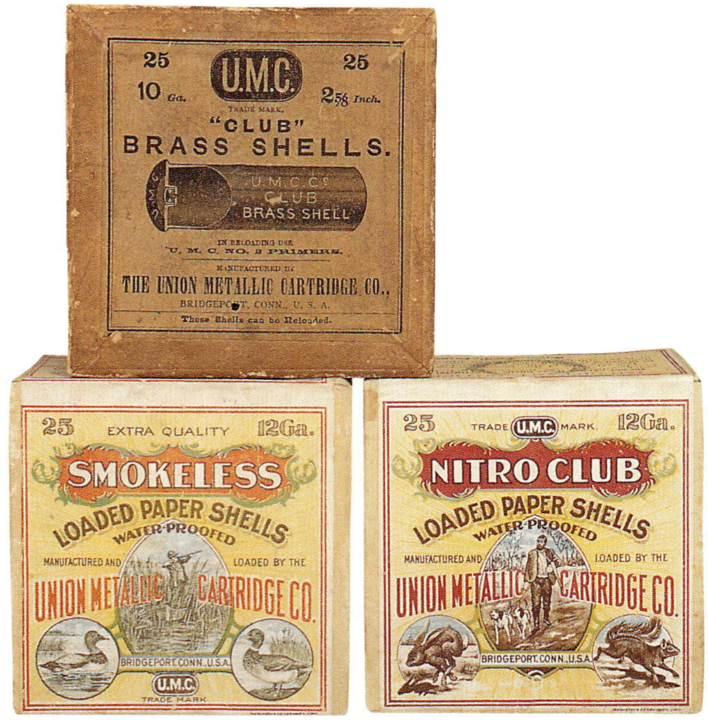

Union Metallic Cartridge Co. shell boxes, circa 1920: top, U.M.C. Club, 10 gauge, brass shot shell box, $200; left, U.M.C. Smokeless Loaded Paper Shells, 12 gauge, $500; right, U.M.C. Nitro Club Loaded Paper Shells, 12 gauge, $700.

Advertising button, Annie Oakley, extremely rare, Union Metallic Cartridge Co., circa 1890, $500.

Union Metallic Cartridge Co., U.M.C. Nitro Club shot shell box, 12 gauge, circa 1920, $250.

Union Metallic Cartridge Co. High Base Loaded Paper Shells, 12 gauge, circa 1920, $750. (*Collection of Lee Schultz*)

Countertop felt, United Metallic Cartridge Shot Shells, $400. (*Collection of Lee Schultz*)

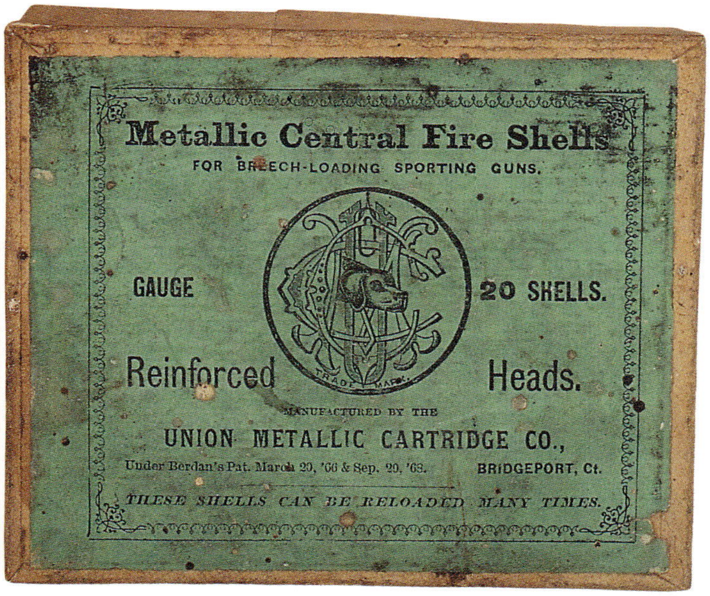

Union Metallic Cartridge Co., Metallic Center Fire Shells, loaded brass shells, rare, circa 1880, $1,000.

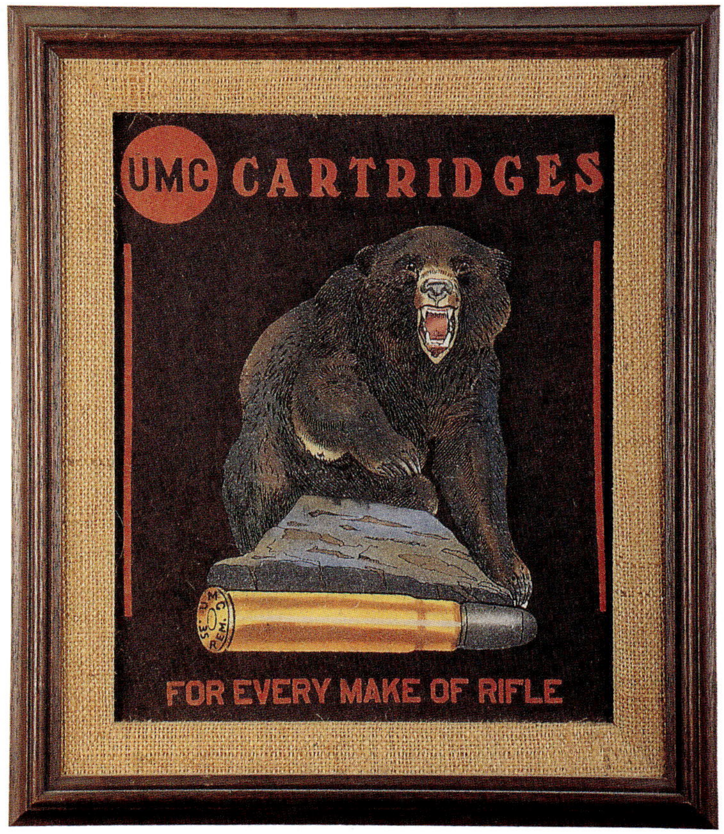

Countertop felt, United Metallic Cartridges, $800.

Left: Shot shell boxes, 410 gauge: top, United Metallic Cartridge Co., U.M.C. paper loaded shot shells, $200; left, Gambles Stores, Gambles shot shells, $150; and right, Montgomery Ward Inc., Xtra Range Sport Loads, $100. (*Collection of Lee Schultz*)

Variations in United States Cartridge Co. Defiance shot shell boxes, one piece, circa 1930, left to right: Trap load, circa 1920, $400; Special Skeet Load, $500; Shot shells, circa 1920, $400. (*Collection of Lee Schultz*)

United States Cartridge Co. shell boxes, circa 1920: Climax Shot Shells, 12 gauge, $100; and Ajax Heavies, one piece box, $400.

Walsrode Co., Walsrode Shotgun Cartridges, $1,000.

Enameled trade sign, two sided, United States Cartridge Co., Black Shells, circa 1910, $700.

Ware Brothers, Spokane, Washington, Championship Shot Gun Loads, $1,500. (*Collection of Ron Willoughby/Photography by Ron Willoughby*)

United States Cartridge Co., Climax Heavies, circa 1920: left; 410 gauge, $200; right, 12 gauge, $400. (*Collection of Lee Schultz*)

Left: A. F. Weiss Brothers Hardware Store, Carlinville, Illinois, hand-loaded shot shells, circa 1910, $400. Right: J. P. Shannon & Sons, Philadelphia, Pennsylvania, Shannon's "Special" Hand Loaded Shells, circa 1920, $800. (*Collection of Lee Schultz*)

Western Cartridge Co., St. Louis, Missouri, left to right: Record shot shell box, $250; wooden shipping crate, $200; New Chief shot shell box, 10 gauge, $400. (*Collection of Lee Schultz*)

Western Sure Shot Paper Shot Shells, two piece, circa 1920, extremely rare, $1,000.

Western Cartridge Co., East Alton, Missouri, left to right: Xpert shot shell box, $200; Xpert shot shell box, $350; Clinton Cartridge Co., Chicago, Illinois, Pointer Sport Load shot shell box, 20 gauge, $450.

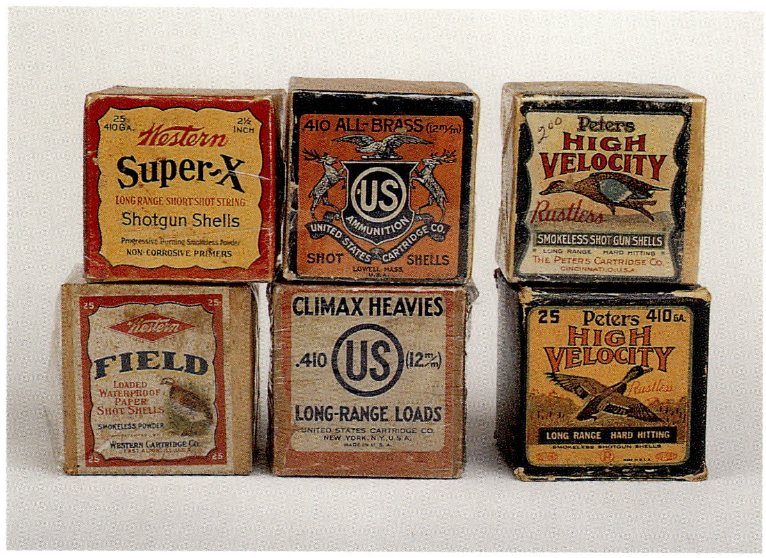

Shot shell boxes, 410 gauge, top row, left to right: Western Cartridge Co., Super X shot shells, $50; United States Cartridge Co., brass shot shells, $75; Peter Cartridge Co., High Velocity Smokeless shot shells, $350. Bottom row, left to right: Western Cartridge Co., Field shot shells, $250; United States Cartridge Co., Climax Heavy Duty, Long Range Loads, $300; Peters Cartridge Co., High Velocity, Long Range—Hard Hitting, $50.

Western Cartridge Co., New Club, 10 gauge, $750. (*Collection of Ron Willoughby/Photography Ron Willoughby*)

Western Cartridge Co., Popper Load, one-piece box, $100; and Winchester Repeating Arms Co., Duck Load, one-piece box, made for export to Canada, $75.

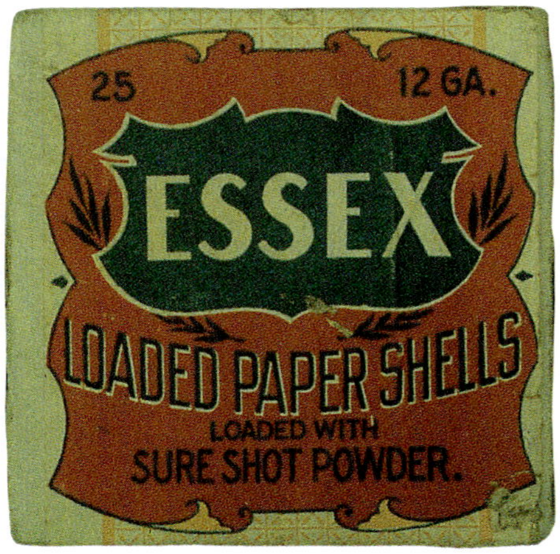

Western Cartridge Co., Essex shells, $1,200. (*Collection of Ron Willoughby/ Photography by Ron Willoughby*)

Side view of Challenge Shot Shells box.

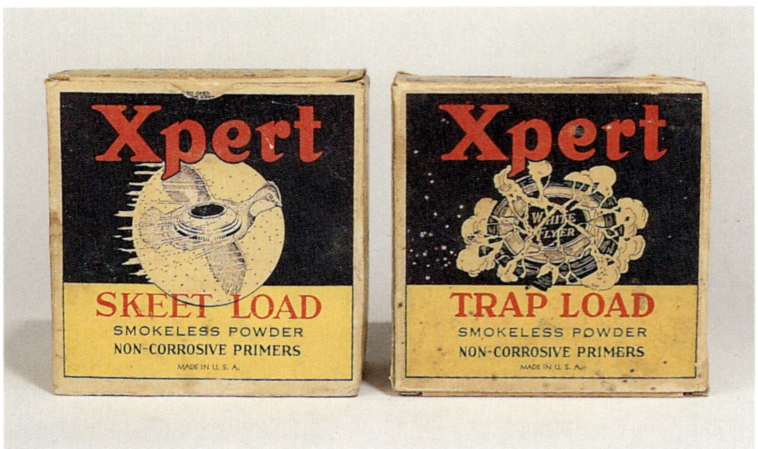

Western Cartridge Co. one-piece shell boxes: Xpert Skeet Load, $125; and Xpert Trap Load, $125.

Advertising button, The Topperweins, Winchester Repeating Arms Co., circa 1920, $50.

Wilson & Wilson Hardware Store, Illinois, hand-loaded Challenge Shot Shells, 12 gauge, circa 1920, $1,500.

Advertising button, Winchester Model 97, circa 1925, $50.

Advertising button, J. R. Taylor, Winchester Repeating Arms Co., circa 1911, extremely rare, $400.

Advertising button; Aldoph Topperwein, Winchester Cartridges, circa 1920, $50

Advertising button, W. R. Crosby, Repeater shot shell, Winchester Repeating Arms Co., circa 1920, $75.

WINCHESTER

Trade Marks Reg. U. S. Pat. Off. and throughout the world

Red

W

CLEANING PREPARATIONS

Gun Grease
Gun and
Machine Oil
Rust Remover
Crystal Cleaner

Will Keep Firearms in Perfect Condition

THE KIND USED AT THE
WINCHESTER WORKS

5-14
2194

Shot shell box advertising insert, $75.

Brass shot shell boxes, Winchester Repeating Arms, circa 1910: 12 gauge, full sealed, $250; 10 gauge, full sealed, $500; 20 gauge, full sealed, $500.

Winchester Repeating Arms Co., advertising buttons and stick pins, $50-150 each. (*Collection of Rick Simmons*)

Winchester Repeating Arms Co., shot shell boxes, circa 1920: top, Nu Black, two-piece box, $200; left, Leader, one-piece box, $400; and New Rival, two-piece box, $150.

Wooden shipping crates: top, Winchester Repeating Arms Co., Ranger Super Trap Loads, 16 gauge, $75; bottom, Star Brand shot shells, $100.

Winchester Repeating Arms Co., variations of Leader Shot Shell two-piece boxes, circa 1920, left to right: plain graphics, 12 gauge, $150; Leader Oval, 10 gauge, circa 1930, $150; Lighting box, 12 gauge, $200.

Winchester Repeating Arms Co., circa 1910: left, New Rival, 12 gauge, $400; right, Rival, 12 gauge, $350.

Winchester Repeating Arms Co., variations of Ranger Shot Shell boxes, left to right: Ranger Staynless, circa 1935, $150; Ranger W, circa 1930, $250; Ranger one-piece box, circa 1940, $75.

Winchester Repeating Arms Co.: one-piece box, Ranger Trap Load, circa 1940, $125; Leader "experimental," full, sealed, two-piece box, $250; Repeater, two-piece box, circa 1920, $125.

Winchester Repeating Arms Co., left to right: Lead Air Rifle Shot, circa 1910, full, sealed, $100; 220 Swift new primed empty shot shells, $25; 410 gauge shot shell box, circa 1920, $125.

Winchester Repeating Arms Co., Winchester Wonder Black Powder Shells, $2,000. (*Collection of Ron Willoughby/ Photography by Ron Willoughby*)

Winchester Repeating Arms Co., Repeater 100 count new primed empty shot shells, two-piece box, circa 1910, $150.

Winchester Repeating Arms Co., Turkey Cartridges, extremely rare, $4,000. (*Collection of Tim Melcher*)

Winchester Repeating Arms Co., Leader, 100 count loaded empty shot shells, circa 1920, $200.

Winchester Repeating Arms Co., Star Paper Shells, extremely rare, $4,000. (*Collection of Tim Melcher*)

Chapter 7

Duck Stamps

Miscellaneous Ducks Unlimited pins; $100-300 each. (*Collection of Dean Dashner*)

Duck Unlimited Brochures, circa 1940s, $20 each.

Duck Unlimited buttons, circa 1974 to present, sold at fund raising functions, $5-20. (*Collection of Dean Dashner*)

Federal Migratory Bird stamp, 1934–present.

Form 3333

FEDERAL MIGRATORY-BIRD HUNTING CERTIFICATE AND STAMP

Issued by Post Office Department under Act of Congress March 16, 1934. For exclusive use of owner whose signature appears on the reverse side hereof

U.S. DEPARTMENT OF AGRICULTURE

VOID AFTER JUNE 30, 1935

MIGRATORY BIRD HUNTING STAMP

Postmarking Stamp Here

W. C. ROBERTSON, Postmaster

Postmaster.

Rare first-day issue card with Federal Migratory Bird Hunting Certificate and Stamp, Postmarked September 6, 1934, Minneapolis, Minnesota, $450.

Duck Unlimited buttons: canvasback, 1947, $100; Canada goose, 1951, $150; blue-winged teal, 1950, $50; wood ducks, 1952, $100; blackduck, 1953, $100; pintail, 1948, $50. (*Collection of Dean Dashner*)

Ducks Unlimited buttons, from top clockwise: 1937, first issue, pintail $500; 1938, pintail, $400; 1962, canvasback, $200; 1966, blackduck, $300; 1951, Canada goose, $125; 1955, mallard, $300; 1950, pintail, $150. Center: 1942, pintail, $250. (*Collection of Dean Dashner*)

Appendix A

Federal Migratory Bird Stamps

On March 16, 1934, the Migratory Bird Conservation Act of 1929 was amended by the Migratory Bird Hunting Stamp Act to provide provisions to procure funds to support the existing National Wildlife Refuge System. Every hunter over the age of 16 was required to annually purchase and carry a duck stamp. These stamps were sold by the U.S. Postal Service and, as of June 28, 1941, all migratory stamps not sold by the end of the fiscal year were turned over to the philatelic agency to be sold to collectors. The duck stamps are popular among both stamp collectors and sportsmen. Their value is largely dependent on condition. Since hunters must carry their stamps on their person when hunting and because they were required to sign their stamps after 1935, these stamps have little value. Serious stamp collectors insist that even the perforated edges of a stamp be totally intact. Many stamps have been devalued because someone has moistened the back, or worse, used glue or tape to affix the duck stamp for display. Most glues have a chemical reaction to the inks used to print the stamp and consequently discolor the image.

When the migratory bird stamp program was started, the federal government commissioned professional artists to create the artwork for the stamp. By the late 1930s, the stamp program took its first step toward the present-day duck stamp competition by inviting several artists to submit designs. Today the duck stamp competition is open to the general public and is a highly sought after prize because the artist retains total rights to his winning design, which is usually reproduced in the lucrative business of limit edition prints.

Year	Title Unused/Used	Medium	Artist	Value
1934-35	Mallards Dropping In	ink	J. N. "Ding" Darling	$400/$85
1935-36	none (canvasbacks)	etching	Frank W. Benson	$400/$100
1936-37	Coming In (Canada geese)		Richard E. Bishop	$200/$50
1937-38	none (great scaup)		Joseph D. Knap	$160/$27.50
1938-39	none (pintail)	etching	Roland H. Clark	$160/$35
1939-40	none (green-winged teal)	graphite pencil	Lynn Bogue Hunt	$115/$15
1940-41	none (blackducks)	black and white wash	Francis Lee Jaques	$110/$15
1941-42	Ruddy Ducks	tempera/wash painting	Edwin R. Kalmbach	$110/$15
1942-43	American Widgeon	dry point etching	Alden L. Ripley	$110/$14
1943-44	Federal Duck Stamp Design, 1943 (wood duck)	dry point etching	Walter E. Bohl	$47.50/$15
1944-45	White-front Geese	black and white wash	Walter A. Weber	$40/$14
1945-46	Spoonbills	black and white wash	Owen J. Gromme	$35/$10
1946-47	Redheads	ink drawing with wash	Robert W. Hines	$32.50/$9
1947-48	Far Beyond the North Wind (snow geese)		Jack Murray	$35/$9
1948-49	Buffleheads Aloft	wash/tempera	Mayard Reece	$32.50/$9
1949-50	American Goldeneyes	black and white wash	Roger E. Preuss	$37.59/$8
1950-51	Trumpeter Swans	black and white wash	Walter A. Weber	$45/$7
1951-52	Gadwalls	tempera	Mayard Reece	$45/$5
1952-53	Harlequin Ducks	black and white wash	John H. Dick	$45/$5
1953-54	Early Express-Blue-winged	Teal ink wash	Clayton B. Seager	$45/$5
1954-55	Ring-necked Duck	monochromatic watercolor	Harvey D. Sandstrom	$45/$4.75
1955-56	Blue Geese	ink and pencil on scratch board	Stanley Streans	$45/$4.75
1956-57	American Mergansers	monochromatic watercolor	Edward J. Bierly	$45/$4.75
1957-58	American Eider	gouache	Jackson Miles Abbott	$45/$.75
1958-59	Canada Geese	black and white wash	Leslie C. Kouba	$45/$4.75
1959-60	King Buck (black Labrador)	wash and watercolor	Mayard Reece	$60/$4.75
1960-61	Redhead Ducks	black and white wash	John A. Ruthven	$60/$4
1961-62	Nine Mallards	black and white wash	Edward A. Morris	$60/$4
1962-63	Pintails	black and white wash	Edward A. Morris	$70 $5.50

1963-64	American Brant	black and white wash	Edward J. Bierly	$65/$5.50
1964-65	Nene High Among the Lava Flows (nene geese)	black and white wash, gouache	$65/$5.50	
1965-66	Canvasbacks	black and white wash	Ron Jerkins	$65/$5.50
1966-67	Whistling Swans	black and white wash	Stanley Streans	$65/$5
1967-68	Old Squaw-Tree River N.W.T.	black and white wash	Leslie C. Kouba	$65/$5
1968-69	Poised (hooded mergansers)	black and white wash	Claremont Gale Pritchard	$40/$5.50
1969-70	White-winged Scoters	black and white wash	Mayard Reece	$40/$4.50
1970-71	Ross' Geese	watercolor	Edward J. Bierly	$40/$4
1971-72	Cinnamon Teal	color wash	Mayard Reece	$27.50/$3.75
1972-73	Emperor Geese	watercolor	Arthur M. Cook	$17/$3.75
1973-74	Stellar's Eider	opaque watercolor	Lee LeBlanc	$17/$3.75
1974-75	Wood Ducks	oil	David Maass	$14/$3.75
1875-76	Canvasback	watercolor	James E. Fisher	$10/$3.75
1976-77	Canada Geese	ink on scratch board	Alderson Magee	$9.50/$3.75
1977-78	Ross' Geese	acrylic	Martin R. Murk	$9.50/$3.75
1978-79	Hooded Merganser	opaque watercolor	Albert Earl Gilbert	$9.50/$3.75
1979-80	Green-winged Teal	gouache	Ken Michaelson	$12/$4
1980-81	Mallards	acrylic	Richard W. Plasschaert	$12/$4
1981-82	Ruddy Ducks	gouache	John S. Wilson	$12/$4
1982-83	Canvasbacks	oil	David Maass	$12/$4
1983-84	Pintails	acrylic	Phil V. Scholer	$12/$4
1984-85	Widgeon	acrylic	William C. Morris	$12/$4
1985-86	Cinnamon Teal	opaque watercolor	Gerald Mobley	$12/$4
1986-87	Fulvous Whistling Duck	acrylic	Burton E. Moore	$14/$4
1887-88	Redheads	unknown	Arthur G. Anderson	$14/$4
1988-89	Snow Geese	unknown	Daniel Smith	$14/$4
1989-90	Lesser Scaup	gouache	Neal R. Anderson	$17/$3.50
1990-91	Black Bellied Whistling Duck	?		$20/$3.50
1992-93	King Eiders	?		$20/$4
1993-94	Spectacled Eider	?		$20/$4
1994-95	Red-breasted Merganser			$20/$4

Appendix B

Gunpowder Companies

Company	City, State
A.F. & Company	
American E.C. & Schultze Powder Co.	Oakland, NJ
American Powder Mills	Boston, MA
American Wood Powder Co.	Jersey City, NJ
Austin Powder Co.	Glenwillow, OH
Bracketts Sporting Powder	Winchester, MA
California Powder Works	Santa Cruz, CA
Canada Industries Limited	Montreal, Canada
Curtis & Harvey	London, England
E.I. DuPont de Nemours & Co.	Wilmington, DE
Eureka Powder Co.	New Durham, NH
Hamilton Power Co.	Ontario/Manitoba
Hazard Powder Co.	New York, NY
Hercules Powder Co.	Wilmington, DE
Kings Great Western Powder Co.	Cincinnati, OH
King Powder Co.	Kings Mills, OH
Laflin & Rand Powder Co.	Esopus, NY
Miami Powder Co.	Xenia, OH
Orange Powder Mills	New York, NY
Oriental Powder Co.	South Windham, ME
Oriental Powder Mills	Portland, ME
Robin Hood Powder Co.	Swanton, VT
A.C. Thompson Co. Ltd.	North Sydney
Warren Powder Mills	Boston, MA
White Mountain Powder Co.	Concord, NH

Appendix C

Decoy Manufacturers

Company	Dates	City, State
Acme Folding Decoy/St. Louis Brass Manufacturing Company	circa 1895–1910	St. Louis, MO
Adams Decoy Company	?	Hickman, KY
Airflate Decoy Company	circa 1940s	Kansas City, MO
Airtite Decoy Company	circa 1920s	Danville, IL
Animal Trap Decoy Company/Victor Decoy Company	circa 1896–1940	Lititz, PA
Animal Trap Decoy Company	circa 1939–1946	Pascagoula, MO
Armstrong Cork Company	circa 1920–1930	Pittsburgh, PA
Armstrong Featherweight Decoys	1930–1940	Houston, TX
Bate's Decoys	?	Cambridge, MA
Bayco Decoy Company	circa 1920	New Orleans, LA
L. L. Bean, Incorporated	circa 1935	Freeport, ME
Benz decoys	?	Jefferson City, MO
Best Duck Decoy Company, Incorporated	?	New York, NY
Boyd Martin Decoy Company	circa 1930	Delphi, IN
Brinkop Duck Decoy/Montgomery Ward Catalog	circa 1895	Chicago, IL
Bucklure Company	?	Newark, MO
Builders Woodwork Company	circa 1930	Burlington, IO
Burkhard's Decoys	?	St. Paul, MM
Canvas Decoy Company	circa 1886–1923	Union City, TN
Cape May Company	?	Cape May, NJ
Custom Bilt Decoys	circa 1946–1948	San Diego, CA
Joseph Coudon & Company	circa 1890–1910	Aikin, MD
Dans Duck Factory	?	Quincy, IL
Danz Company	circa 1880–1907	St. Paul, MN
Deancoys	circa 1941–1950	Kansas City, MO
Decoys Delux	circa 1935	Staples, ME
Decoys Unlimited	circa 1961	Erie, PA
Deeks, Incorporated	circa 1940–1950	Salt Lake City, UT
C. E. Dellenbarger Company	circa 1930	Joliet, IL
Delmarva Decoys	circa 1890	Herndon, VA
Dewey's Metal Folding Decoys	circa 1920	Elkhart, IN
J. N. Dodge Decoys Company	circa 1884–1894	Detroit, MI
Down East Sportcraft	circa 1940	Freeport, ME
Dunster Sporting Goods Company	circa 1940	Seattle, WA
The Evans Decoy Company	circa 1921–1940	Ladysmith, WI
E-Manufacturing Company	circa 1930	East Dedham, MA
Fibro-Lite Products Company	circa 1930–1940	Minneapolis, MN
Flap-o-matic	circa 1955	Chicago, IL
Flyway Decoys	circa 1955	Wading River, NJ
Folduck	circa 1940	Broken Bow, NE
G & H Goose Decoy Company	circa 1940	Henryette, OK
General Fibre Company	circa 1945–1960	St. Louis, MO
Galdwin Decoy Works	?	Frederick, MI
B. Graves Decoy Company	circa 1936–1946	Peoria, IL
C. W. Grubbs Manufacturing Company	circa 1922–1928	Pascagoula, MS
C.W. Grubbs Sporting Goods	circa 1928–1933	Houston, TX
Gundelfinger Woods Products Company	circa 1920–1930	Jefferson City, MO
H. C. Hamman Decoys	circa 1970	Middletown, DE
Hansells Cork Decoys	circa 1930	Minneapolis, MN

Ken Harris Decoys	circa 1945–1981	Woodville, NY
J. M. Hays Wood Products Co.	circa 1920–1930	Jefferson City, MO
The Herter's Manufacturing Co.	circa 1930–1980	Waseca, MN
Herter's Incorporated	circa 1985-present	Beaver Dam, WI
J. C. Higgins	circa 1920	Kansas City, MO
Hudson Decoy Co.	circa 1960	Pascagoula, MS
Ideal Decoy Co.	circa 1930	Klamath Falls, OR
Jackson Industries	circa 1946–1956	Kalamazoo, MI
Wm. R. Johnson Co.	circa 1920–1960	Seattle, WA
K-D Decoys	circa 1920	St. Paul, MN
Lifelike Lures	circa 1949	New Orleans, LA
Majestic Molding Co.	circa 1940	Elyris, OH
Marble & Shattuck Chair Co.	circa 1940	Cleveland, OH
Wm. Mason Decoy Co.	circa 1896–1924	Detroit, MI
Modern Decoy Co.	?	New Haven, CT
Natural Duck Co.	?	Topeka, KS
Neumann & Bennetts	circa 1940–present	Klamath Falls, OR
North American Decoys Co.	circa 1950–1960	Weston, CT
Outing Manufacturing Co.	?	Elkhart, IN
Pascagoula Decoy Co.	circa 1941–1956	Pascagoula, MS
PawPaw Bait Co.	circa 1932–1936	PawPaw, MI
Peterborough Canoe Co.	circa 1910–1940	Peterborough, Ontario
George Peterson	circa 1873–1884	Detroit, MI
Poitavin Brothers Decoys	circa 1928–1940	Pascagoula, MS
William E. Pratt Manufacturing Co.	circa 1920–1939	Joliet, IL
Oscar Quam Co.	circa 1928–1960	Spicer, MN
William Read & Sons	?	Boston, MA
Real-Lite Decoy Co.	?	Kansas City, MO
Realistic Decoy Co.	circa 1932–1944	Kewaukee, WI
J. W. Reynolds Decoy Factory	circa 1904–1950	Chicago, IL
Rex Manufacturing Co.	circa 1930	Morrill, Nebraska
The Rose Folding Decoy	circa 1920	Chicago, IL
W. J. Ruppel Co.	circa 1938–1944	Sheboygan, WI
David C. Sanford Co.	?	Bridgeport, CT
Scott Cork Decoy Co.	circa 1940–1950	Oakland, CA
Soules & Swisher	circa 1940	Decatur, IL
Paul A. Sherry Decoys	circa 1920	New Haven, CT
Harvey A. Stevens Decoys	circa 1880–1902	Weedsport, NY
Sibley Decoy Co.	circa 1899–1901	Whitehall, MI
Strater & Sohier	circa 1974	Boston, MA
W. D. Trimble	circa 1880–1890	Baltimore, MD
Tru-Dux	circa 1939–1949	Chicago, IL
Tryon Co.	?	Philadelphia, PA
Tuf-Skin Decoy Co.	circa 1930–1940	Minneapolis, MN
Tuveson Manufacturing Co.	circa 1920–1930	St. James, MN
Tux-dux	circa 1930–1940	Madison, CT
Van Fleet Manufacturing Co./Makutchan Roller B. Co.	circa 1920	Joliet, IL
Waterloo Decoy Co.	circa 1940	Waterloo, IO
M. C. Wedds	circa 1880	Rochester, NY
C.V. Wells	circa 1936–1944	Milwaukee, WI
Wildfowler Decoys/Ted Mullikens	circa 1939–1958	Old Saybrook, CT
Wildfowler Decoys/Robert Stanford	circa 1958–1961	Quoque, NY
Wildfowler Decoys/Charles Birdsall	circa 1961–1976	Point Pleasant, NJ
Wildfowler Decoys/Amel Massa	circa 1976–present	Babylon, NY
Wizard Co. (Duck-in Decoy)	circa 1937	St. Louis, MO

Appendix D

Ammunition Manufacturers

Co.	City, State
American Ammunition Co.	Chicago, IL
Austin Cartridge Co.	Cleveland, OH
Blatchford Cartridge Co.	Chicago, IL
Califorinia Powder Works	San Francisco, CA
Chamberlain Cartridge & Target Co.	Cleveland, OH
Chicago Shot Tower Co.	Chicago, IL
Clinton Cartridge Co.	Chicago, IL
Cussins & Fearn Co.	Columbus, OH
Dominion Co.	Montreal, Canada
Federal Cartridge Corporation	Minneapolis, MN
Hibbard, Spencer & Barrlett Co.	Chicago, IL
Kirkwood Brothers	Boston, MA
A.S. Kleinman	Chicago, IL
Liberty Cartridge Co.	Chicago, IL
Meridan Firearms Co.	Meridan, CT
Montgomery-Ward Co.	Chicago, IL
Peoria Gun Co.	Peoria, IL

Co.	City, State
Peters Cartridge Co.	Cincinnati, OH
Remington-U.M.C.	Bridgeport, CT
REM-UMC	Bridgeport, CT
Remington-Peters	Bridgeport, CT
Robin Hood Powder Co.	Swanton, VT
Robin Hood Ammunition Co.	Swanton, VT
Sears-Roebuck & Co.	Chicago, IL
Selby Smelting & Lead Co.	San Francisco, CA
Standard Cartridge Co.	Chicago, IL
Union Metallic Cartridge Co.	Bridgeport, CT
United States Cartridge Co.	Lowell, MA
VonLengerke & Antoine Co.	Chicago, IL
VonLengerke & Delmold Co.	New York, NY
Walsrode Co.	
Western Cartridge Co.	East Alton, IL
Winchester Repeating Arms Co.	New Haven, CT

Appendix E

Glass Target Balls

Brogardus, patented 1877, amber, fishnet pattern with Brogardus and shooter printed in center, $150

W.W. Greener's Mary Works, Birmingham, England, purple, fishnet pattern, $200 each

Ira Paines, patented 1877, amber, $250 each

Berth, NB Glass Works, pale green, $150 each

Berth NB Glass Works, clear, fishnet pattern with embossed name in center, $125 each

Berth NB Glass Works, cobalt blue, fishnet pattern with name in center, $125

Unknown maker, dark amber, horizontal raised ribs, $150 each

Unknown maker, amber, plain blown, $50 each

Unknown maker, pitch, black, pottery, $150 each

Unknown maker, light purple, plain blown, $75 each

Unknown maker, cobalt blue, fishnet pattern, $100 each

Van Gutsem, cobalt blue, fishnet pattern with "A St. Quentin" printed in center band, $200 each

Appendix F

Periodicals

Decoy Magazine, P. O. Box 787, Lewis, Delaware 19958

Sporting Collector's Monthly, R. W. Publishing Company, P.O. Box 305, Camden, Delaware 19934

Wildfowl Carving and Collecting, 500 Vaughn Street, Harrisbug, Pennsylvania 17110

Appendix G

Organizations

Back Bay Wildfowl Guild, P.O. Box 805, Virginia Beach 23451

Canadian Decoy & Outdoors Collectible Association, 22-635 Richmond Road, Ottawa, Ontario, Canada K2A-0G6

Chincoteague Decoy Carvers and Artist Association, Reggie Birch, 5332 Matthew Lane, Chincoteague, Virginia 23336

Duck Call Collector and Makers Association, 5145 Deland Road, Flushing, Michigan 48433

International Ammunition Association, P.O. Box 721793, Houston, Texas 77272

Long Island Decoy Collectors Association, 516-757-8040

Louisiana Wildfowl Carvers and Collectors Guild. P.O. Box 10883, New Orleans, Louisiana 70281

Midwest Decoy Collector's Association, Herb Desch, 3006 Fox Glen Court, St. Charles, Illinois 60174

Minnesota Decoy Collector's Club, 1515 Byrd Avenue South, Golden Valley, Minnesota 55422

Pacific Southwest Wildfowl Arts, 12834 Carriage Road, Poway, California 92064

Ohio Decoy Carvers and Collectors Association, P.O. Box 499, Richfield, Ohio 44286

Shot Shell Collectors Historical Society, 222 Redfield Heights, Lodi, Ohio 44254

Sioux Empire Cartridge Collector Association, 2275 26th Avenue South, St. Cloud, Minnesota 56301

Ward Brothers Foundation, 909 S. Schumaker Drive, Salisbury, Maryland 21801

Wisconsin Decoy Collectors, 3792 Leonard Point Road, Oshkosh, Wisconsin 54904

Appendix H

Auction Houses

Classic Sporting Collectibles Auctions, c/o Blue Book Publications, Inc., One Appletree Square, Minneapolis, Minnesota

Decoys Unlimited, Inc., 2320 Main Street, West Barnstable, Massachusetts 02668

Dixie Sporting Collectibles, 1206 Rama Road, Charlotte, North Carolina 28211

Gary Guyette & Frank Schmidt Decoy Auction House, RR #1, Box 540, West Baldwin, Maine 04091

James Julia Inc., P.O. Box 830, Fairfield, Maine 04937

Frank & Frank Sporting Collectibles, 424 Lakewood-Farmington Road, Howell, New Jersey 07731

Lang's Sporting Collectibles Inc., 31R Turtle Cove, Raymond, ME 04071

Victorian Images, P.O. Box 284, Marlton, New Jersey 08053

Bibliography

Barber, Joel, *Wild Fowl Decoys*. New York, New York, Dover Publications, 1934.

Berkey, Barry R., Velma, and Richard E., *Pioneer Decoy Carvers: A Biography of Lemuel and Stephen Ward*, Cambridge, Maryland, Tidewaters Publishers, 1977.

Barrett, Harry B., *Lore & Legends of Long Point*. Edited by Lenore D'Anjou. Don Mills, Ontario, Burns & MacEachen Ltd., 1977.

Bosworth, T. Thompson and Jeffery R Hayes, Ph.D., *Whistling Wings, Whittled Ducks & Wetlands* museum catalog. Milwaukee, Wisconsin, Milwaukee Public Museum, 1996.

Bourne, Richard A., *The Rare Decoy Collection of George Ross Starr, Jr.* Hyannis Port, Massachusetts, Private printing, 1986.

Decoy auction catalogs. Circus Promotions. Jefferson, Maine.

Decoy auction catalogs. Dixie Sporting Collectibles, Charlotte, North Carolina.

Decoy auction catalogs. Guyette/Julia Inc.

Decoy auction catalogs. Guyette/Schmidt Auction House.

Decoy auction catalogs. Jame Julia Inc., Fairfield, Maine.

Decoy auction catalogs. Richard A. Bourne Company, Hyannisport, Massachusetts, private printing 1970–1987

Brisco, R. Paul, *Waterfowl Decoys of Southwestern Ontario*. Erin, Ontario, Boston Mills Press, 1986

Buckwater, Harold R., *Susquehanna River Decoys*. Edited by Nancy Brown. York, Pennsylvania, Maple Press, 1978.

Caldwell, Russell H., *Reelfoot Lake—History—Duck Call Makers—Hunting Tales*. Private printing, 1988.

Cheever, Bryon, *L.T. Ward & Bro.* Heber City, Utah, North American decoys, 19??.

Cheever, Byron, *Mason Decoys*. Spanish Fork, Utah, Hillcrest Publications, 1974.

Cheramie, Brian, *Louisiana Lures and Legends*. Golden Meadows, Louisiana, REM Corporation, 1997.

Chesapeake Decoys. Edited by R. H. Richardson. Cambridge, Maryland, Crow 3 Haven Publishers, 1973.

Christensen, Robert D., *Duck Calls of Illinois*. DeKalb, Illinois, Northern Illinois University Press, 1994.

Classic Sporting Collectibles, auction sales catalogs, Minneapolis, Minnesota.

Connett, Eugene, V., ed., *Duck Shooting Along the Atlantic*. New York, New York, Boaza Books, 1947.

Crandell, Bernard, W. "Barney," *Decoying: St. Clair to the St. Lawrence*. Erin, Ontario, Boston Mills Press, 1988.

Coykendall, Ralf, *Duck Decoys and How to Rig Them*. New York, Chicago, San Francisco; Holt, Rinehart, and Winston, 1955.

Cullity, Brian, *The Songless Aviary: The World of A. E. Crowell & Son*. Heritage Plantation of Sandwich, Hyannis, Massachusetts, The Patriot Press, 1992.

Decoy Collector's Guide. Edited by Hal Sorenson. Burlington, Iowa, Hal Sorenson, 1963–1977.

Delph, John, *Firearms & Tackle Memorabilia: A Collector's Guide*. West Chester, Pennsylvania, Schiffer Publishing Ltd., 1991.

Delph, John & Shirley, *Factory Decoys of Mason, Stevens, Dodge, and Peterson*, Atglen, Pennsylvania, Schiffer Publishing Ltd., 1980

Delph, John & Shirley, *New England Decoys*. Atglen, Pennsylvania, Schiffer Publishing Ltd. 1981

Earnest, Adele, *The Art of the Decoy: American Bird Carvings*. New York, New York, Bramhall House, 1965.

Fleckenstein, Henry A. Jr., *American Factory Decoys*. Atglen, Pennsylvania. Schiffer Publishing Ltd., 1981.

Fleckenstein, Henry A. Jr., *Decoys of the Mid-Atlantic Region*. Atglen, Pennsylvania, Schiffer Publishing Ltd. 1979.

Fleckenstein, Henry A. Jr., *Southern Decoys of Virginia and the Carolinas*. Atglen, Pennsylvania, Schiffer Publishing Ltd., 1993.

Fleckenstein, Henry A. Jr., *New Jersey Decoys*. Atglen, Pennsylvania, Schiffer Publishing Ltd., 1983.

Fleming, Patricia, *Traditions in Wood*. Edited by Thomas Carpenter. Ontario, Camden House Publishing, 1987

Frank, Charles W. Jr., *Louisiana Decoys*. New Orleans, Louisiana, Harvey Press, Inc. 1975.

Gates, Bernie, "Ontario Decoys: Some Carvers and Regional Styles." *The Upper Canadian* magazine. Ontario, 1982.

Goldberger, Russ J. and Alan G. Haid, *Mason Decoys*, Decoy Magazine. Burtonsville, Maryland, 1993.

Guyette, Gary and Dale, *Decoys of Maritime Canada*. Schiffer Publishing Ltd., Atglen, Pennsylvania, 1983.

Haid, Alan G., *Decoys of the Mississippi Flyway*. Atglen, Pennsylvania, Schiffer Publishing Ltd., 1981.

Hall, Michael and Ronald Swanson, *Decoys as Folk Sculpture*, exhibition catalog. Bloomfield, Michigan, Cranbrook Academy of Art Museum, 1987

Harlan, Howard L. and W. Crew Anderson, *Duck Calls: An Enduring American Folk Art*. Nashville, Tennessee, Harlan-Anderson Press, 1988.

Harlan, Howard L., *Turkey Calls: An Enduring American Folk Art*. Edited by W. Crew Anderson. Nashville, Tennessee, Harlan-Anderson Press, 1994.

Harrell, Dr. Loy S., *Decoys of Lake Champlain*. West Chester, Pennsylvania, Schiffer Publishing Ltd., 1986.

Decoys a Cultural Interpretation, Philadelphia Wildfowl Exposition catalog. Edited by Bernard Herman and David Orr.

Philadelphia, Pennsylvania, The Academy of Natural Sciences of Philadelphia, 1979.

Hornaday, William T., *Our Vanishing Wildlife*, New York, New York, New York Zoological Society, 1913.

Huster, H. Harrison and Doug Knight, *Floating Sculpture; Decoys of the Delaware River*. Spanish Forks, Utah, Hillcrest Publications, 1982.

Iverson, Robert J., *The Shotshell in the United States*. Jefferson, Maine, Circus Promotion Corporation, 1988.

Benj. J. Schmidt: A Michigan Decoy Carver. Edited by Lowell Jackson. Private publication.

The Bird Decoy. Edited by Paul A. Johnsgard. Lincoln, Nebraska, University of Nebraska Press, 1976.

Johnson, Archie, *Canvas Decoys of North America*. Burtonsville, Maryland., Decoy Magazine, 1994.

Johnson, Archie and Bud Coppedge, *Gun Clubs & Decoys of Back Bay & Currituck Sound*. Virginia Beach, Virginia, CurBac Press, 1991.

Kangas, Gene and Linda, *Decoys*. Paducah, Kentucky, Collector Books, 1992.

Kangas, Gene and Linda, *Decoys: A North American Survey*. Spanish Fork, Utah, Hillcrest Publications, Inc., 1983.

Lacy, Ann Tandy, *Perdew: An Illinois River Tradition*. Edited by Nancy Baxter. Muncie, Indiana, David Galliher (private printing) 1993.

Lacy, Tandy, *The Wooden Bird*. Washburn, Illinois, Sun Foundation, 1989.

Lawson, Genn, *Lem Ward*. West Chester, Pennsylvania, Schiffer Publishing Ltd. 1984.

Levinson, John M. and Somers G. Headley, *Shorebirds: The Birds, the Hunter, the Decoys*. Centerville, Massachusetts, Tidewater Publishers, 1991.

Lui, Alan J., *The American Sporting Collector's Handbook*. Tulsa, Oklahoma, Winchester Press, 1982.

Mackey, William J. Jr., *American Bird Decoys*. New York, New York, E. P. Dutton & Co., 1965.

Mackey, William J. Jr., *The Decoy Maker's Art* exhibition catalog. Minneapolis, Minnesota, St. Paul Art Center, and Oshkosh, Wisconsin, Paine Art Center. Edited by Patricia Heikenen. St. Paul, Minnesota, North Central Publishing Company, 1967.

McGrath, Brain J., *Duck Calls and Other Game Calls*. Plano, Texas, The Thomas B. Reel Company, 1988.

McKinney, J. Evans, *Decoys of the Susquehanna Flats and Their Makers*. Hockessin, Delaware, The Holly Press, 1978.

Merkt, Dixon with Mark H. Lytle, *Shang: A Biography of Charles E. Wheeler*. Edited by Ruth Wolfe. Spanish Forks, Utah, Hillcrest Publications, 1984

Mickel, Earl, *Turkey Call Makers—Past and Present: Mick's Picks*. Edited by Mary Heaton. Beach Lake, Pennsylvania, private printing, 1994.

Miner, Jack, *Jack Miner: His Life and Religion*. Kingsville, Ontario, The Jack Miner Migratory Bird Foundation, 1969.

Murphy, Stanley, *Martha's Vineyard Decoys*. Boston, Massachusetts, David R. Godine, 1978.

Musgrove, Jack W. and Mary R., *Waterfowl in Iowa*. DesMoines, Iowa, The State of Iowa, 1943.

Parmalee, Paul W. and Forrest D. Loomis, *Decoys and Decoy Carvers of Illinois*. DeKalb, Illinois, Northern Illinois University Press, 1969.

Ridges, Bob, *Decoy Ducks*. New York, New York, W.H. Smith Publishers Inc., 1988.

Robarts, Ronnie and Bill Birkbeck, ed., *The Red Book of Sporting Collectibles*. Conway, New Hampshire, private printing, 1996.

Robinson, Jimmy, *Forty Years of Hunting*. Minneapolis, Minnesota, Jimmy Robinson, 1947.

Shaw Robert, *Call to the Sky: The Decoy Collection of James McCleery, MD*. Houston, Texas, Gale Publishing Company, 1992.

Stadt, Ronald W., *Winchester Shotgun and Shotshells*. Tacoma, Washington, Armory Publication, 1984.

Stansbury, Henry H., *Lloyd J. Tyler: Folk Artist, Decoy Carver*. Burtonsville, Maryland, Decoy Magazine, 1995.

Starr, George Ross, Jr., *Decoys of the Atlantic Flyway*. New York, New York, Winchester Press, 1974.

Strauss, Bob & Beverly, *American Sporting Advertising, Volume I: Posters and Calendars*. Jefferson, Maine, Circus Promotion Corporation, 1987.

Strauss, Bob & Beverly, *American Sporting Advertising, Volume II: Posters and Calendars*. Jefferson, Maine, Circus Promotion Corporation, 1989

Townsend, E. Jabe, *Gunner's Paradise: Waterfowling and Decoys on Long Island*, Stony Brook, New York, Museums at Stony Brook, 1979.

Traff, Cliff Jr., and John Lindgren, *Last of the Prairie Carvers*. Private printing, 1970.

The Postal Service Guide to U.S. Stamps, 20th edition. Crawfordsville, Indiana, R. R. Donnelley & Sons Company, 1994.

Walsh, Clune Jr. *Waterfowl Decoys of Michigan and the Lake St. Clair Region*. Edited by Lowell G. Jackson. Detroit, Michigan, Gale Graphics, 1983.

Walsh, Harry M., *The Outlaw Gunner*. Centerville, Maryland, Tidewater Publishers, 1971.

Webster, David S. and William Kehoe, *Decoys at Shelburne Museum*. Burlington, Vermont, The Lane Press, 1961.

Wildfowl Decoys. Edited by Joseph Engers. San Diego, California, Thunder Bay Press Inc. 1990.

Index